Studies in German Literature, Linguistics, and Culture
The Intellectual Contexts of Kafka's Fictions

The Intellectual Contexts of Kafka's Fictions

Arnold Heidsieck

The Intellectual Contexts of Kafka's Fiction: Philosophy, Law, Religion

CAMDEN HOUSE

Published by Camden House, Inc.
Drawer 2025
Columbia, SC 29202 USA

Printed on acid-free paper.
Binding materials are chosen for strength and
durability.

ISBN:1-879751-66-6

Library of Congress Cataloging-in-Publication Data

Heidsieck, Arnold, 1937-
    The intellectual contexts of Kafka's fictions : philosophy, law, religion /
Arnold Heidsieck.
        p.   cm. -- (Studies in German literature, linguistics, and culture)
    Includes bibliographical references and index.
    ISBN 1-879751-66-6 (alk. paper)
    1. Kafka, Franz, 1883-1924--Criticism and interpretation.
    I. Title. II. Series.
    PT2621.A26Z746225   1994
    833'.912--dc20   94-8230
                                                                    CIP

Acknowledgements

MY WORK ON THIS book was supported by grants from the Faculty Innovation and Research Fund of the University of Southern California and the German Academic Exchange Service, with each grant covering one month of travel and research in Austria or Germany. Materials from my Kafka articles in *The Dove and the Mole*, ed. Moshe Lazar and Ronald Gottesman (1987), *Philosophy and Literature* (1987), *Poetica* (1989), and *German Quarterly* (1989) are used here by permission of the editors. Quotations from Kafka's works in English translation are reprinted here with permission from Schocken Books, New York.

I wish to thank the following colleagues for their support during the eight years of conceiving and writing this book. During my research at the "Forschungsstelle und Dokumentationszentrum für österreichische Philosophie" (Graz, Austria) in the spring of 1989, its director, Rudolf Haller (University of Graz), and deputy director, Reinhard Fabian, gave generous help, as well as permission to quote from materials in the Center's custody. Edwin McCann and, especially, Brian Loar, both in the School of Philosophy at U.S.C., were generously available, during the mid to late 1980s, to discuss with me issues in the philosophy of mind and language. Andreas Kemmerling (University of Munich) provided information on twentieth-century German philosophy of language in several conversations. Rolf-Peter Janz invited me in 1984, 1987, and 1989 to lecture on Kafka at the Free University Berlin. Clemens Knobloch (University of Siegen) sponsored my German Academic Exchange Service travel grant. Margarita Pazi (Tel-Aviv University), Hans-Gerd Koch (University of Wuppertal) and Peter Simons (University of Salzburg) answered queries on Max Brod's diaries, Kafka's personal library, and Anton Marty's theory of judgment. Jerold Frakes (U.S.C.) and, especially, Professor Stephen Dowden (Yale University), reader for Camden House, made important comments on an earlier draft of this book. Marliss Desens and Philip Dematteis, copyeditor for Camden House, provided invaluable editorial assistance. James Hardin, managing editor of *Studies in German Literature, Linguistics, and Culture*, was untiringly and generously available to help with the intricacies of formatting this book. Thien Nguyen and Roger Stewart helped to resolve computer software problems.

I also would like to thank two groups of people who made it easier for me to persist with this project over such a long time. Well over a hundred undergraduate and graduate students put up with my fascination with Franz Kafka and wrote term papers or exams about aspects of his work. The staffs of the main and philosophy libraries at U.S.C., and the research library of the University of California, Los Angeles, responded to my bibliographic curiosity about Kafka' intellectual contexts as well as let me keep a legion of books for years on end. Finally, I would like to express my profound gratitude to Deborah Ensign for her support during the many years of writing this book.

Contents

Preface

ALL QUOTES FROM GERMAN materials in the main text are given in English translation, with Kafka quotes from the Schocken Books editions — specifically, where available, the Schocken Kafka Library paperbacks. The translations of Kafka's aphorisms and literary fragments in his blue octavo notebooks are quoted from their first paperback edition, published by Exact Change. In order to render the original meaning of Kafka's writing as closely as possible when making a critical point, I have made occasional adjustments, indicated by square brackets, within these published translations. I have also translated a few passages from Kafka's "Description of a Struggle," omitted from the version in *The Complete Stories,* as well as other brief Kafka texts not available in translation. Abbreviated passages from the original text of Kafka's fictions and personal writings are offered in footnotes. All these German Kafka passages, with the exception of those from "Description of a Struggle," are cited from the paperback version of the first complete edition of Kafka's German works, published by Fischer Verlag. Max Brod originated this edition after Kafka's death; beginning in 1950 he reissued many of the volumes and added new ones. Additional volumes of Kafka letters were edited later by others. I have cited from the Fischer Taschenbuch (paperback) version of this complete edition because all its volumes are available in print and, thus, most accessible to the general reader. Whenever desirable, I have quoted or referred to emended passages from the as yet incomplete critical edition published by Fischer Verlag since 1982.

I have kept the main text free of bibliographical references and abbreviations; they are in footnotes. Wherever available (and they are in almost all cases) I have documented Kafka's works in both their German and English versions. References employ the abbreviations given in the List of Abbreviations and are distinguished in the following manner: the page number in the original-language paperback edition is given before the semicolon, the one in the English translation after it; if a quotation from an English translation is documented (even one consisting of a single word), its page number is given first, the one in the German edition second.

Bibliographical references other than those in the List of Abbreviations are given in full at their first appearance in a footnote. Unless otherwise noted, translations of all unpublished and some published German materials, other than the Kafka texts, are mine. I have frequently corrected or changed phrases and passages in published English translations of such materials, indicating that I have done so either in the accompanying footnote or by using square brackets. Materials in German, mainly of interest to the more academic audience, are provided in the appendix, without English translation.

List of Abbreviations

A   Franz Kafka, *Amerika*, trans. Willa and Edwin Muir (New York: Schocken, 1946; 1974). Schocken Kafka Library, 1962.

APNDX   Appendix of German-Language Sources.

B   Franz Kafka, *Briefe 1902–1924*, ed. Max Brod (Frankfurt: Fischer, 1958). Fischer Taschenbuch [1575], 1975.

BK   Franz Kafka, *Beschreibung eines Kampfes: Novellen, Skizzen, Aphorismen aus dem Nachlaß*, ed. Max Brod (Frankfurt: Fischer, 1954). Fischer Taschenbuch [2066], 1980.

BN   Franz Kafka, *The Blue Octavo Notebooks*, ed. Max Brod, trans. Ernst Kaiser and Eithne Wilkins (Cambridge, Mass.: Exact Change, 1991) [reprinted from DF 33–135].

C   Franz Kafka, *The Castle*, trans. Willa and Edna Muir (New York: Schocken, 1954; 1982). Schocken Kafka Library, 1988.

CS   Franz Kafka, *The Complete Stories*, ed. Nahum Glatzer (New York: Schocken, 1971). Schocken Kafka Library, 1988.

D 1   Franz Kafka, *The Diaries 1910–1913,* trans. Joseph Kresh (New York: Schocken, 1948). Schocken Paperback, 1965.

D 2   Franz Kafka, *The Diaries 1914–1923,* trans. Martin Greenberg (New York: Schocken, 1949). Schocken Paperback, 1965.

DF   Franz Kafka, *Dearest Father: Stories and Other Writings*, ed. Max Brod, trans. Ernst Kaiser and Eithne Wilkins (New York: Schocken, 1954). [Kafka, "Letter to His Father," 138–96].

E   Franz Kafka, *Sämtliche Erzählungen*, ed. Paul Raabe
                     (Frankfurt: Fischer, 1970). Fischer Taschenbuch [1078], 1970.

EF 1   Max Brod and Franz Kafka, *Eine Freundschaft*, ed. Malcolm
                     Pasley, vol. 1, *Reiseaufzeichnungen* (Frankfurt: Fischer,
                     1987).

EF 2   Max Brod and Franz Kafka, *Eine Freundschaft*, ed. Malcolm
                     Pasley, vol. 2, *Ein Briefwechsel* (Frankfurt: Fischer, 1989).

F   Franz Kafka, *Briefe an Felice und andere Korrespondenz aus
                     der Verlobungszeit,* ed. Erich Heller and Jürgen Born
                     (Frankfurt: Fischer, 1967). Fischer Taschenbuch [1697], 1976.

FE   Franz Kafka, *Letters to Felice*, trans. James Stern and Eliza-
                     beth Duckworth (New York: Schocken, 1973).

GW   Franz Kafka, *The Great Wall of China: Stories and Reflec-
                     tions*, trans. Willa and Edna Muir (New York: Schocken,
                     1946).

H   Franz Kafka, *Hochzeitsvorbereitungen auf dem Lande und
                     andere Prosa aus dem Nachlaß*, ed. Max Brod (Frankfurt:
                     Fischer, 1953). Fischer Taschenbuch [2067], 1980.

K   Franz Kafka, *Beschreibung eines Kampfes: Die zwei Fas-
                     sungen. Parallelausgabe nach den Handschriften*, ed. Ludwig
                     Dietz (Frankfurt: Fischer, 1969).

L   Franz Kafka, *Letters to Friends, Family, and Editors*, trans.
                     Richard and Clara Winston (New York: Schocken, 1977).
                     Schocken Kafka Library, 1977.

M   Franz Kafka, *Briefe an Milena,* ed. Jürgen Born and Michael
                     Müller (Frankfurt: Fischer, 1983). Fischer Taschenbuch
                     [5307], 1986.

MA   Anton Marty, *Descriptive Psychology: Nach den Vorlesungen
                     des Prof. Dr. Marty*, mimeographed course transcript (333 p.)
                     on microfilm, in custody of the "Forschungsstelle und
                     Dokumentationszentrum für österreichische Philosophie"
                     (Graz, Austria).

MI   Franz Kafka, *Letters to Milena*, trans. Philip Boehm (New
              York: Schocken Kafka Library, 1990).

P   Franz Kafka, *Der Prozeß: Roman*, ed. Max Brod (Fischer:
              Frankfurt, 1950). Fischer Taschenbuch [676], 1979.

PKA 1   Franz Kafka, *Der Proceß*, ed. Malcolm Pasley (Frankfurt:
              Fischer, 1990) [Franz Kafka, *Schriften - Tagebücher - Briefe:
              Kritische Ausgabe*, ed. Jürgen Born, Gerhard Neumann, Mal-
              colm Pasley, and Jost Schillemeit (Frankfurt: Fischer, 1982-)].

PKA 2   Franz Kafka, *Der Proceß: Apparatband* [Kritische Ausgabe],
              ed. Malcolm Pasley (Frankfurt: Fischer, 1990).

S   Franz Kafka, *Das Schloß: Roman,* ed. Max Brod (Frankfurt:
              Fischer, 1951). Fischer Taschenbuch [900], 1968.

SKA 1   Franz Kafka, *Das Schloß* [Kritische Ausgabe], ed. Malcolm
              Pasley (Frankfurt: Fischer, 1982).

SKA 2   Franz Kafka, *Das Schloß: Apparatband* [Kritische Ausgabe],
              ed. Malcolm Pasley (Frankfurt: Fischer, 1982).

T   Franz Kafka, *Tagebücher 1910–1924*, ed. Max Brod
              (Frankfurt: Fischer, 1951). Fischer Taschenbuch [1346], 1973.

TKA 1   Franz Kafka, *Tagebücher* [Kritische Ausgabe], ed. Hans-Gerd
              Koch, Michael Müller, and Malcolm Pasley (Frankfurt:
              Fischer, 1990).

TKA 2   Franz Kafka, *Tagebücher: Apparatband* [Kritische Ausgabe],
              ed. Hans-Gerd Koch, Michael Müller, and Malcolm Pasley
              (Frankfurt: Fischer, 1990).

TKA 3   Franz Kafka, *Tagebücher: Kommentarband* [Kritische Aus-
              gabe], ed. Hans-Gerd Koch, Michael Müller, and Malcolm
              Pasley (Frankfurt: Fischer, 1990).

TR   Franz Kafka, *The Trial*, trans. Willa and Edwin Muir (New
              York: Schocken, 1956; 1984). Schocken Kafka Library, 1988.

V   Franz Kafka, *Amerika: Roman [Der Verschollene]*, ed. Max
                    Brod (Frankfurt: Fischer, 1953). Fischer Taschenbuch [132],
                    1956.

VKA 1   Franz Kafka, *Der Verschollene* [Kritische Ausgabe], ed. Jost
                    Schillemeit (Frankfurt: Fischer, 1983).

VKA 2   Franz Kafka, *Der Verschollene: Apparatband* [Kritische Aus-
                    gabe], ed. Jost Schillemeit (Frankfurt: Fischer, 1983).

Introduction

THIS STUDY TRACES THE development of Franz Kafka as a writer of enduring modern fiction and an incisive critical observer of his time. Max Brod, his closest friend, believed that Kafka had no interest in theories and wrote exclusively from intuitive imagination. Some critics since have tried to lend credence to Brod's view, denying Kafka's fiction any theoretical insight or intent. I will argue that the author used not only his unique intuition — idiosyncratic, existential, aesthetic, fictionalizing, or however it may be viewed — but also a broad conceptual way of thinking and writing to achieve the analytical and metaphorical force for which his work is known. I also hope to show that the author had a wide-ranging knowledge of the human sciences, from physiology and semantics to jurisprudence and ethics, which he used for evolving his narrative themes and structures. His fictional descriptions of consciousness and his single-character point of view radically altered the approach to storytelling, yet he did not join in the literary avant-garde's widespread rejection, around 1900, of science and utilitarianism.[1] Although he explores the uncertainty of objective knowledge and the paradoxical outcomes of norms, he always appeals to our linguistically shaped intersubjective rationality. Thus, he affirms social institutions, science, law, and literate culture as conditions for the possibility of shareable knowledge, nonparadoxical norms, and individualism.

It is true that Kafka's fictional works are shaped by personal interests: an unrelenting introspection (painstakingly recorded in diaries and letters), overscrupulous interactions with others (his father and women friends, especially), and a devotional pursuit of truth through writing. Yet they are also informed by nonintrospective, nonaesthetic, impersonal discourses drawn from academic and public debates during the first decade of the twentieth century on physiology; perceptual, cognitive, and linguistic psychology; the philosophy of mind and language; positive law and natural-law theory; criminal

---

[1]The Austrian literary avant-garde remained part of the liberal middle-class culture (Carl Schorske, *Fin-de-Siècle Vienna: Politics and Culture* [New York: Vintage, 1981] 299).

procedure; ethics; and religion. Kafka encountered these discourses during his formative years as a writer through friends and teachers and made free thematic and formal use of them. Sometimes they appear reflected in minute details of his work, leaving us wondering what purpose such reflections could possibly serve. At other times they appear fictionally reconstructed on a large scale and in such ways as to reveal their novelty and far-reaching aims.

At the time of Kafka's birth in 1883 the predominant nineteenth-century paradigm in prose fiction, representational or mimetic realism, was on the wane. Its main feature was to mirror the bourgeois economic and intellectual order objectively and critically, while supporting its basic values.[2] In the theater Henrik Ibsen's existentially probing realism had come to focus on self-deceptions, idealistic rationalizations, and moral compromises within the professional classes. The naturalists (Emile Zola, later Gerhart Hauptmann) outdid realism with strident, determinist, incipiently sociological descriptions of middle-class corruption and urban and working-class alienation. The last decade of the century produced a panorama of literary experiments and styles. In Vienna the impressionists Hugo von Hofmannsthal and Arthur Schnitzler — influenced by a philosophical climate of radical epistemological subjectivism[3] — sympathetically or critically depicted a middle-class culture besieged by narcissism and resignation. All across Europe writers retreated from the bourgeois faith in utilitarian progress and objective or scientific knowledge. They cultivated decadent themes and styles such as aestheticism, mysticism, exoticism, and occultism. They gave voice to a determinist sense of devolution, physiological fatigue and degeneration, apocalyptic crisis and decay.[4] During the same decade, however, early modern writers such as August Strindberg, Anton Chekhov, Joseph Conrad, and Thomas Mann, wielding a clinical, existential, or ironic (Nietzschean) psychology, steered away from determinism, mysticism, and aestheticism. They recorded and impugned their characters' idealistic conceits and vacillations among individualism, narcissism, and class-bound egotism as pathogenic adjustments to a self-satisfied bourgeois culture.

It was in the context of these modes of writing at the turn of the century that Kafka produced two mostly unpublished novelistic fragments, the kaleidoscopic "Description of a Struggle" (1904–1906) and the more realistic

---

[2]See Erich Auerbach, *Mimesis: The Representation of Reality in Western Literature* (Princeton UP, 1953) 454–524.

[3]Ernst Mach's associationism and phenomenalism (Allan Janik and Stephen Toulmin, *Wittgenstein's Vienna* [New York: Touchstone, 1973] 133–38). See chapter 1 of the present book for Kafka's response to non-Machian versions of these theories.

[4]Jens Malte Fischer, *Fin de siècle: Kommentar zur einer Epoche* (Munich: Winkler, 1978). *Decadence and Innovation: Austro-Hungarian Life and Art at the Turn of the Century,* ed. Robert B. Pynsent (London: Weidenfeld & Nicolson, 1989).

"Wedding Preparations in the Country" (1907). They are saturated with youthful autobiography and the geography of Prague and share certain stylistic elements with the impressionists and the writers of fin-de-siècle decadence.[5] Yet they also mimic and ironically subvert features of realist representation[6] and naturalist determinism.[7] Several years later Kafka's first major story, "The Judgment" (1912), achieves the analytical and metaphorical force of his mature style. Here a figure narrates, in the third person, his own cognitions, inferences, and beliefs about the world. By writing a letter to and discussing a self-exiled friend whose actual existence remains in doubt throughout, this figural narrator emphasizes the subjective nature of his knowledge of others. His attempt at self-affirmation through business success and marriage is condemned by his father and himself as, ambiguously, a pathological, moral or existential failing. After "The Judgment" Kafka's predominant point of view is the central character's third-person self-narration concerning his own conscious cognitions and beliefs. The reader is offered the fictive world solely through this figure's continuously attentive, cognitively enervated self-narration. Such a stance has little in common with the mystical self-explorations of fin-de-siècle writers nor the psychological probings of the early modernists. In short, Kafka's mature style cannot be traced to his immediate literary precursors or contemporaries. Instead, his innovations gain insight from psychological, linguistic, and ethical theories of how perceptions, cognitions, and beliefs — including those reflecting desires, moral values, and self-attributions of guilt — arise in consciousness. His characters analyze and narrate their beliefs, yet due to their subjectivist outlook they are not sure how to deal with the ambiguities of knowledge and normative paradoxes. They overcome self-inflicted guilt and cognitive disorientation through the shock of disillusion and, often, self-destruction.

Kafka's fictive descriptions occasionally provide, within realistic everyday settings, supernatural entities and events: people living after their deaths or riding in the air; animals and inanimate objects that think or talk; ubiquitous

---

[5]Mark M. Anderson sees Kafka reacting to fin-de-siècle styles as well as to the turn-of-the-century *Jugendstil* (*Kafka's Clothes: Ornament and Aestheticism in the Habsburg Fin-de-Siècle* [Oxford: Clarendon, 1992]). For Kafka's mature work this was no longer the case.

[6]This subversion is suggested for all of Kafka's work: realism's modernist "crisis in representation ... reaches its peak in Kafka" (Stephen D. Dowden, *Sympathy for the Abyss: A Study in the Novel of German Modernism: Kafka, Broch, Musil, and Thomas Mann* [Tübingen: Niemeyer, 1986] 23).

[7]A related interest has been suggested for his much later letter to his father which resembles the naturalist "document of a strict determinist" (Walter H. Sokel, "The Programme of K.'s Court: Oedipal and Existential Meanings of *The Trial*," *On Kafka: Semi-Centenary Perspectives*, ed. Franz Kuna [New York: Barnes & Noble, 1976] 19).

court offices accessible through the attic of every house; a person metamorphosed into a giant insect. What the supernatural distortions of reality mean on a symbolic level remains to be seen. Regardless of whether fantastic or realistic entities are described, time and again the narrators introduce for themselves, and thus for the reader, difficulties of distinguishing between what merely appears to exist or happen and what actually does. In other words, nothing is revealed beyond the characters' perceptions, illusions, and surmisings, which threatens to make the reader's understanding largely subjective as well. As will emerge from discussions of Kafka's use of cognitive, semantic, legal, and ethical theorems, however, the subjective narrative perspective does not, by itself, entail a rejection of the possibility of shareable knowledge for narrator or reader.

Kafka research over the last several decades has generated three methods of interpretation: the search for literary influences, the examination of biographical motivations, and the exclusive focus on the text. The first approach studies writers whom Kafka considered his literary ancestors — Heinrich von Kleist, Charles Dickens, Gustave Flaubert, and Feodor Dostoyevsky — as well as his literary contemporaries (decadents, impressionists, and expressionists) and identifies unilateral or mutual intertextual dependencies with respect to motifs and style. The second elicits the author's experiences and intellectual interests from his personal writings, life circumstances, and cultural background and links them developmentally (sometimes causally) to the production of his fictional texts. Among the text-oriented approaches, the New Criticism and structuralism investigate the generic features, intertextual structural homologies, multiple metaphorical meanings, and palimpsestlike leitmotifs within these works. The poststructuralist method alleges the fictional text's indifference to the referential efficacy of language. It proposes undecidable or, at best, infinitely deferable and differentiable meanings for all such texts. Despite the extremely varied, and frequently combined, use of these methods, important features of Kafka's style have remained enigmatic. It is my hope that explorations of his fictional use of psychological and philosophical theorems, law, and religion will shed new light on them.

Previous scholarship has shown that Kafka's descriptive precision was partly influenced by the scientific observation and description taught in his high-school science courses and textbooks.[8] Scant attention has been given, however, to the full-fledged explanatory theories into which he inquired and which helped him to direct his painstaking search for themes, narrative structures, valid ethical perspectives, and historical and fictional truth. During his last high-school year (1900–1901) students received four weekly hours of

[8]Klaus Wagenbach, *Franz Kafka: Eine Biographie seiner Jugend* (Bern: Francke, 1958) 54. Hartmut Binder, "Der Mensch," *Kafka-Handbuch*, ed. H. Binder, 2 vols. (Stuttgart: Kröner, 1979) 1: 213.

instruction in philosophy and were required to own copies of the books used. The opening chapters of the psychology textbook used in this instruction summarized up-to-date physiological research on the nervous system, sensations, and perception. For Kafka's class especially, philosophy meant elementary physiology and cognitive psychology, since his philosophy teacher, Emil Gschwind, was a former student of the well-known experimental psychologist Wilhelm Wundt.[9] During his second university semester, the summer of 1902, Kafka enrolled in a lecture course on descriptive (philosophical) psychology by Anton Marty, one of the chairholders in philosophy at the German University of Prague. As part of his law studies Kafka was required to take an oral test on the material covered by a philosophy course, and he chose this one for the examination.[10] Because Marty's lectures were extremely abstract and difficult to follow, it is conceivable that Kafka studied a mimeographed transcript of this course to prepare himself for this test. This would help to explain why some of the ideas Marty advanced on these subjects appear reflected in the early prose fragments and stories.[11]

According to Max Brod, from late 1902 until the end of 1905 Kafka attended meetings of the philosophers' club or *Louvre-circle* along with Brod himself, who joined shortly after him.[12] The group consisted of the three academic lecturers and several students from the university's philosophy department, all of them closely associated with their teacher, Marty. The meetings, conducted like extracurricular graduate seminars, were intellectually

[9]About the particulars of gymnasial philosophy instruction see David Lindenfeld, *The Transformation of Positivism: Alexius Meinong and European Thought* (U of California P, 1980) 65. Wilhelm Hemecker, "Sigmund Freud und die herbartianische Psychologie des 19. Jahrhunderts," *Conceptus* 21.53-54 (1987): 219. Hugo Hecht, "Zwölf Jahre in der Schule mit Franz Kafka," *Prager Nachrichten* 17.8 (1966): 5–6.

[10]It was administered by Marty himself; Kafka did not pass it (Hugo Bergman, "Erinnerungen an Franz Kafka," *Universitas* 27 [1972]: 745). For a description of Marty's corpus of lecture courses see Johann Christian Marek and Barry Smith, "Einleitung zu Anton Martys *Elemente der Deskriptiven Psychologie*," *Conceptus* 21.53–54 (1987): 33–47.

[11]The course, or one very much like it, has survived as a 333-page mimeographed transcript: *Descriptive Psychologie: Nach den Vorlesungen des Prof. Dr. Marty* (in custody of the "Forschungsstelle und Dokumentationszentrum für österreichische Philosophie" in Graz, Austria) [= MA]. Lecture transcripts were readily available; Kafka used them in preparing for his law examinations (Max Brod, *Streitbares Leben 1884–1968* [Munich: Herbig, 1969] 165, 159; Brod, *Über Franz Kafka* [Frankfurt: Fischer, 1974] 394).

[12]Brod, *Streitbares Leben* 163–77. The name derives from the Café Louvre, where the meetings took place. See also Peter Neesen, *Vom Louvrezirkel zum Prozeß: Franz Kafka und die Psychologie Franz Brentanos* (Göppingen: Kümmerle, 1972) 21–29.

dominated, though never attended, by Marty himself and his former teacher, Franz Brentano, who had retired from the university of Vienna in 1895. As will be detailed later, Kafka learned a great deal from the core group of the club: the lecturers Alfred Kastil, Oskar Kraus, and Josef Eisenmeier; his former high-school classmates Hugo Bergmann and Emil Utitz, who both took their doctorates with Marty at the end of 1905; and Max Lederer, a Marty student and Prague judge. Three other students of Marty's, Kafka's former classmate and friend Oskar Pollak, Berta Fanta (later the hostess to a well-known literary salon), and her sister Ida Freund attended these gatherings.[13] At an October 1905 meeting of the club, Utitz accused Brod of slandering Brentano in a short story he had just published about a womanizing civil servant who claims adherence to Brentano's rationalist theism. Brod was barred from attending further club meetings and, by his own account, was traumatically shaken by the ceremonious disciplinary proceedings. In relating this story many years later he pokes fun at a remark from Marty's lecture course on practical philosophy, which passingly defined beauty as the value or richness of an artwork's representational content. As Brod had realized during the club gatherings, Utitz was impressed by this (for Brod, empty) definition. In fact, Utitz referred to it in his dissertation, stressing Marty's contention that beauty lies solely in the perfection and scope of the ideas represented by the artwork. In apparent protest against his expulsion, Brod published an extremely formalist (anti-Brentanoan) aesthetics in the same weekly in which the alleged slur had appeared.[14] The fact that Utitz still talked about the incident[15] in the late 1940s suggests that it had a strong emotional significance for him as well. A partial explanation of his zealousness as a Brentano defender on this occasion was that he and Bergmann had just returned from a visit with Brentano at his residence in Lower Austria, a redesigned monastery building high above the Danube. The house appeared

---

[13]See Wagenbach, *Franz Kafka* 108–9. Binder, in *Kafka-Handbuch* 1: 288. Kafka met with Lederer as late as March 1910 (B 79; L 63; for a slightly different dating of Kafka's letter see EF 2: 78). Chapter 6 provides more information about Lederer. In late 1903 Pollak took a tutorial position in the countryside (B 497; L 426), but he attended club meetings when in Prague during holidays.

[14]Brod, *Streitbares Leben* 167. Utitz, *J. J. Wilhelm Heinse und die Ästhetik zur Zeit der deutschen Aufklärung* (Halle: Niemeyer, 1906) 9, 63. Brod, "Zur Ästhetik," *Die Gegenwart* (17 Feb. 1906): 102–4; (24 Feb. 1906): 118–19 [discussed in chapter 1]. Brod's story, consisting mainly of two letters between friends, was "Zwillingspaar von Seelen," *Die Gegenwart* (7 Oct. 1905): 220–21.

[15]Hans Demetz, "Meine persönlichen Beziehungen und Erinnerungen an den Prager deutschen Dichterkreis," *Weltfreunde: Konferenz über die Prager deutsche Literatur*, ed. Eduard Goldstücker (Prague: Academia, 1967) 141. Brod writes that out of friendship Kafka left the meeting with him that evening and, expressing lack of interest in the club's activities, never returned. This was hardly the case (see below).

to Utitz like a "fairy tale castle," and he experienced a feeling of "deepest veneration" for the philosopher. Bergmann was no less impressed by Brentano during this visit.[16] For many years Marty, Kraus, Kastil, and Eisenmeier had been frequent visitors at Brentano's house and at his winter residence in Florence. Although Bergmann and Utitz were to stay with him for more extended periods in the coming years, this first brief encounter was important because in the eyes of Marty and the lecturers it admitted these two doctoral candidates to the ranks of the academic Brentano school.

The account so far of the philosophers' club, and its possible importance for Kafka, is taken entirely from published sources. Additional information about the club is available, however, in unpublished letters that form part of Franz Brentano's literary estate. The relevant letters are among those from Anton Marty, Christian von Ehrenfels, Oskar Kraus, and Emil Utitz to Franz Brentano, and from Brentano to Marty, Ehrenfels, and Kraus. They never mention Kafka's name but reveal a good deal about the members and activities of the club that he frequented over a number of years. In the following I will refer to, quote from, or paraphrase many of these letters. A few days after Bergmann and Utitz had returned from their visit with Brentano, Marty wrote Brentano that the two had received the most favorable impression and now understood that Brentano and his followers were greater philosophical innovators than the fashionable idols in the philosophy chairs at Leipzig, Vienna, or Munich.[17] As the correspondence also shows, Berta Fanta and Ida Freund had visited Brentano in the spring of 1904, while Oskar Pollak and Max Lederer traveled to see him in the summer of 1906. Since all were students in his seminars, Marty, in letters to their host, gave advance notice of their arrival along with short reports on each of them. It appears that Kafka and Brod, probably due to their largely literary interests, were the only members of the club not to have met Brentano in person.

According to Brod, the club began meeting as early as 1902. Marty also suggests an early date when he asks in 1903 that Brentano send him copies of all his letters to third parties for the present and future benefit of "our little local congregation." In early 1905, however, Marty provides a new, conflicting date in his statement that Alois Höfler and Christian von Ehrenfels, his

---

[16]Emil Utitz, "Erinnerungen an Franz Brentano," *Wissenschaftliche Zeitschrift der Universität Halle-Wittenberg: Gesellschafts- und sprachwissenschaftliche Reihe* 4 (1954–55): 76. "Briefe Franz Brentanos an Hugo Bergmann," ed. H. Bergmann, *Philosophy and Phenomenological Research* 7 (1946–47): 83.

[17]The Brentano correspondence, in the custody of the "Forschungsstelle und Dokumentationszentrum für österreichische Philosophie" (Graz), will be published as part of a forthcoming critical edition of his works. Longer quotations from these letters (along with those from other German-speaking sources) are offered in an appendix [= APNDX], without English translation. Marty to Brentano, 15 Sept. 1905 (APNDX 1).

rivals in the Prague philosophy department, unsuccessfully tried to start a philosophical society of their own and that a philosophical club in the Brentanoan spirit had formed in the winter semester 1904-1905. This puzzlingly late date for the club's beginnings can be explained in the following way. In 1904 Berta Fanta, inspired by her visit with Brentano and perhaps also in reaction to Höfler's attempt to found a rival society, had started to sponsor "parallel" meetings and parties for the club at her house.[18] Since the Fantas were socially prominent members of Prague's business class, her sponsorship (the fledgling *Fanta-circle*) gave the hitherto purely academic philosophers' club greater visibility. If initially Marty was sympathetic to Mrs. Fanta's efforts to boost the club socially, in 1906 he encouraged the separation of the club from her circle, insisting that the club must have an academic purpose rather than one based on friendship. He also mentioned that Bergmann and the three lecturers regularly attended. Brentano expressed his satisfaction over this change. Several months earlier, from the Fantas' summer house in Podbaba at which he was staying as a guest, Marty had explained to Brentano that Bergmann had met his bride, Berta Fanta's daughter, through the club, which had often met there or at the Fanta residence in Prague. By using the past tense, he appears to indicate that Mrs. Fanta no longer belonged to the club, and that she had ceased to sponsor parallel meetings. When Bergmann received his doctorate in December of 1905, Berta Fanta and other club members (including Kafka) presented him with a book. Its personal dedication to the memory of their common studies perhaps suggests that the philosophers' club and the Fanta circle were expected to go off on separate paths.[19] The historical reconstruction given here agrees with Brod's report that after his leaving the club in October 1905, the philosophical gatherings at the Fanta house (which for some time he also avoided) continued for many years but were no longer influenced by Brentano.

Brod's related statement that the meetings of the philosophers' club (the *Louvre-circle*, in his words) ceased entirely in 1906, however, is false. Letters from Marty, Kraus, and especially Utitz to Brentano confirm that the club continued to exist vigorously at least until late 1907, with breaks between

---

[18]"Unserer hiesigen kleinen Gemeinde" (Marty to Brentano, 10 Nov. 1903). Marty to Brentano, 13 Mar. 1905 (APNDX 2). Brod, *Streitbares Leben* 169–70; Brod uses the term *parallel*. It appears that the three lecturers (*Privatdozenten*) and Utitz attended events only at the Café Louvre (172), Felix Weltsch, a friend of Brod's and Kafka's, only those at the Fantas' (175). A New Year's Eve party was held at the Fantas' in 1904 (Wagenbach, *Franz Kafka* 108; Binder, in *Kafka-Handbuch* 1: 288).

[19]Marty to Brentano, 19 Oct. 1906 (APNDX 3). "I am pleased if the philosophers' club in Prague gets itself organized better" (Brentano to Marty, 26 Oct. 1906). Marty to Brentano, 20 Aug. 1906 (APNDX 4). "In memory of our common striving" (Bergman, "Erinnerungen" 745). Nothing is known about Leopold Pollak, another signer and apparent club member. Marty never mentions him as a student.

academic semesters. This revised chronology is much less at odds with Bergmann's curious statement that the philosophers' club grew out of the social meetings at the Fantas' than with Brod's claim.[20] Two events intensified the club's activities in 1906 and 1907. Höfler's second attempt at founding a society in the summer of 1906 was successful (Marty reported on a meeting of that society the following May),[21] and soon thereafter Höfler accepted a position in Vienna. Marty's efforts to replace him with one of the lecturers in his department, or at least someone sympathetic to the Brentano school, boosted the club members' spirits. Brentano pressured Ehrenfels to go along with Marty in trying to appoint such a person by reminding him that he, Brentano, had a moral right to his school survival's in Austria. Accordingly, Marty instilled in all his students a sense of urgency about this survival. Kraus once told Brentano that he wanted to become the St. Paul of the Brentanoan gospel, and years later he claimed that Prague remained the only "fort held by" Brentanoan philosophers. Utitz declared that as an academic teacher he would want to preach the Brentanoan doctrine and recruit students. Many years later he called Brentano the "disputatious ecclesiastical prince" of his own church.[22]

In addition to Brentano's and Marty's writings and lecture courses, it was the books, articles and book reviews of the members themselves that served as the main subjects for club discussions. Additional topics were theories — physiological, psychological, cognitive, linguistic, and semantic — of Brentano's academic friends and foes: Hermann von Helmholtz, Ewald Hering, Wilhelm Wundt, Carl Stumpf, Alexius Meinong, and Edmund Husserl. As their correspondence with each other shows, Brentano and Marty, sympathetically or critically, were thoroughly preoccupied with these theorists. Many of Kafka's early works evidence his familiarity with a number of them, though not necessarily with their published work. His curiosity did not take him much beyond what he could glean from the discussions among club members. In many cases this knowledge helped him to direct his fictions' thematic *foci* and invent modulelike linguistic and aesthetic structures for them. As the first four

[20]Brod, *Streitbares Leben* 172–77. Utitz details three club meetings in 1906 and 1907 (APNDX 5). "[We met] now and then in the 'salon' at the Fanta residence, out of which later grew the philosophical circle which called itself *Louvre-circle*" (Bergman, "Erinnerungen" 745). Bergmann was welcome in both circles after their separation.

[21]Utitz to Brentano, 7 June 1906. Marty to Brentano, 14 May 1907 (APNDX 6).

[22]"You asked me ... to remain mindful of your moral right to have your teachings continued in Austria" (Ehrenfels to Brentano, 5 Dec. 1907). "I would wish to receive the strength to become the Paul of the gospel which you preach" (Kraus to Brentano, dated as "before 9 Oct. 1901"). Kraus to Brentano, 31 Dec. 1908. "It is truly my favorite plan to be appointed at another university and to recruit disciples" (Utitz to Brentano, 26 May 1907). Utitz, "Erinnerungen an Brentano" 84.

chapters of the present work will show, for instance, his narratives' descriptive precision conforms to turn-of-the-century psychological and philosophical research on perception, cognition, belief, and language. Thus, his narrators strive for quasi-scientific, exhaustive descriptions of the environments in which they find themselves. They describe and narrate the fictional locales and events as filtered through their own cognitively astute beliefs. In other words, what gets narrated in these fictions is almost exclusively what impinges on the main figures' perceptual fields (vision, hearing, etc.) and whatever else occurs in their minds, such as memories,[23] inferences, beliefs, desires, and the like. Perceptual, phenomenological (sensory input-interpreting), inferential, and emotive criteria of selection and attention in the figural consciousness provide the basic condition for a predominantly monoperspectival (monoperceptual as well as single-minded) narrative point of view. These theories reverberate also within the fictional characters themselves — in their physiological, psychological, and behavioral dispositions and attitudes (such as conscious awareness, curiosity, attentiveness, and fatigue), as well as in their understanding of speech and pantomimic or gestural modes of communication.

Other, more clearly philosophical issues are explored in the third and fourth chapter: the epistemic and ontological separation of the mind from the body; the intentional, reflexive, perspectival, and linguistic structure of consciousness; the fallibility of perception; the gaps between what is factual and what is believed; the possibility of alternate states of affairs. New Critics, along with many others, pretend to an abstinence from conceptual generalizations and dismiss philosophical readings of literature. As I hope to show through textual details and reconstructed contexts, Kafka's fictions invite the conceptual approach. Despite their descriptive specificity, they often can be seen to reflect abstract frameworks of thought — Cartesian epistemology, Husserl's early phenomenology, and aspects of the philosophy of mind and language — that greatly add to our critical understanding of them. Why Kafka should have based some of his thematic and stylistic innovations on his friends' philosophical concerns is unclear, but several possible explanations stand out. Initially, for him as for Bergmann, their high school's emphasis on experimental and philosophical psychology made these fields appear contemporary endeavors which warranted continued interest. Once he had joined the philosophers' club in 1902, another rationale for continuing these contacts emerged. The German-speaking countries, especially Germany, made it extremely difficult for Jews to attain academic teaching credentials and espe-

---

[23]Kafka's characters turn their scrutinizing gaze on their immediate environment, they "self-narrate." Memory is far less important for them than for those in the works of, for instance, Marcel Proust or James Joyce.

cially professorial rank.[24] Marty's doctoral candidates in the club, Bergmann, Utitz, and Pollak, were Jews. They sought Marty's tutelage in their pursuit of a philosophical career because, like Brentano, he was free of racial prejudice. Brentano hoped that it might be possible for Marty's Jewish students to succeed, if not in Germany, then at least in the Austrian university system.[25] Marty and Brentano prompted not only Kraus but also Utitz and Bergmann to undergo Protestant baptism to facilitate their careers.[26] While they failed with Bergmann,[27] they succeeded with the other two. Kraus received his associate professorship in 1909,[28] the year after his baptism, and Utitz obtained the lecturer accreditation after he was baptized.[29] Bergmann and Utitz were perceived by their older colleagues as guarantors of the Brentano school's survival. This, as well as their promotion of Brentano's philosophical agenda through scholarly publications, gave them the reasonable expectation of becoming accepted into the (non-Jewish) academy and the culture at large. Their professional zeal and fledgling publishing success aroused Kafka's ambition and feelings of solidarity. His perhaps decisive rationale to stay in touch with members of the club is the subject of this book. Kafka had a profound curiosity about conceptual and linguistic problems,[30] patiently learned

---

[24]Max Weber in 1919 characterized it as hopeless ("Wissenschaft als Beruf," *Gesammelte Aufsätze zur Wissenschaftslehre* [Tübingen: Mohr, 1922] 530).

[25]Brentano to Marty, 17 Nov. 1908 (APNDX 7). On Marty's advice, Pollak pursued a doctorate in art history instead of philosophy (Marty to Brentano, 2 Feb. 1907).

[26]"Es ist ein rechtes Kreuz mit diesem Confessionalismus und seinem Druck auf die philosophische Karriere" ["What a thorough burden denominationalism is on a career in philosophy"] (Marty to Brentano, 11 Sept. 1906). Of the three lecturers, apparently only Kraus was Jewish.

[27]Bergmann developed a strong Jewish national (Zionist) identity, and thus Marty (and Stumpf in Berlin) lost interest in sponsoring him. See Brentano's letters to Bergmann ("Briefe Franz Brentanos an Hugo Bergmann" 101–5, 128–33). Also Schmuel Hugo Bergman, *Tagebücher und Briefe*, ed. Miriam Sambursky, 2 vols. (Königstein: Athenäum, 1985) 21–22, 43–53.

[28]"His early marriage and his late conversion to Christianity have badly hurt his [Kraus's] career" (Brentano to Marty, 31 May 1908). In 1916, after Marty's retirement, Kraus acceded to his chair. In letters to Brentano Kraus expresses great sadness that he had to accept "conversion," and thus give offense to many who love him (Kraus to Brentano, 4 Apr. 1908; 19 May 1908), "in the service of philosophy" (Kraus to Brentano, 12 May 1908).

[29]Utitz treats his baptism as an utterly pragmatic matter, opting for Protestantism in the hope of making a career at a north German university (Utitz to Brentano, 1 July 1908). He received his accreditation (Habilitation) at the University of Greifswald.

[30]This view opposes Brod's: "Kafka did not love the theories. He spoke in images because he thought in images" (*Über Franz Kafka* 268; similarly 169); "Kafka had little knowledge of systematic philosophy" (*Streitbares Leben* 169. On rare occasions

to master them, and worked them into his fictions. A certain feature of "The Metamorphosis" and an extended passage from *The Trial* indicate that, until the spring of 1907, their author was well familiar with topics discussed in the club. Later that year he accepted his first professional employment, with a private insurance agency, which made great demands on his time. Even as late as 1910, when Brod and Weltsch participated in Marty's seminar on the philosophy of language in preparation for their book on cognitive psychology and conceptual analysis, *Intuition and Concept*, Kafka expressed interest in their project.[31] It would take him until 1912, about eight years longer than Brod, to achieve his desired literary style and establish his independence as a Jewish-German writer of fiction.

The fifth chapter looks at some recent work on Kafka's fictionalizing method and narrative perspective. It reads "The Judgment" and "The Metamorphosis" in light of the biographical-discursive contexts sketched earlier and explores their nascent conceptions of moral guilt. Finally it discusses the inconsistent, occasionally contradictory, belief system of Josef K., the narrator of *The Trial*. The sixth chapter's jurisprudential explorations result in an extensive new reading of this novel. By drawing on the letters of the Brentano circle and publications by Oskar Kraus, especially with regard to positive and natural law, it shows Kafka to tackle difficult issues in law, jurisprudence, criminal investigation, and procedure. The seventh chapter shows how, through the writing of "Before the Law" and "In the Penal Colony," the author deciphers his self-condemning guilt as an ethical self-contradiction. It also retrieves from his aphoristic reflections of 1917 a philosophically astute essay on the relationship between guilt, ethics, and individualism. The eighth chapter deals with the author's life from 1917 on — matters such as his illness, relationships with women, sexual and existential fears — and the majority of stories written during 1917. If the earlier work — excessively descriptive, rationalizing, transparently linear — expresses a fixation with internalized guilt, the works of this middle period address more ambiguous, even inscrutable aspects of our temporal experience and knowledge of self. They amount to resigned, spiritual, universalizing contemplations of the individual's life as journey and fate. The last chapter discusses *The Castle*, Kafka's most complex, enigmatic work. It is read along New Critical and structuralist lines

Kafka himself claimed that he found it difficult to think conceptually (F 275, 400; FE 174, 270).

[31]In "The Metamorphosis" the registry of sensory pain reflects on a debate that took place in the club in early 1907 (see the last section of chapter 1). Titorelli's discussion of types of acquittal in a criminal trial echoes Lederer's study of the U.S. juvenile court system on which he addressed the club in the spring of 1907 (Utitz to Brentano, 1 May 1907 [APNDX 5]; for details see chapter 6. B 125; L 104. F 327; FE 214. See the last two sections of chapter 2.

but, above all, against the background of the author's most important theoretical interests during his remaining years: the theological and cultural rivalry between Judaism and Christianity, the parasitical connection between religion and prejudice, the dynamics of Jewish assimilation and Zionism, as well as the Jews' threatened legal equality under the increasing anti-Semitic pressures during and after the Great War.

The interpenetration of reconstructed explanatory discourses familiar to Kafka with critical readings of his fiction departs from the established methods, such as the biographical interpretation, the New Criticism, and recent poststructuralist readings. This last method, for instance, casts suspicions on the explanatory roles of individual (and certainly, transcendental) consciousness and of propositional, referential language. What I am proposing instead is that paradigms of perception, consciousness, referential and propositional knowledge, positive law, natural law, and ethics remain central to an understanding of Kafka's work. This view does not preclude that any of his textual networks of metaphorical and symbolic meanings may disclose paradoxical features within such paradigms. By reflecting, and playing on, modern philosophical explanations of mind and language, law and moral value, Kafka's fiction expands our view of literary modernism. Furthermore, due to its linguistic and conceptual complexness and ambiguity, it enriches our understanding of literary truth.

1: Perception and Narrative Description

KAFKA'S INTEREST IN PHYSIOLOGICAL psychology partly accounts for his early work's intense formal experimentation and its development toward a monoperspectival point of view. Echoes of important psychological paradigms reverberate through the first decade of his writing: thought association, phenomenalist perception, the interdependence of sensory threshold and receptivity, pain as a type of perception. The common turn-of-the-century epistemological framework for these kinds of psychological paradigms was the assumption of (Cartesian) psychophysical dualism. The self can be certain only about its own thoughts and the impingements of sensory qualities (such as color) and feelings (such as pain), because these phenomena are exactly as they are thought, seen, or felt. They are logically independent of any external (physical, sense-perceptible) object they might be caused by or attributed to. The psychologists who shared this framework agreed that both kinds of objects should be studied: the subjective phenomena just listed and, dualist skepticism notwithstanding, the physical world. Those who studied the subjective phenomena insisted — although they claimed that they also somehow produced knowledge about physical things — on the subjective, perspectival, and limiting (privative) origin of that knowledge. They were aware that the perception of a sense-perceptible thing can be mistaken, can be an illusion or hallucination. Those who studied the physical world insisted that, despite the subjective nature of sensory phenomena and individual inferences, they produced objective knowledge of that world.

Association-based Narration

For some time into his writing career Kafka was intrigued with a model of the mind that predated the turn-of-the-century revolution in psychology. The second half of Gustav Lindner and Franz Lukas's *Textbook of Psychology*, which was used in Kafka's high-school philosophy class, dealt with ideas (representations), memory, and feelings. It was a rather feeble revision by

Lukas[1] of the textbook's previous version that had been written by Lindner. By staying close to Lindner's outmoded Herbartian psychology, Lukas perpetuated the notion of the mind's passive, association-bound nature. Johann Herbart had taught that ideas compete with one another for a place in consciousness which has only limited space for them. By ideas he meant experienced or reproduced sensations and intuitions (ostensive, sense-derived representations) as well as concepts. Kafka used the Herbartian (originally Lockean) term *narrowness of consciousness* as late as 1920.[2] Herbart called the admission of new ideas into consciousness through assimilation, as well as the conscious reproduction of repressed ideas, *apperception*. Ideas continually strive to ascend to and remain suspended in conscious awareness while squeezing all others below the threshold into the apperceptive mass, the collection of impeded ideas in the unconscious mind. Repressed ideas may regain strength, push through the threshold, and associate with and assimilate some newly received idea. Apperception keeps the constant struggle among accumulated as well as new ideas — their combining and reinforcing, counteracting and impeding — in a state of equilibrium. The high-school textbook, offering variations on these themes, distinguishes between a new idea's unaltered (perception) and altered (apperception) absorption into consciousness. Apperception entrenches knowledge, which always outweighs new information and sometimes prevents its acknowledgment.[3]

Herbartian psychology provided a rich reservoir of imagery for Kafka's work. In "The Judgment," for instance, Georg Bendemann makes it a practice in his occasional letters to his friend who lives in voluntary exile in St. Petersburg not to change what the friend remembers about their hometown: "So Georg confined himself to giving his friend unimportant items of gossip such as [accumulate] at random in the memory when one is idly thinking things over .... All he desired was to leave undisturbed the idea of the hometown

[1]Gustav A. Lindner and Franz Lukas, *Lehrbuch der Psychologie* (Vienna: Gerold, 1900). This revision, in fact, was authored by Lukas alone (cf. *Allgemeine deutsche Bibliographie*, vol. 51 [Leipzig: Duncker & Humblot, 1906] 739). The more substantial reworking of the first part draws on standard works in physiology such as *Handbuch der Physiologie*, ed. Ludimar Hermann, 6 vols., 12 parts (Leipzig: Vogel, 1879–83) and Wilhelm Wundt, *Grundzüge der physiologischen Psychologie*, 2nd ed., 2 vols. (Leipzig: Engelmann, 1880).

[2]*Enge des Bewußtseins* (BK 220; the English translation of this phrase ["question of conscience" - GW 273] is based on an earlier, mistaken reading of this passage). Cf. "The law of the narrowness of our consciousness has inexorable force" (Hugo Bergmann, "Über Bücher und über das Lesen," *Herder-Blätter* [J. G. Herder Vereinigung, Prague] 1.1 (1911–12): 5. Bergmann did not consider Herbart "old hat"; he was interested in editing his work (*Tagebücher und Briefe* 1: 42).

[3]Johann F. Herbart, *Sämtliche Werke*, ed. G. Hartenstein, 12 vols. (Leipzig: Voss, 1850–52) 5: 15–21; 6: 188–205. Lindner and Lukas, *Lehrbuch* 91–94 (APNDX 8).

which his friend must have built up." The information he gives is insignificant to the point of being misleading; it reinforces the friend's well-entrenched but outdated knowledge about the place. In another scene the father tries to cow his son with declarations of regained strength that echo another Herbartian notion: ideas continually strive to rise up into consciousness through bonding with sympathetic others and suppressing and dividing competing ones: "I am still much the stronger of us two. All by myself I might have had to give way, but your mother has given me so much of her strength [and I have] established a fine connection with your friend .... Just take your bride on your arm and try getting in my way! I'll sweep her from your very side, you don't know how!"[4] Upon its completion, Kafka wrote that for him ."The Judgment" appeared connected to Freud. Despite his extensive exposure to Brentanoan psychology, which denies unconscious mental events, Kafka may well have continued to find Herbart's psychology convincing to the degree that it assumed an unconscious part of the mind, thus accommodating Freud's view. Furthermore, the tendency of so many of his fictional characters, such as Gregor Samsa after his metamorphosis, to remind themselves in the face of uncertainty or adverse feelings "that cool reflection, the coolest possible, was much better than desperate resolves," may have something to do with Herbart's view that it is always within a person's intellectual powers to return to a state of mental balance. Even as late as 1920, a distinctly Herbartian metaphor crops up in Kafka's thought. In a diarylike note he recalls sitting on a Prague hillside as a young man reviewing his wishes for the future. The most alluring wish was to gain a perspective on life in such a way that it, "while still retaining its full-bodied rise and fall, would simultaneously be recognized no less clearly as a nothing, a dream, a dim hovering." The picture of life's descent, ascent, and suspension mirrors Herbart's metaphor for describing the mind's internal dynamic.[5]

Implicitly following the tradition from Aristotle to Locke, Hume, Herbart, and Mill, Kafka's high-school textbook distinguishes two basic types of associations which accumulate over time into series. The temporal contiguity (simultaneity) in the acquisition of ideas, as well as the spatial contiguity of their

---

[4]CS 79; "[Vorfälle] wie sie sich, wenn man ... nachdenkt, in der Erinnerung ungeordnet aufhäufen. Er wollte nichts anderes, als die Vorstellung ungestört lassen, die sich der Freund von der Heimatstadt ... wohl gemacht [hatte]" (E 25). *Aufhäufen* echoes the *apperceptive mass*. CS 86; "Allein hätte ich vielleicht zurückweichen müssen, aber so hat mir die Mutter ihre Kraft abgegeben, mit deinem Freund habe ich mich herrlich verbunden" (E 31).

[5]T 184; D 1: 276. CS 93; E 60. GW 267; "[Eine Ansicht,] in der das Leben zwar sein schweres Fallen und Steigen bewahre, aber gleichzeitig ... als ein Schweben erkannt werde" (BK 217–18). Herbart, *Werke* 6: 74–75. The images of rising and falling occur throughout Kafka's early works, especially in "Children on a Country Road" (CS 379; E 7).

referents, constitute the causal type of association. The similarity and contrast
between ideas constitute the logical type. Due to its narrowness, consciousness
can contain only a single idea at a given moment. Memory stores ideas passing through consciousness in serial patterns in accordance with the two associative mechanisms. Thus, any idea can be reproduced in consciousness by
hitting on the starting point of the respective series and scanning it. Kafka
occasionally uses these techniques of association, but the claim that they determine all aspects of plot advancement in his fictions cannot be supported.[6] The
novel *Amerika* (1912) assembles more association-based passages than any
other of his works but, curiously, often lets them run into dead ends. Just
before Karl Roßmann's disembarkation in New York, the walking stick of an
acquaintance reminds him that he has left his umbrella (a sort of walking stick)
below deck, so he goes downstairs to recover it. Because of a barred short cut,
he attempts to retrace a longer passageway which he has used only once or
twice before. He loses his way and chances to stop at the door of a small
cabin, where he makes the acquaintance of a stoker. The series of contiguous
associations (retraced steps and familiar objects along the way), triggered by
the sight of a walking stick, does not lead to the recovery of his umbrella but
to his chancing to stop. The umbrella is the first in the series of the things
Karl keeps acquiring and losing. The trunk his father gave him or a photo-
graph of his parents first connect him with, then, when lost, disconnect him
from his past. They are, like the feelings regarding his seduction by the maid,
removed into a contiguously, serially ordered "vanishing past."[7]

In the following two passages Kafka ironically inverts the two association
mechanisms sketched above, thus rendering them pointless. The first presents
an association-relation based in similarity. The writing desk in his uncle's
house is equipped with a crank and a rotary mechanism to move, enlarge, or
make smaller its many compartments: "By turning a handle you could produce
the most complicated combinations ... the transformation took place slowly or
at delirious speed according to the rate at which you wound the thing round."
The mechanism reminds Karl of a crank-operated Christmas panorama in his
hometown: "[He had been] closely comparing the movement of the handle,
which was turned by an old man, with changes in the scene, the jerky advance
of the Three Holy Kings, the shining out of the Star." The trigger for Karl's
associative chain is the revolving device which determines the changes in both

---

[6]Lindner and Lukas, *Lehrbuch* 79–84; 85–86 (APNDX 9). Jürgen Kobs, *Kafka:
Untersuchungen zu Bewußtsein und Sprache seiner Gestalten*, ed. Ursula Brech [Bad
Homburg: Athenäum, 1970] 267.

[7]A 27; "Im Gedränge einer immer mehr zurückgestoßenen Vergangenheit" (V 29).
Since the novel is told from Karl's point of view, his stopping (*stocken* - V 10)
could conceivably be triggered, through association, by his search for his walking
stick (*Stock*).

writing desk and Christmas panorama according to the speed at which it is operated. Karl then remembers that he used to point out to his mother various changes in the panorama, and he concludes his train of recollections with the following thought: "The desk was certainly not made merely to remind him of such things, yet in the history of its invention there probably existed some vague connection similar to that in Karl's memory."[8] In other words, since the writing desk's revolving device admittedly had not been built to evoke memories of his past, Karl contrives a historical connection between them: the invention of the mechanical panorama serves as a remote cause for the invention of the writing-desk mechanism. Karl thus converts a logical into a causal-spatial association-relation.

When he later visits Mr. Pollunder's home on Long Island, Karl wants to return to his uncle's house in Manhattan. He recalls the images which entered his mind on his journey to Long Island in terms of their spatial connectedness, though in reverse order of their acquisition. Karl sees their historical connection as something stringent and immutable: "The road leading to his uncle through that glass door, down the steps, through the avenue, along the country roads, through the suburbs to the great main street where his uncle's house was, seemed to him a strictly ordered whole." The failure to retrace a series of associations to its origin (the place where Karl lost his umbrella) as well as the inverse applications of the two types of associations indicate that Kafka was not aiming to construct fiction out of ever more complex associative (metonymic) concatenations. Karl's insight about the stoker's unstructured, confused complaint before the captain is a reflection of Kafka's own choice as an author: "Everything demanded haste, clarity, exact statement; and what was the stoker doing? ... from all points of the compass complaints about Schubal streamed into his head ... all he could produce for the Captain was a wretched farrago in which everything was lumped together."[9] As the following sections will illustrate, Kafka prevents his narratives, unlike that of the stoker, from becoming a mere series of associations. Instead he aims at devising precise descriptions of thoughts, character dispositions, and actions, as well as varying cognitive strategies to capture a complex reality.

---

[8] A 41; "Man konnte durch Drehen an der Kurbel die verschiedensten Umstellungen [erreichen] ... alles ging, je nachdem man die Kurbel drehte, langsam oder unsinnig rasch vor sich" (V 39). A 41; "[Er hatte] die Kurbeldrehung ... mit den Wirkungen im Krippenspiel verglichen, mit dem stockenden Vorwärtskommen der Heiligen Drei Könige" (V 39). A 42; "In der Geschichte der Erfindungen bestand wohl ein ähnlich undeutlicher Zusammenhang wie in Karls Erinnerungen" (V 39).

[9] A 82; "[Der Weg] durch die Glastüre, über die Treppe, durch die Allee, über die Landstraßen ... erschien ihm als etwas streng zusammengehöriges" (V 71). A 17; "Aus allen Himmelsrichtungen strömten ihm Klagen über Schubal zu ... aber was er dem Kapitän vorzeigen konnte, war nur ein trauriges Durcheinanderstrudeln aller insgesamt" (V 20–21).

Sensory Physiology and Perception

The opening chapters of Kafka's psychology textbook, more thoroughly revised than the later ones, offered up-to-date information on the physiology of the nervous system, sensations (sensory stimuli), and perception. The explanations of psychophysical interaction — the causal connection between mind and body despite their underlying duality — ran roughly as follows: the centripetal nerve fibers enable mechanical, chemical, or electromagnetic stimuli received by the body's peripheral nerve endings (receptors) to be transformed into electrical energy and to travel to the spinal cord and brain. There they create sensory phenomena, in other words, conscious sensations and intuitions (ostensive representations). In turn, the centrifugal nerve fibers transmit electrical impulses from the brain to the muscles, where they generate contractions and bodily movements. Since we are able to sense our muscle states internally, we become aware of our bodily movements before, or even without, experiencing them through our external senses. The textbook further taught, following Helmholtz, that our knowledge of the world is completely inferential. Sensory qualities do not copy external things but rather substitute as constant signs for them. Sensory qualities (colors, sounds, tastes) are merely phenomenal; they only appear to us as what they are due to the specific makeup of our sense organs. In actuality, they are something entirely different — electromagnetic fields, light or sound waves, or chemical processes. We can make everyday inferences about things and their properties, however, by projecting sensory qualities onto specific places inside or outside the body. For instance, cutaneous sensations help to generate our awareness of space: when a knife edge or metal plate touches our skin, we also sense a spatial extension of the skin area being touched. Ultimately, spatiality results from our projections onto the things that appear to induce such spatial sensations. Above all, the textbook discusses inferences in the field of optics. For instance, the muscles attached to the eyeball turn it in such a way that the light reflected from the object searched for is received in the optimum area of the retina. They also flatten or thicken the lens to focus it on the chosen object. These muscle contractions are sensed internally, memorized, and permanently associated with locations in the two-dimensional field of vision and, by extension, in the depth of visual field which becomes related to our tactile perceptions.[10]

Kafka's developing cognitive and linguistic practices will go far beyond this sensory model of knowledge. His early fragments and the shorter stories, up to the time of "The Metamorphosis" (1912), are replete with references to

[10]Lindner and Lukas, *Lehrbuch* 16, 53, 61 (APNDX 10); 62–71 (APNDX 11).

such physiological insights. For instance, the stimulations of retinal points and their concomitant evocations (via memory traces) of external eye movements are complemented by mental images of the moving (touching) hand. Kafka approaches this insight in the vignette "On the Tram," published in 1908: "[A girl] is so distinct to me as if I had run my hands over her ... her nose, slightly pinched at the sides, has a broad round tip .... Her small ear is close-set, but since I am near her I can see the whole ridge of the whorl of her right ear."[11] Many passages of the novel fragment "Wedding Preparations in the Country" (1907) give illustrations of a fully developed three-dimensional optical sense. One describes, as if mimicking an experiment in the psychology of perception, how the focus of vision is moved along with its intended object:

As soon as the carriage had passed Raban, some bar blocked the view of the near horse drawing the carriage; then some coachman — wearing a big top hat — on an unusually high box was moved across in front of the ladies — this was now much farther on — then their carriage drove around the corner of a small house that now became strikingly noticeable .... Raban followed it with his gaze, his head lowered, resting the handle of his umbrella on his shoulder to see better.[12]

Three further examples (the last one from 1916) demonstrate an interest in rendering visual depth linguistically: "Through the windowpane of a ground-floor café, close to the window, gentlemen could be seen sitting .... Beyond these window tables all the furniture and equipment in the large restaurant were hidden by the customers." "The official had put his right hand on his hip, and through the triangle formed by the arm and the body Raban saw the girl." "Through the vacant window and door openings of a café one could see two men quite at the back drinking their wine. The proprietor was sitting at a table in front." The textbook also offers a physiological explanation of visual and auditory hallucinations, for example, voices of people who are not present.[13] The middle section of "Description of a Struggle" (1904–1906), enti-

[11]See Lindner and Lukas, *Lehrbuch* 70–71. Wundt, *Physiologische Psychologie* 2: 296. CS 388–89; "[Ein Mädchen] erscheint mir so deutlich, als ob ich sie betastet hätte ... [ich sehe] den ganzen Rücken der rechten Ohrmuschel" (E 16).

[12]CS 57; "Gleich als der Wagen an Raban vorüber war, verstellte irgendeine Stange den Anblick des Handpferdes dieses Wagens, dann wurde irgendein Kutscher ... vor die Damen geschoben" (E 237).

[13]CS 60; "Sah man eng beim Fenster ... Herren sitzen .... Hinter diesen Fenstertischen war ... jedes Möbel und Gerät durch die Gäste verdeckt" (E 239). CS 68; "Durch das Dreieck, das zwischen dem Arm und dem Körper entstand, sah Raban das Mädchen" (E 246). CS 226; E 285. Lindner and Lukas, *Lehrbuch* 76 (APNDX 12).

tled "Diversions," deals with a series of hallucinatory experiences. One episode reverses the relation between one's body (which is always within reach) and the depth of visual field by having the body expand beyond it: "Meanwhile the banks of the river stretched beyond all bounds, and yet with the palm of my hand I touched the metal of a signpost which gleamed minutely in the far distance ... my impossible legs lay over the wooded mountains .... They grew and grew! They already reached into the space that no longer owned any landscape, for some time their length had gone beyond my field of vision." Another scene describes a landscape as if projected onto a two-dimensional plane, since everything in it appears equidistant from the eye. The narrator visualizes a faraway mountain but sees himself on that mountain: "I caused to rise an enormously high mountain whose plateau, overgrown with brushwood, bordered on the sky ... I, as a small bird on a twig of those distant scrubby bushes, forgot to let the moon come up."[14] The idea of projecting objects onto, as it were, a two-dimensional plane in front of the eye or inside it (on the retina) appears linked to another feature of the early works, allusions to phenomenalist research amassed by late-nineteenth-century experimental psychology.

The Phenomenalist Basis of Perception

Phenomenalist research stresses the subjective aspects — the phenomenal qualities — in perception that are not necessarily attributable to the external objects. In 1905 Josef Eisenmeier published his thesis for certification as academic lecturer on Ewald Hering's treatment of the brightness and darkness of colors. Hering, professor of physiology in Prague until 1895, was famous for his elaborate studies of vision. He conducted them not with respect to the perceived external objects but in terms of their phenomenal or mental representedness, their being seen. The spatial proportions of seen things, for instance, can be very different from those of the corresponding real things. The moon or sun are seen as small flat disks not much farther away than the most distant mountain, although we know them actually to be spherical and in outer space. When we look at a piece of white cardboard with a zigzag-edged hole, positioned over a dark open box, we see either a three-dimensional hole or a

---

[14]CS 46; "[Ich berührte] das Eisen eines in der Entfernung winzigen Wegzeigers mit der Fläche meiner Hand ... meine unmöglichen Beine lagen über den bewaldeten Bergen ...! Schon ragten sie in den Raum der keine Landschaft mehr besaß, längst schon reichte ihre Länge aus der Sehschärfe meiner Augen" (K 126-28). CS 22; "Ziemlich weit meiner Straße gegenüber ... ließ ich einen hohen Berg aufstehn, dessen Höhe mit Buschwerk bewachsen an den Himmel grenzte... [ich schaukelte] als ein kleiner Vogel auf den Ruten dieser entfernten struppigen Sträucher" (K 48).

black patch on the cardboard; yet the retinal image causing both appearances is the same. The blurred retinal impression of a fly in close proximity to our eyes may at first blush (re)produce the image of a bird at a distance — a mere buzzing sound turns it instantly into the image of a fly. Utitz gave expression to the phenomenalist emphasis Hering had imparted to Brentano and his school: "The psychologist deals only with the 'seen things,' not with what corresponds to the sense-perceptible qualities in reality. His attention is focused on what we 'experience,' what occurs in our consciousness."[15] Passages in "Description" suggest that Kafka was aware of the phenomenalist distinction between real and seen things. He describes the moon as lying behind a mountain and a cloud as lying in front of the sun. The evening sun appears flat and illuminates the objects in its seeming proximity at the horizon: "And now the evening sun's [flat shine] broke forth from behind the rims of the great cloud and illuminated the hills and mountains [at the edge of the field of vision], while the river and the region beneath the cloud lay in an uncertain light." In "Wedding Preparations," tram cars nearby are big, those further away blurred: "Electric tramcars moved past, huge and very close; others, vaguely visible, stood motionless far away in the streets." In "Description," the supplicant expresses the insight that things are known only as appearing, not as actual: "I grasp the things around me only in transitory ideas ... I have a great desire to see what they are like before they appear to me."[16]

Among Hering's most influential work was the analysis of color vision. He demonstrated, for instance, that brightness and darkness of colors have nothing to do either with the presence or absence of light or with admixtures of white and black but are indigenous properties in their own right (i.e. yellow is brighter than blue, etc.). He defined black as a positive color (instead of as mere absence of light), equal to the other two neutral colors (white, gray). Black reaches its highest degree of saturation (its full darkness) when contrasted with something white or bright — that is, when the retina is partly lit. Brentano and his school were committed to this view. In his lecture course on

---

[15]Josef Eisenmeier, *Untersuchungen zur Helligkeitsfrage* (Halle: Niemeyer, 1905). Ewald Hering, "Der Raumsinn und die Bewegungen des Auges," *Handbuch der Physiologie*, ed. L. Hermann, 3.1: 343–45; 573–74; 570. Eisenmeier received this handbook in compensation for secretarial services to the nearly blind Brentano (Marty to Brentano, 14 Jan. 1903). Emil Utitz, *Grundzüge der ästhetischen Farbenlehre* (Stuttgart: Enke, 1908) 1 (APNDX 13).

[16]CS 28; "Da brach aus den Rändern der großen Wolke der flache Schein der abendlichen Sonne ... an der Grenze des Gesichtskreises" (K 66). CS 58; "Wagen der elektrischen Straßenbahn fuhren groß in der Nähe vorüber, andere standen weit in den Straßen undeutlich still" (E 238). "Ich erfasse nämlich die Dinge um mich nur in so hinfälligen Vorstellungen .... Immer, lieber Herr, habe ich eine so quälende Lust, die Dinge so zu sehen, wie sie sich geben mögen, ehe sie sich mir zeigen" (K 90). The English translation (CS) does not include this last passage.

descriptive psychology (which Kafka took in 1902) Marty said: "If you place a white rectangle on a black surface, you will notice immediately that around its edge the black appears especially saturated, and vice versa."[17] In his thesis for accreditation as academic lecturer in philosophy, Eisenmeier defended Hering's analysis of black. He subsequently summarized it in a review of Hering's new book on physiological optics as follows: "A saturated black occurs only if at the same time other and especially adjacent areas of the field of vision appear white or grey; the more, up to a certain limit, the rest of the visual field is lit, the more saturated the black gets."[18]

In "Wedding Preparations" and other works descriptions occur that suggest that Kafka was familiar with the fact that a contrasting white or bright color or light source creates a saturation condition for black. Raban, inside a horse-drawn bus at night, lights a candle, which makes the walls and windows appear washed in black: "It was bright enough, the darkness outside made it appear as though the omnibus had black distempered walls and no glass in the windows." Another passage describes shops, with their lights already turned on, around a city square at dusk. The monument in its center is made somewhat darker "by the light around the edge." Similarly, "a statue of a saint stood out in black relief only because of the light from a [small] shop." A similar observation crops up in *The Trial*, where a single candle in one area of the cathedral makes everything around it look darker: "It was lovely to look at, but quite inadequate for illuminating the altarpieces ... it actually increased the darkness." Hering also taught that three-dimensional vision is not learned but is native to human perception, and that even darkness (the absence of light) is seen as something three-dimensional or material that covers the visual object, actually fills the space between it and the eye.[19] In the following passage from "Description" the narrator describes the afterimage of a perception (and along with it, darkness) as spatial: "Perhaps it was that short quiet lull between night and day ... when everything ... disappears; we remain

[17]Franz Brentano, *Untersuchungen zur Sinnespsychologie* (Leipzig: Duncker & Humblot, 1907) 10. Eisenmeier, Utitz and Bergmann were familiar with this book since they helped edit it. "Wenn man auf einen schwarzen Grund ein weißes Quadrat legt, so bemerkt man sofort, daß am Rande das Schwarz besonders intensiv auftritt, ebenso umgekehrt" (MA 242).

[18]Eisenmeier, *Untersuchungen zur Helligkeitsfrage* 13–14. Eisenmeier, rev. of *Physiologische Optik*, by Ewald Hering (*Handbuch der gesamten Augenheilkunde*, ed. A. K. Graefe and Th. Saemisch, vol. 3, pt. 1), *Deutsche Arbeit* 5 (1905–1906): 156.

[19]CS 69; "Es war genügend hell, die Dunkelheit draußen machte, daß man schwarzgetünchte Omnibuswände ohne Scheiben sah" (E 246). CS 56; "Durch das Licht am Rande etwas verdunkelt" (E 236). CS 70; "Eine Heiligenstatue trat nur durch das Licht eines Kramladens schwarz hervor" (E 248). TR 204; P 175. Hering, "Der Raumsinn" 573 (APNDX 14).

alone, our bodies bent, then look around but no longer see anything ... we cling to the memory that a certain distance from us stand houses with roofs and with fortunately angular chimneys down which the darkness flows through garrets into various rooms." The motif of darkness as something three-dimensional is taken up again in *The Trial*. Josef K. walks up to the great pulpit and examines it: "the carving of the stonework was very carefully wrought, the deep caverns of darkness among and behind the foliage looked as if caught and imprisoned there."[20] It becomes apparent from examples such as these that Kafka's interest in the phenomenalist explanation of visual perception contributed to the precision of his fictional descriptions. In "Wedding Preparations" a portrayal of a cityscape scrupulously duplicates what meets the eye from a distance: "On the side of the square along which they were walking, there was an uninterrupted row of houses, from the corners of which two — at first widely distant — rows of houses extended into the indiscernible distance in which they seemed to unite." In *Amerika* Karl Roßmann, upon entering the passenger steamer's pay-office, registers the various persons present. An intermittent movement of the captain's interlocutor discloses to him part of a row of decorations on the captain's chest. Through the distant window he sees large ships and smaller boats between them. After he crosses the room to the window he is able to see the interlocutor's red face, "which was now in his line of vision for the first time," as well as the smaller boats that are close by. The novel's careful attention to the character's perceptual point of view establishes a physiological basis for its unilateral narrative perspective. Karl's tale transmits nothing that has not first appeared within his perceptual field.[21]

Sensory Reception of Novelty and Beauty

Herbart taught that the constant struggle among accumulated as well as new ideas generates feelings of pleasure and displeasure in the apperceiving consciousness. When an idea newly entering into consciousness is repressed, displeasure arises in proportion to the idea's vividness. Pleasure derives from

---

[20]CS 43; "In gewissem Abstand von uns [stehn Häuser] mit Dächern und ... Schornsteinen, durch die das Dunkel in die Häuser fließt, durch die Dachkammern in die verschiedenartigen Zimmer" (K 112). TR 205; "Das tiefe Dunkel zwischen dem Laubwerk und hinter ihm schien wie eingefangen und festgehalten" (P 176).

[21]CS 60; "Auf der Seite des Platzes, an der entlang sie weitergingen, stand ein ununterbrochener Häuserzug, von dessen Ecken aus zwei voneinander zuerst weit entfernte Häuserreihen in die unkenntliche Ferne rückten, in der sie sich zu vereinigen schienen" (E 239). V 17; A 12–13. A 14; V 18.

an idea's release and unimpeded ascent into consciousness. As mentioned
earlier, in 1906 Max Brod used the Herbartian tradition as a springboard for
an essay on beauty and aesthetic feeling. Since Kafka raised objections to it,
a brief outline of Brod's treatise,[22] and of the nineteenth-century aesthetic
tradition from which it emerges, appears in order. Brod modifies Herbart's
general model of feelings to suit his own idiosyncratic aesthetics. He agrees
that the assimilation of new ideas upsets the balance within the apperceptive
mass. Modifying Herbart, he claims that apperception generates pleasure or
displeasure according to the tolerance each individual has for this imbalance
— or rather for novelty. Some intellects are geared toward routine: the more
novel their sensory input, the greater their displeasure; the more often something has been experienced before, the greater their pleasure. Others, however, experience pleasure from new and unusual ideas. Thus, for each person
there is a specific threshold of novelty in apperception which affords him or
her the greatest pleasure. In a further, reductionist move, Brod defines pleasure and displeasure as exclusively aesthetic feelings, ascribing to the things
that elicit them the property of beauty or ugliness. Beautiful is anything that
enables a person to apperceive it with a feeling of pleasure. In each person the
"aesthetic zone," the area between the lowest and highest amount of novelty
pleasurably apperceived,[23] takes a specific position relative to degrees of
artistic novelty. These degrees are not based in the historical development of
the arts but in individual dispositions of reception that change even within each
individual. For example, a person familiar with music only up to Haydn will
experience an extremely high and thus unpleasant degree of novelty when
listening to Gustav Mahler or Richard Strauß, whereas someone who has
learned to appreciate Richard Wagner would be much more disposed to enjoy
these two contemporary composers. It is clear that Brod's subjectivism provides objective criteria neither for describing changes in literary or music
history such as modernism nor for beauty. All artistic styles and aesthetic
values are of equal worth or indifferent.[24]

[22]Herbart, *Werke* 5: 32, 70–78, 333; 6: 73–80. Brod, "Zur Ästhetik," *Die Gegenwart* (17 Feb. 1906): 102–104; (24 Feb. 1906): 118–19. Brod quotes the Herbartian
Wilhelm F. Volkmann, *Grundriß der Psychologie* (Halle: Fricke, 1856) 124.

[23]In his story "Tod den Toten" Brod introduces a proviso to this concept: "What is
new can never make an aesthetic impression on us. By that I mean, what is completely new: since it finds nothing in our soul to attach itself to …. When it finds
within us something similar to itself, it will nestle against us …. The apperception
completes itself, and only as long as this happens, the feeling of pleasure lasts"
(Brod, *Tod den Toten: Novellen des Indifferenten (1902–1906)* [Berlin: Juncker,
1906] 24).

[24]Brod's "indifferentism" (relativism) regarding values was derived from Schopenhauer (Margarita Pazi, *Max Brod: Werk und Persönlichkeit* [Bonn: Bouvier, 1970]
25–39). In "Zur Ästhetik" Brod also insists, with Schopenhauer, that aesthetic

Brod's radically individualist aesthetics was due not only to his relativism and eager experimentation with new poetic themes and structure during his early years as a writer but also to the widespread contemporary (though less relativist) practice of analyzing beauty and ugliness in terms of the two feelings to which they presumably give rise. In mid-nineteenth-century Germany a contest was waged between, on the one hand, the Herbartian (formalist or intellectualist) theory of aesthetic feeling — which ignores the representational content of ideas in favor of their dynamic interaction — and the Hegel-school's historicist emphasis on an artwork's representational materiality, on the other. Gustav Fechner proposed to resolve this conflict through an empirical-psychological aesthetics which based appreciation of art on both its representational aspects and the dynamic within the individual psyche. Aesthetic pleasure results from both a *direct factor* — the artwork's formal qualities by way of ideas presented to consciousness — and an *associative factor* — the percepts' or ideas' associations with (analogies to) one's past experiences and imaginary life. Fechner's investigations, along with the growing interest in sensory physiology and psychology, the Brentano school's stress on phenomenological description, and the intense study of aesthetic empathy were important to turn-of-the-century psychological aesthetics.[25] Brod's essay represented a throwback to a merely formalist (Herbartian) position because it effectively emptied associations and experience of their representational content, changing them into a criterion for tolerance toward novelty.

Later, Kafka will gain greater awareness that his narratives contribute to his generation's project of reshaping a literary tradition. In this early response he bases his critique of Brod's reductionist notions on physiological considerations. For one, tolerance toward novelty as the primary aesthetic criterion is relativist because the psychological makeup of each individual, as Brod readily admits, changes all the time. Furthermore, Brod does not account for those things that are pleasing or displeasing for other than aesthetic reasons. Although Kafka first considers pleasure the satisfaction of intellectual inquisitiveness (an Aristotelian notion), he soon links it to the physiological state of freshness. Tolerance is less a disposition toward psychological content than the physiological condition of being rested, attentive, ready for activity and new experience; it is the opposite of fatigue and habituation. Thus, lack of tolerance is not merely an opposition to novelty but occurs, Kafka states, in all mental or physical activities, such as learning, mountain climbing, and eating. The second part of his text refers to Fechner's particular view, an updated statement of Herbart's concept of the mind's threshold that ideas need to rise

appreciation is divorced from the will and desire.

[25]Gustav Th. Fechner, *Vorschule der Ästhetik*, 2 vols. (Leipzig: Breitkopf & Härtel, 1876) 1: 86–183. Ernst Meumann, *Einführung in die Ästhetik der Gegenwart* (Leipzig: Quelle & Meyer, 1908) 40–79 ("Die Psychologie des ästhetischen Gefallens").

above to become conscious. Fechner empirically demonstrated that sensory impressions and their concomitant feelings require a minimal (noticeable) intensity to enter into consciousness. He applied this concept to aesthetics and introduced the term *aesthetic threshold,* which Kafka is using here as well.[26] Kafka then directly refers to Fechner's theorem that a dulling of the senses occurs when two pleasurable sensations follow each other too closely.[27] Bergmann, discussing Fechner, points out that strong stimuli, such as loud noises, raise the physiological threshold through an increase in dulling: "The quickening decrease in sensory input due to sharply increasing stimulation protects us. The threshold phenomenon of consciousness affords us the opportunity for rest, which we could not enjoy if every stimulus could rush at us." Kafka's late story, "A Hunger Artist," explains the fading of the spectators' interest in the hunger artist — at a time when public fasting had gone into a steep decline — as a kind of mental fatigue, a falling below the threshold of attention: "[The hunger artist] was only an impediment on the way to the menagerie. A small impediment, to be sure, one that grew steadily less. People grew familiar with the strange idea that they could be expected, in times like these, to take an interest in a hunger artist, and with this familiarity the verdict went out against him."[28] As will be shown shortly, the claims Kafka and his friends made about the relativity of receptiveness and dulling, attention and fatigue take on greater importance when applied to more complex forms of cognition and to consciousness.

[26]Brod discovered Kafka's incidental text among his own papers and published it in his *Der Prager Kreis* (Stuttgart: Kohlhammer, 1966) 94–95 (APNDX 15). Kafka replaces Fechner's term *ästhetische Schwelle* (threshold, limen) [*Vorschule der Ästhetik* 1: 49] with *ästhetische Kante* (aesthetic edge).

[27]Fechner, *Vorschule der Ästhetik* 2: 240–46. Kafka's phrase is: "Müdigkeit (die es eigentlich nur zur Liebhaberei der knapp vorhergehenden Zeit gibt)" (APNDX 15). He tells the fledgling art historian Pollak in 1903 that he reads Fechner (B 20; L 10). Oskar Kraus's long-standing interest in Fechner's theory of sensory threshold and dulling through physiological exhaustion (*Zur Theorie des Wertes: Eine Bentham-Studie* [Halle: Niemeyer, 1901] 44–57) may explain further why Kafka was so familiar with it.

[28]Bergmann, rev. of *Psychophysik: Historisch-kritische Studien über experimentelle Psychologie,* by Constantin Gutberlet, *Philosophische Wochenschrift* 3 (1906): 116 (APNDX 16). CS 276; "Man gewöhnte sich an die Sonderbarkeit, in den heutigen Zeiten Aufmerksamkeit für einen Hungerkünstler beanspruchen zu wollen, und mit dieser Gewöhnung war das Urteil über ihn gesprochen" (E 170).

Pleasure and Pain in "The Metamorphosis"

Kafka's psychology textbook reflected the impact late-nineteenth-century physiology had on the question of pleasure and displeasure, distinguishing three types of this pair depending on their point of origin in the body. The body as a whole experiences well-being or pain. By contrast, smell and taste locate pleasure and displeasure partly in the object being sensed and partly in the sensory organ itself (nose or tongue). Vision and hearing attribute sensory qualities and their concomitant pleasure or displeasure predominantly to the external objects that appear to project those qualities.[29] In his lecture course on descriptive psychology Marty disclaimed any interest in physiology and experimental psychology. Even though he discussed related issues, such as the internal sensing of one's own muscle contractions,[30] the central role of cutaneous sensibility for spatial perception, and the different sensitivity of spatial measurement on tongue, finger, lips, forehead, and arm, he reduced them to purely phenomenal data. The mind is aware of them — brightness, hardness, burning, cutting, or woundedness — in the form of qualities or sensations. Utitz stated that the intensity of the physical quality within one's perceptual field equals the intensity of one's sensory activity, while its lack (nondistinctness) equals the lack of such activity: "To each saturated part of the perceptual field there corresponds a saturated part within our sensory capacity. Each empty part of the perceptual field is matched by a partial privation of our senses."[31] Marty grouped the bodily feelings together with the lower sensory activities (touching, tasting, smelling) as a third sense, the *common feeling*. This multiple sense localizes its sensed qualities not so much in the outside world as within the sensing organ itself or the body as a whole. In a departure from the prevailing consensus, however, for Marty and Brentano feelings of pleasure and displeasure (or pain) are not localized in the body (as part of the common feeling), nor do they originate within the outside world. They are not

[29]Lindner and Lukas, *Lehrbuch* 128–33. They also discussed physiological and mental fatigue, dulling, and satiety.

[30]MA 36, 187. From the *Handbuch der Physiologie* (3.2: 372) Marty cites experiments with patients whose internal muscle sense was paralyzed, who could grasp objects only as long as they looked at their hands (MA 187–88). In *Amerika* the stoker's behavior could echo this: "He brought his fist several times down on the table, never taking his eyes from it while he flourished it" (A 7; V 12).

[31]MA 192–99. "Jedem Teil des erfüllten Sinnesraumes [entspricht] ein darauf bezüglicher Teil unseres Empfindens" (Utitz, rev. of *Untersuchungen zur Sinnespsychologie,* by Franz Brentano, *Philosophische Wochenschrift* 8 (1907): 389.

sensations in any direct sense but rather affective-intellectual acts of loving or hating.[32]

In early 1907 Carl Stumpf, professor in Berlin and Brentano's oldest student, published an article on sensory feelings which showed that feelings of pleasure and pain are neither diffused throughout the body, nor affective colorings of regular sensations (as the traditional theories, including Wundt's, would have it), nor mainly intellectual in origin, as Brentano and Marty held. Rather, they are themselves sense-perceptible qualities that can be localized experimentally in specific pleasure- or pain-sensing receptors and nerve fibers. Brentano immediately chided this deviation from his teachings, and Marty intoned the school's dogma that pleasure and pain are not sensory qualities but rather mental attitudes about such qualities.[33] As was to be expected, Stumpf's theory caused a debate in the philosophers' club. Bergmann probably was immediately sympathetic to this view, since he was thoroughly familiar with Helmholtz's claim that each distinct tone is assigned a specific kind of fiber of the membrane, each basic color a specific kind of optic nerve. In a letter to Brentano, Utitz became emboldened enough to agree with Stumpf that there are distinct receptors which sense pain without at the same time sensing an additional quality. Examples he gave were the pain of an infected wound and the rising body temperature yielding to the sensation of pain, neither pain depending on the concomitant sensing of other qualities.[34] A few months later Kraus sought assurances concerning the validity of Brentano's arguments against Stumpf that Brentano had been able to add to his recent book. The club members asked whether pleasure and pain are sensations or mental attitudes and, in effect, embraced Stumpf's view.[35]

Kafka's descriptions of bodily well-being and pain in "The Metamorphosis" are opposed to Brentano's and Marty's and in broad agreement with

---

[32]MA 192–213. Roderick Chisholm discusses Brentano's uncoupling of affective mental attitudes from sensory qualities (*Brentano and Intrinsic Value* [Cambridge: UP, 1986] 24–27). See also Chisholm, "Brentano's Theory of Pleasure and Pain," *Topoi* 6 (1987): 59–64.

[33]Carl Stumpf, "Über Gefühlsempfindungen," *Zeitschrift für Psychologie und Physiologie der Sinnesorgane* 44 (1907): 1–49. "Es ist eine arge Verwirrung, wenn Stumpf meint, daß Schmerz und Lust keine Gemütsbewegungen seien" ["it is a gross confusion for Stumpf to claim that pain and pleasure are not intellectual emotions"] (Brentano to Marty, 15 Jan. 1907). Marty to Brentano, 2 Feb. 1907 (APNDX 17).

[34]Bergmann, rev. of *Johannes Müllers philosophische Anschauungen*, by Karl Post, *Philosophische Wochenschrift* 2 (1906): 186–88. Utitz to Brentano, 12 Jan. 1907 (APNDX 18). Utitz soon adopted Stumpf's position publicly ("Kritische Vorbemerkungen zu einer ästhetischen Farbenlehre," *Zeitschrift für Ästhetik und allgemeine Kunstwissenschaft* 3 [1908]: 339).

[35]Kraus to Brentano, 6 Sept. 1907. Brentano, *Untersuchungen zur Sinnespsychologie* 121–25. Utitz to Brentano, 19 Oct. 1907 (APNDX 19).

Stumpf's claim about the sensory nature of pleasure and displeasure. Gregor Samsa notices an unpleasant itching on his belly, locates the spot and wants to touch it. He perceives pain as a localized sensation: "He had cut one finger a little with a knife and had still suffered pain from the wound only the day before yesterday. Am I less sensitive now? he thought." He experiences bodily pleasure as distinct from sensations of touch and temperature: "He was struck by the picture of the lady muffled in so much fur and quickly crawled up to it and pressed himself to the glass, which [stuck firmly to] and comforted his hot belly." Pain is sensory in that it is localized ("in the lower part of his body"), has a specific intensity and duration ("Gregor wanted to drag himself forward, as if this startling, incredible pain could be left behind him"), and can be discerned as hallucinatory or real ("He had felt small aches and pains ... which had proved purely imaginary"). The following scene illustrates most vividly that pain is not the same as touch, that both are raw sensations of distinct kinds: "When finally, almost wild with annoyance, he gathered his forces together and thrust out recklessly, he had miscalculated the direction and bumped heavily against the lower end of the bed, and the stinging pain he felt informed him that precisely this lower part of his body was at the moment probably the most sensitive."[36] The story's allusions to the properties of the (so-called) five senses and to Stumpf's views about bodily well-being and pain suggest that Kafka's interest in empirical physiology and its discussions in the club was geared toward developing a state-of-the-art precision in describing what one conceivably could perceive. The story's unique thoroughness in this regard helps to explain why until this day, eight decades after its conception, it leaves the reader with such strong impressions of sensory experience.

---

[36]CS 90; "Er fühlte ein leichtes Jucken ... fand die juckende Stelle" (E 57). CS 108; E 72. CS 118; "Er preßte sich an das Glas, das ihn festhielt und seinem heißen Bauch wohltat" (E 81–82). CS 98; "die Schmerzen im Unterleib" (E 64). CS 122; E 84. CS 92; E 59. CS 93; E 59.

2: Noticing, Memory, and Language in Narration

IN HIS EARLY NARRATIVES and personal writings Kafka explores cognitive procedures of increasing complexity, such as the relationships between perceptual focus and consciousness, gesture and speech, awareness and memory, the narrowness and spaciousness of consciousness. His narrators assess their perceptions, integrate them with their beliefs, preserve them in memory, and communicate them to others. In sustained reflections on these issues in diary and letters, Kafka recognizes that his narrators' cognitive performances are derived from what he, the author, personally perceives, acknowledges, believes, remembers, and tries to communicate. He probes ways of opening the narratives up to what lies beyond the characters' singular perspective, to the worlds they inhabit. Explorations by Brod and their mutual friend Felix Weltsch of the relationship between what we subjectively know and what we communicate to others help Kafka to understand the roles of reference and belief for telling a story. His early view of them as modes of perceptual-cognitive attentiveness yields to a complex linguistic one.

In his influential work on physiological psychology, Wundt criticized Herbart's theory of association and impeding and replaced it with one of attentiveness or apperception. Associationism cannot explain the dominance of certain contents over others in consciousness. Wundt believed that apperception is spontaneous, a function of the brain's "apperceptive center" — ultimately, the will — that brings one's sensations and ideas into focus and thus to full awareness, clarity, and comprehension.[1] Marty accepted the psychological role of attention, as well: "When something attracts our attention, we cease to think about what we had been thinking about." Although in 1886 he had criticized Wundt's failure to distinguish between attentiveness (deliberate focusing) and apperception (noticing, discerning judgment), his use of *apperception* in his 1902 lecture course covers both Wundt's notion of a particular experiential awareness (attentiveness) and his own stress on logically discern-

---

[1] Wundt, *Physiologische Psychologie* 2: 316; as late as 1905 Ernst Mach considered thought association a central scientific concept: *Erkenntnis und Irrtum: Skizzen zur Psychologie der Forschung* (Leipzig: Barth, 1905). Wundt, *Physiologische Psychologie* 1: 218; 2: 205–219.

ing knowledge.[2] On the one hand, apperception originates in perception, depends on attention, and is easily obstructed by physiological and mental states. On the other hand, in contrast to perception as a mere awareness of something phenomenally or physically appearing, apperception is the conscious discernment and explicit acknowledgment of the percept.[3] A vignette in "Wedding Preparations" indicates that consciousness consists of sequences of events — for instance, of attention, focusing, perception, discernment, remembering, redirection of attention, forgetting: "He looked down on a little girl's hat, which was made of plaited red straw and had a little green wreath on the wavy brim. He went on remembering this even when he was in the street, which went slightly uphill in the direction he wished to follow. Then he forgot it, for now he had to exert himself a little." In another passage the task of counting change and putting it away is temporarily interrupted by incidental perceptions and apperceptions: "Raban took the money that he had received from the cashier out of his waistcoat pocket and counted it over. He held up each coin firmly between thumb and forefinger for a long time and also twisted it this way and that on the inner surface of his thumb with the tip of his forefinger. He looked for a long time at the Emperor's image, then he was struck by the laurel wreath .... At last he found the sum was correct and put the money into a big black purse."[4]

Apperception is hampered by various physiological and mental states. Of these, the most obvious are sleep and dreams. Waking states, however, such as disinterest, boredom, satiety, affects, prejudice, lack of concentration and practice, distraction by competing perceptions, excessive narrowness of consciousness, and mental and physical (especially the central nervous system's) fatigue, also disrupt apperception. Many of Kafka's works of fiction offer some observation concerning the dynamics of apperception and fatigue. Since the narrator of "Description" occasionally displays a mysterious power to change his physical environment by merely imagining (apperceiving) such changes, fatigue will make things vanish: "I felt overcome by an intense drowsiness caused, I assumed, by the [exertions of the day which, I admit, I could no longer remember]. I wandered on for a while with closed eyes,

[2]"[Die Folge ist], daß man von etwas anderem, womit man sich beschäftigte, abgezogen wird, nicht mehr daran denkt" (MA 33). Marty, *Gesammelte Schriften,* ed. Josef Eisenmeier, Alfred Kastil, and Oskar Kraus, 2 vols., each vol. in 2 parts (Halle: Niemeyer, 1916–20) 1.2: 64–110.

[3]MA 25–28 (APNDX 20). For a contemporary view of this distinction see Brian O'Shaughnessy, "Consciousness," *Studies in the Philosophy of Mind,* ed. Peter French, Theodore Uehling, and Howard Wettstein (Minneapolis: U of Minnesota P, 1986) 50.

[4]CS 55; E 235. CS 64–65; "drehte es auch mit der Spitze des Zeigefingers auf der Innenseite des Daumens hin und her" (E 243).

keeping myself awake only by a loud and regular clapping of my hands. But then, as the road threatened to slip away from under my feet and everything, as weary as I myself, began to vanish, I summoned my remaining strength."[5] Once asleep, he playfully contemplates the notion that sleep restricts one's apperception but (in accordance with Marty) allows a degree of perception sufficient to generate memory: "Although I did not dream, my sleep was not free from a continuous slight disturbance. All night long I heard someone talking beside me. The words I could hardly hear ... and I remember that even in my sleep I rubbed my hands with pleasure at not being obliged to recognize single words, since I was asleep." In another example, from *The Castle*, the point is entirely explicit: "K. was asleep, it was not real sleep, he could hear Bürgel's words perhaps better than during his former dead-tired state of waking, word after word struck his ear, but the tiresome consciousness had gone." Secretary Bürgel later hints at how detrimental the close link between fatigue and diminished comprehension has been for K.: "No, you don't need to apologize for being sleepy, why should you? One's physical energies last only to a certain limit. Who can help the fact that precisely this limit is significant in other ways too?" A counterfactual situation in "The Burrow" paradoxically shows apperception and sleep to occur at the same time: "[It is as if I were looking] at myself sleeping, and had the joy of being in profound slumber and simultaneously of keeping vigilant guard over myself."[6] In "Resolutions," the narrator describes the making of a decision and a subsequent series of physiological actions designed to facilitate comprehension of what others are saying: "To lift yourself out of a miserable mood, even if you have to do it by strength of will, should be easy. I force myself out of my chair, stride around the table, [make my head and neck nimble,] make my eyes sparkle, tighten the muscles around them." This description resembles Brentano's observations about noticing: "If you want someone to notice something that is difficult to notice, you have to place him into circumstances which incline him to notice by habit: walking up and down in his study, opening his eyes wide, lifting his head, pricking up his ears, sensing his muscles in his accustomed environment at an accustomed hour."[7]

[5]MA 23–46. Concentration and distraction in Kafka's protagonists are discussed by Walter H. Sokel, *Franz Kafka: Tragik und Ironie. Zur Struktur seiner Kunst* (Munich and Vienna: Langen & Müller, 1964) 299–310. CS 23; K 48–50.

[6]"[It is false that] in half-sleep our ability to notice vanishes. It is well-known that one can direct a dreamer's attention through ... spoken suggestion" (MA 31). CS 23; K 52 (the narrator hears his own previously used words - K 24). C 342; "Wort für Wort schlug an sein Ohr" (S 249). C 351; S 255. CS 334; E 367.

[7]CS 398; "[Ich] mache Kopf und Hals beweglich, bringe Feuer in die Augen, spanne die Muskeln um sie herum" (E 12). Brentano, *Deskriptive Psychologie*, ed. Roderick Chisholm and Wilhelm Baumgartner [Hamburg: Meiner, 1982] 39; on noticing and

For Wundt, moving one's head and flexing one's eye muscles was the prime example for demonstrating the link between perception and apperception, which he metaphorically saw as a focusing of the mind's eye: "The entry of an idea into the internal field of vision is called perception, its entry into the focal point apperception."[8] Passages from "Wedding Preparations" and *Amerika* allude to such links: "He looked at Raban as he glanced up and ... did not turn his face away from Raban, as one gazes steadily at a point in order not to forget anything of what one wants to say." "While Mr. Pollunder's eyes followed Karl to the door with a friendly look, Mr. Green, though as a rule one's eyes involuntarily follow those of the man one is talking to, did not once glance round at Karl." As mental concentration and focusing by their very nature are exclusionary, they must actively impede or marginalize whatever else is in the perceptual and mental field. One passage states this almost as an experimental observation: "[The elderly gentleman from time to time] glanced toward Raban, even though to do so he had to twist his neck sharply. Yet he did this only out of the natural desire ... to observe everything exactly, at least in his vicinity. The result of his aimless glancing hither and thither was that there was a great deal he did not notice." In *Amerika* the porter at the information desk of the hotel Occidental "neither looked at the counter, where he was perpetually handing things out, nor at the face of this or that questioner, but straight in front of him, obviously to economize and conserve his strength."[9] Since the narrative focus on the external world is restricted to Karl's phenomenal awareness, it expresses itself also through his auditory perception:

The stoker's voice no longer dominated the room, which was a bad sign. The gentleman in civilian clothes was the first to show his impatience by bringing his bamboo stick into play and tapping, though only softly, on the floor ... the Head Purser, who now thought he had won the day, heaved a loud ironical sigh ... the gentleman with the bamboo cane came over to Karl and asked, not very loudly yet clearly enough to be heard above the stoker's ravings: "By the way, what's your name?"

apperception see 31–65 and 162.

[8] Wundt, *Physiologische Psychologie* 2: 206. Also quoted by Marty (*Gesammelte Schriften* 1.2: 75). Wundt later postulated a "law of correspondence between apperception and fixation" (*Grundzüge der physiologischen Psychologie*, 5th ed., 3 vols. [1902–1903] 2: 533).

[9] CS 63; E 242. A 66; "obwohl man doch schon unwillkürlich sich den Blicken seines Gegenübers anzuschließen pflegt" (V 58). CS 72–3; E 249–50. A 196; V 162.

Given the monoperceptual viewpoint in this novel, Karl's attentiveness, required to survive in the New World — "he suffered from an actual longing for sleep, probably in consequence of the unremitting attention which he had to exercise all day long"[10] — meshes with his attentiveness as narratorial consciousness or agency. Although Kafka goes beyond the straightforward descriptivism of *Amerika* to the complex cognitive and linguistic structuring of his later works, the concept of attentiveness will remain central to his narratorial concerns up to his last stories.

Psychology of Gestures and Language

In December of 1902 Kafka appears to fictionalize Marty's basic view that we use language to communicate our thoughts: words become little gentlemen, wearing patent-leather shoes and ties, who leave the speaker's mouth and cram themselves into the ears of the listener.[11] Whereas Marty's psychology course discussed language only cursorily in the context of apperception and memory, his linguistic theory introduced the following distinctions: an originally natural sign imitating the sound of a thing or animal (a bark, e.g.) becomes the conventional linguistic term denoting such sounds: it serves both a conceptual and a communicative function. As language evolves, the term extends metonymically to the animal or thing that creates the sound. Through further analogical or metaphorical (associative) extension, many terms acquire additional conceptual meanings that apply to mental acts or abstract objects. In other words, a term's literal (ostensive) meaning may take on more figurative (abstract) ones.[12] One of Marty's examples for the analogical or metaphorical abstracting process was swaying as applied to a thing (a wooden beam) and extended to a person's indecisiveness in judging or willing. The fat

[10]A 16–20; E 20–23. A 45; V 42. Karl's need for close attention also causes him headaches (A 198; V 164). The relation of monoperspectivism to the character-narrator's narrowness of consciousness is discussed by Peter U. Beicken ("*Berechnung* und *Kunstaufwand* in Kafka's Erzählrhetorik," *Franz Kafka*, ed. Maria Luise Caputo-Mayr [Berlin: Agora, 1978] 216–34).

[11]This was five months after taking Marty's oral examination and shortly after joining the philosophers' club. The little fable is the bulk of a letter to Pollak (B 15-16; L 6).

[12]Language is derived from the mental designation of things ("innerliches Benennen der Gegenstände" - MA 58). Marty's linguistic theory is contained in his lecture course "Grundfragen der Sprachphilosophie," *Psyche und Sprachstruktur*, ed. Otto Funke [Bern: Francke, 1940] 75–117. It was offered in 1904 and became a common reference point for club members. Its basic ideas are Lockean; they predate Ferdinand de Saussure's structuralism.

man in "Description" gathers both analogical meanings of the term into a straightforward simile: "The landscape disturbs my thought ... It makes my reflections sway like suspension bridges." Another of Marty's examples is the metaphorical link between the ostensive and abstract meaning of *to grasp*. In the opening scene of *Amerika,* the stoker asks Karl Roßmann why he felt he had no choice but to come to the United States. Karl dismisses the story, literally throwing it away "with a wave of the hand."[13] As was typical for theories predating linguistic structuralism and modern language philosophy, Marty allowed for mental acts such as apperceiving and remembering to be effected without the help of language. But through its associative and ultimately referential operation, language enhances apperception: "when I refer to something, it becomes apperceived. The more accurate the designation, the more precise the apperception." This consideration helps us to understand a scene from "Description" in which the narrator suddenly imagines that he is loved by a girl in a beautiful white dress. He is repeating the phrase *white dress,* seemingly denoting a girl, in order to preserve her in his apperception. As he had feared, when his companion talks to him, his obsessive thinking of the phrase lapses, and the girl escapes from him as a "white gleam."[14]

In earlier articles Marty had treated a broad range of linguistic questions. He especially took issue with Wundt, who assumed, regarding the mind-body relation, psychophysical parallelism: each elementary psychological event coexists, without a causal link, with an elementary bodily event. From this assumption Wundt derived his version of the so-called nativist theory of language: a person is born with a complete set of psychophysical correlations between his or her mental states (sensations, thoughts, feelings) and their physical expressions. The latter are body and facial movements (gestures) and, in evolutionary terms, the latest and most sophisticated movements — articulations of sound (speech). In his major linguistic work, *Language* (*Die Sprache*), Wundt expounded in elaborate detail the ironclad coordination between

---

[13]Marty, "Grundfragen der Sprachphilosophie" 92–93, 96. The word for both swaying and indecisiveness is *schwanken*. CS 25; "Die Landschaft ... läßt meine Überlegungen schwanken" (K 60). The man's swaying reflections also hint at his desire to ferry across the river: the word for reflecting and ferrying across is *überlegen*. A 6; "[er] warf die ganze Geschichte mit der Hand weg" (V 11); cf. the similar phrase: "Er sah zu ihr [the Statue of Liberty] auf und verwarf das über sie Gelernte" (VKA 2: 123); this is in analogy to the way physical *greifen* becomes a mental *begreifen*.

[14]MA 48 (APNDX 21). "Und so wiederholte ich angestrengt und unaufhörlich 'weißes Kleid, weißes Kleid' um wenigstens durch dieses eine Zeichen mir das Mädchen zu erhalten ... in dem Augenblick, als ich anfing seine Worte zu verstehn, hüpfte ein weißer Schimmer zierlich am Brückengeländer entlang, strich durch den Brückenthurm und sprang in die dunkle Gasse" (K 40; E 205). This passage does not appear in the English translation of "Description."

mental activities and the body's various movements. He explored their whole range: involuntary body changes (breathing, circulation, respiration), involuntary facial and pantomimic expressions (as externalizations of affects), intentional pantomime and gestures, gestural languages (of deaf-mutes and others), and spoken languages as expressions of thought. In the case of conventional gestures and speech, he introduced a volitional element: we impede certain involuntary affective expressions and instead "imitate" or act out perceptual representations derived from vision, touch, and the internal experience of one's own bodily movements (such as parrying, warding off, or striking someone). In other words, we sense, learn, and develop our own and other people's body articulations into conventional gestures and linguistic abilities (speaking and understanding).[15] Wundt gave prominence to the gestural language of, among others, the people of Naples, the "homeland of plastic gesticulation." A scene from *The Trial* may allude to this theorem. Josef K., listening to a businessman from southern Italy, is unable to place his gestures within a linguistic convention he recognizes: the man was "once raising his arms with loosely fluttering hands to explain something which K. found it impossible to understand, although he was leaning forward to watch every gesture."[16]

In 1901 Bertold Delbrück made Wundt's *Language* the subject of a widely read critical study, and Wundt published a lengthy rejoinder. Posthumously published manuscripts of Marty's show that from 1900 on he was working on a refutation of Wundt's study and was aware of Delbrück's book.[17] In line with his earlier criticism of Wundt's (nonconventionalist) nativism, Marty sets out in the linguistics course of 1904 to demonstrate that there exists no isomorphism whatsoever between mental states, on the one hand, and expressive movements such as gestures or sounds, on the other. Mental states adhere to a logic of their own within the principal Brentanoan structure of representation, judgment, and desire, and they adopt various "natural" (heteromorphic or conventional) languages for the purpose of external communication and internal memory. Marty defines language as *sign* — something that stands for

[15]Marty, *Gesammelte Schriften* 1.2: 35–199. Wilhelm Wundt, *Völkerpsychologie*, vol.1, *Die Sprache*, 2 pts. (Leipzig: Engelmann, 1900) 1.1: 37–359. Wundt developed the physiological basis for his linguistic theory in *Physiologische Psychologie* (2: 418–40; 1: 296, 430). See also Karl Bühler, "The Psychophysics of Expression of Wilhelm Wundt," *in* Wilhelm Wundt, *The Languages of Gestures*, ed. Arthur Blumenthal (The Hague: Mouton, 1973) 30–54.

[16]Wundt, *Die Sprache* 1.1: 147–91 ("Heimat des plastischen Gebärdenspiels" - 190). TR 200–201; P 171–72. Thomas Mann's *The Magic Mountain* attributes to Settembrini's speech a similar plastic gesturing.

[17]Bertold Delbrück, *Grundfragen der Sprachforschung* (Straßburg: Trübner, 1901). Wundt, *Sprachgeschichte und Sprachpsychologie* (Leipzig: Engelmann, 1901). Marty, *Über Wert und Methode einer beschreibenden Bedeutungslehre*, ed. Otto Funke (Reichenberg: Stiepel, 1926) 25–65.

something else — and, in a more specifically Lockean fashion,[18] as an extra-mental sign for mental states. Such a sign can be an involuntary expression of an affect (laughter), an action (eating, walking) or an intentional and finally conventional expression such as a gesture or articulation of sounds. The following excerpts, first from Marty's course and then from Delbrück's book, show that many turn-of-the-century linguists explored expressive movements with Wundt's parallelist assumptions in mind:

> A scream of horror or fear, a call of joy, an involuntary laughter, weeping, turning pale, blushing, sparkling of the eye, opening and twisting of the mouth .... These also are signs of mental events, and thus constitute a language in a broader sense. This is the most natural "language," innate and thus understood by all — even by those who speak very different conventional languages.

> Among the *movements* of the *body* we first notice the bows. How many sentiments do they express and how many relations between people do they mirror in their long gradation from the stiff compliment, which moves half the body, to the confidential nodding of the head and eventually the barely noticeable movements of the eyelids .... Of immense expressibility is the play of the eyes which can suddenly radiate ... question and answer, implore and refuse, entreat and threaten.

A scene from "Description" appears to be written in the spirit of the quotation from Delbrück: "At about midnight a few people rose, bowed, shook hands .... The hostess stood in the middle of the room and made graceful bowing movements." Kafka referred to mimic expressions and gestures in his earliest letters. He certainly understood the premise that people not only use language but other expressive movements to communicate their thoughts and feelings.[19] Kafka is clear about what distinguishes involuntary from voluntary expressions. In *The Trial* Josef K. — in observing his subordinate "Kaminer with his insupportable smile, caused by a chronic muscular twitch" — is

---

[18]Marty, "Über Sprachreflex, Nativismus und absichtliche Sprachbildung," *Gesammelte Schriften* 1.2: 266. For a discussion of Marty's views within the context of German-speaking linguistics cf. Clemens Knobloch, *Geschichte der psychologischen Sprachauffassung in Deutschland von 1850 bis 1920* (Tübingen: Niemeyer, 1988) 273–85 and passim.

[19]Marty, "Grundfragen der Sprachphilosophie" 79–80. Delbrück, *Grundfragen der Sprachforschung* 49–50. CS 9; K 10. B 9–13; L 1–5. Hartmut Binder (*Kafka in neuer Sicht: Mimik, Gestik und Personengefüge als Darstellungsformen des Autobiographischen* [Stuttgart: Metzler, 1976] 133–37) dismisses any possible influence of Brentano's view of language and gesture.

obliged to admit "that Kaminer's smile was not intentional, that the man could
not smile intentionally if he tried." But he sometimes inverts or plays with
these distinctions. Facial gestures commonly understood as involuntary become deliberate pathways for affects ("For a little while I let my mouth hang
open, so that my agitation could find a way out") or speech: "I screwed up my
mouth, this being the best preparation for resolute speech." In "Description"
and other early stories there are numerous episodes in which the protagonists'
expressive movements help to propel the action by precisely revealing their
mental states: "He gazed at me in astonishment and parted his wet lips." "He
winked at me, suggesting some agreement which I had apparently forgotten."
"A characteristic movement in such a condition is to run your little finger
along your eyebrows."[20] The story "Bachelor's Ill Luck" alludes to the qua-
si-linguistic observation that "in anger we clasp our hands against our fore-
heads to lament that we forgot something": "That's how it will be, except that
in reality, both today and later, one will stand there with a palpable body and
a real head, a real forehead, that is, for smiting on with one's hand." In
another story the narrator has studied thoroughly the behavior patterns of
urban confidence tricksters but he has not yet caught on to their intentions.
Only the trickster's smile gives him away: "I did not wait to see the end of
that smile, for shame suddenly caught hold of me. It had needed that smile to
let me know that the man was a confidence trickster." In the later stories less
gets communicated through mere gestures. A scene from "In the Penal Colony" (1914) illustrates that perceptions of pointing hand movements must be
supplemented by linguistic explanations to be understood: "[The prisoner]
directed his gaze wherever the officer pointed a finger ... apparently listening
with all his ears in an effort to catch what was being said. Yet the movement
of his blubber lips ... showed clearly that he could not understand a word ...
his uncertain eyes were trying to perceive what the two gentlemen had been
looking at, but since he had not understood the explanation he could not make
head or tail of it." The story "An Old Manuscript" (1917) questions the
universal meaning of gestural languages. Foreign nomads invade the narrator's
home country. They screech like jackdaws but are completely blind to gestures: "They are unwilling to make sense even out of our sign language. You
can gesture at them till you dislocate your jaws and your wrists and still they
will not have understood you and will never understand. They often make
grimaces ... but they do not mean anything by that."[21] As the following will

---

[20]TR 15–16; P 17. CS 391; E 19 (identically also in "Description" - K 29). CS 29;
K 78. CS 10; K 12. CS 12; K 19. CS 398; E 12. Cf. also "So brauchte ich ja bloß
meinen Kopf zu schütteln, um ihm zu zeigen, daß ich es nicht wußte" (K 90).

[21]CS 395; "[Also auch eine] Stirn, mit der Hand an sie zu schlagen" (E 13); cf.
"[Wir schlagen uns] im Ärger mit der Hand an die Stirn" (Delbrück, *Grundfragen
der Sprachforschung* 59). CS 396; E 10. CS 144–48; E 102–6. CS 416; E 130.

show, by this time Kafka has recognized that meaning and reference require, beyond attentiveness and gestural ostension, complex linguistic expressions.

Ostensive Ideas, Concepts, and Reference

In preparing for their book *Intuition and Concept* — the title refers to the relations between ostensive (perception-derived) ideas, traditionally called *intuitions*, and conceptual thought — Max Brod and Felix Weltsch in 1910 participated in a Marty seminar on the philosophy of language. Brod recalls reading Locke's *Essay Concerning Human Understanding* in this seminar.[22] Marty shared Locke's belief that language translates "mental discourse into spoken words" and passes awareness of the same psychic event from the speaker to the listener.[23] He further taught that language does not express ostensive ideas (presentations or reproductions of sensory particulars) but rather concepts: "[The words of language denote] only a conceptual content ... never anything ostensive; because an ostensive idea ... cannot be communicated through language and words." "Exactly because linguistic communication in a strict sense occurs only when the speaker generates the *same* psychic event in the listener, the infinitely variable ostensive ideas representing physical entities are excluded from it."[24] These statements contain an explanatory difficulty and a logical confusion. First, Marty has a Lockean, nominalist, psychological view of the origin of concepts. They are products of our individual mental activity, the abstracting from ostensive ideas, "singling out in attention some one feature given in direct experience ... and ignoring the other features."[25] And yet they are thought to be objective and communicable. Second, the last line of the longer quote shows that Marty tends to confuse

[22]See Margarita Pazi, "Franz Kafka, Max Brod und der *Prager Kreis,*" *Kafka und das Judentum*, ed. Karl Erich Grözinger, Stéphane Mosès, and Hans Dieter Zimmermann (Frankfurt: Athenäum, 1987) 89. Brod, *Streitbares Leben* 168.

[23]Ian Hacking, *Why Does Language Matter to Philosophy?* (Cambridge UP, 1975) 44. Roy Harris aptly calls this aspect of the Lockean theory *telementation* (*Reading Saussure: A Critical Commentary* [London: Duckworth, 1987] 205).

[24]Marty, "Grundfragen der Sprachphilosophie" 116. Marty, *Untersuchungen zur Grundlegung der allgemeinen Grammatik und Sprachphilosophie* (Halle: Niemeyer, 1908) 433.

[25]Peter Geach's summary of Locke's view (*Mental Acts: Their Content and Their Object* [London: Routledge & Kegan Paul, 1957] 18). See also Barry Smith, "Brentano and Marty: An Inquiry into Being and Truth," *Mind, Meaning and Metaphysics: The Philosophy and Theory of Language of Anton Marty*, ed. Kevin Mulligan (Dordrecht: Kluwer, 1990) 133.

ostensive (subjective) presentations of things and communicable (objective) references to them. The next two chapters will provide more extensive discussions of this difference and its importance to Kafka. In an entry in his travel diary from October 1910, an early thumbnail sketch of his and Weltsch's book, Brod falls into both traps. He states that if the speaker's utterance is to generate "exactly the same idea" in the listener, this idea conceivably can only be a concept, since ostensive ideas are subjective and cannot be communicated. In other words, he sees no difficulty in accepting both the psychological origin and the objectivity of concepts. And just a little later in this one-and-a-half-page text he ponders whether he objectively identifies (makes reference to) Dr. Weltsch by having formed a singular ostensive idea (memory image) of him based on his most recent visit with him, or a generalized memory image, one that is "intermittent" with respect to the several occasions on which he has met him: "Is the intermittence of the memory image the same as that of A + x? What is memory image: when I present to myself 'Dr. Weltsch' or 'Dr. Weltsch at a specific moment during [my] most recent visit with him?'"[26]

Brod duplicates Marty's logical error in failing to distinguish between ostensive presentation and singular reference. He leaves open the question of whether he identifies (refers to) Dr. Weltsch through one (presumably non-communicable) ostension or through a generalized (abstracted), thus communicable reference term. Brod's sketch is a rudiment of his and Weltsch's published theory, which seeks to overcome the gulf between the privacy of ostensive ideas and the publicly shared meanings of concepts and referential terms. The book's contradictory way of bridging this gap is that ostensive ideas, concepts, and reference all work in much the same way. They all ultimately derive from and, thus, function like perception, which itself is partly modeled on the abstraction-theorem of concepts. Perceptions require the blurring (removing from focus) of what is not, and the abstracting (focusing on, noticing) of what is conceptually or referentially important for perceiving that object. Reference, just like perception, is a subjective mental activity: "[The special memory image,] which retains in memory a singular, temporally and spatially completely determined occasion, for instance, my friend in a specific, unique position that is meaningful to me, in a moment made noticeable by some chance ... depends on the distribution of attention within perception [which always] presents a blurred image (K + x)."[27]

[26]Brod, "Reise nach Paris und Rouen," EF 1: 37–51; 47. Dr. Theodor Weltsch was Felix Weltsch's uncle. About *A* + *x* see below.

[27]Max Brod and Felix Weltsch, *Anschauung und Begriff: Grundzüge eines Systems der Begriffsbildung* (Leipzig: Wolff, 1913) 67. (K + x) [*K* for *Kern*, kernel] designates the generalized ostensive representations of *one and the same* thing, where (K) expresses an individuating concept (singular reference). By contrast, the (A) in (A

The book's explanation of concepts runs roughly as follows: in memory we overlay and "blur" ideas of particular things that belong to one class (cats, triangles, etc.) and thereby obtain a generalized memory image that is ostensive and general (conceptlike) at the same time. These generalized ostensive ideas or ostensive concepts (cat, triangle) are called *(A + x)*. Those common classificatory (sortal) properties referred to by (A + x) that the perceiver notices and abstracts from several overlaid singular ostensive ideas make up the conceptual kernel (A). Those properties referred to by (A + x) that remain divergent upon comparison constitute (x), the mass of impeded (though retrievable and noticeable) ostensive ideas. In a further step the authors claim that the conceiver can adjust at will the distribution of the representational (ostensive) and the conceptual elements in the application of ostensive concepts such as (A + x): the larger (more encompassing) the kernel (A) is conceived, the smaller the class of things referred to; the larger the (x) is conceived, the more general is the concept. The notion of distribution also implies that the ostensive concept (A + x) provides the conceiver — in line perhaps with Brod's previous Herbartian sympathies — with a potential access to whole chains of impeded (unconscious) ostensive ideas that he can reproduce at will. Contradicting their earlier thesis that concepts are structured like perceptions, the authors eventually claim that concepts shape perceptions: "(A + x) functions as a distributor of attention and in this way shapes perception."[28] This claim puts the cart before the horse — even if it be allowed, with traditional and contemporary cognitive psychology,[29] that perception requires a conceptual component. The centerpiece of their theory founders on the confusion between the subjective (psychological) and the objective (logical and linguistic). For them concepts and reference are obtained through psychological activity, the accumulating of and then abstracting from ostensive ideas.

+ x) expresses a general concept.

[28]Brod and Weltsch, *Anschauung und Begriff* 153. Of three known reviews one goes along with the book (Aloys Müller, *Archiv für die gesamte Psychologie* 31 [1914]: 39–47); the others criticize the confusion between sensing (ostensive ideas) and thinking (Heinrich Levy, *Kant-Studien* 24 [1920]: 321–25; Henry Watt, *Mind* 15 [1916]: 103–9).

[29]P. F. Strawson, "Imagination and Perception," *Freedom and Resentment* (London: Methuen, 1974) 45–65. George Miller and Philip Johnson-Laird, *Language and Perception* (Harvard UP, 1976) 41, 135.

Description, Memory, and Narration

An entry in Kafka's travel diary of 1911 about his approaching the Zurich railway station reflects on the psychological genesis of perception-based descriptions and concepts: "*Zurich*: coming up of the station out of several blurred stations of the most recent memory — (Max takes possession of it for a + x)." Kafka was aware of his friends' emerging theory of ostensive concepts from conversations and from Brod's diary sketch, since the two discussed and collated their travel diaries for a common literary project.[30] Kafka apparently understood the theory in outline, since he formed a description of the Zurich station — and perhaps at the same time a concept (railway station) — from recollections of previously perceived railway stations. His choice of terms clearly refers to the process of generalized blurring as well as the way a current perception of a thing can be shaped by (abstracted from) past perceptions of similar things. It must have been the linguistic precision of the observation Kafka committed to his diary that prompted Brod to appropriate it for his own theory. In explicitly going beyond Henri Bergson's general theorem that memory shapes perception, Brod and Weltsch claimed that through the employment of memorized and generalized ostensive ideas we can fill in perceptual gaps when perceiving particulars of one and the same class. In *Amerika* there is a somewhat experimental application of the view that memorized ostensive ideas shape or augment perception. From the cashier's office of the ocean liner on which he has made the crossing, Karl Roßmann observes in great detail the large ships in New York harbor: "Great ships crossed each other's courses in either direction .... If one almost shut one's eyes, these ships seemed to be staggering under their own weight." After he has been expelled from Mr. Pollunder's house, Karl and his two traveling companions turn around on their way to Ramses to look at New York harbor from a distance: "To the harbor ... peace had returned, and only now and then, probably influenced by some memory of an earlier view close at hand, did one fancy that one saw a ship cutting the water for a little distance. But one could not follow it for long; it escaped one's eyes and was no more to be found." In the first passage Karl views the harbor from up close and sees the large ships in great detail. In the second he views it from afar, as a calm overall appearance. His generalized image of the harbor, containing vividly remembered images of the ships he had previously perceived, enables him to make out a ship in the distance now and then and to follow it with his eyes for a short

---

[30] "*Zürich*: Heraufsteigen des Bahnhofs aus einigen ineinandergegangenen Bahnhöfen der letzten Erinnerung — (Max nimmt es für a + x in Besitz)" (Kafka, "Reise Lugano — Mailand — Paris — Erlenbach," EF 1: 143–88; 146. Also T 375–76; D 2: 246. See Pasley on their collaboration for "Richard und Samuel" (EF 1: 288–91).

stretch. His present perception of the harbor lacks detail (it is blurred), but since his past ostensive ideas of large ships fill in the perceptual blanks, he is better able to search the visual field and direct his attention. As a result, he briefly apperceives, or so it seems, a ship from afar. The theory behind this passage appears close to the following statement of Brod and Weltsch: "[If the reason] for which we look at something with heightened attention ... [is] a memory image of that thing, its [current or perceptual] image is sharpened above all in the direction indicated by that memory, is abruptly intensified, possibly makes use of a fiction, supposes that aspects already have been seen which the eye cannot see yet, which only memory discloses to it."[31]

The way memory can shape current perception is applied to the auditory sense in Kafka's story "Home-Coming": "And since I am listening from a distance, I hear nothing but a faint striking of the clock passing over from childhood days, but perhaps I only think I hear it." Kafka's applications of his friends' cognitive theorem were experimental and playful. His remark about their book — "I have to force myself to read and understand it; my attention strays too easily when there is nothing there to put one's finger on" — may not (as has been suggested) bespeak an inability to comprehend it but rather a dissatisfaction with its conclusions. The remark echoes his criticism of a lecture on literature which Brod gave at the time he participated in Marty's seminar. In line with his later failure to distinguish between ostensive idea and reference, Brod stated that literature cannot adequately express singular things since it is subject to the conceptual generality of language: "We cannot adequately portray real things and happenings. Cold, precise concepts can never do justice to reality with its infinite range of shades." In the subsequent discussion Kafka insisted on a more adequate definition of language and attributed Brod's complaints about literature's linguistic limitations to his emphasis on abstraction, on longing for a world less diverse, less pluralistic than the existing one: "This imperfection [of literature] results only if your comprehension is abstract .... The speaker is attacking the diversity of the world, not the imperfection [of literature]."[32]

Kafka appears to realize that his friends had arrived at the contradictory notion of ostensive concept through valid insights into what may be common

---

[31]A 11–12; V 16. A 112; V 93. Brod and Weltsch, *Anschauung und Begriff* 51. The quote presumably is about the perception of items of the same class (classification), not of *one and the same* thing (recognition, identification, reference).

[32]CS 445; E 321. FE 207; F 317. Brod, *Der Prager Kreis* 90–91. Brod echoes Hofmannsthal's Lord Chandos: "Die abstrakten Worte, deren sich doch die Zunge naturgemäß bedienen muß, um irgendwelches Urteil an den Tag zu geben, zerfielen mir im Munde" ["The abstract words which our tongues must employ to express any kind of judgment decomposed in my mouth"] (Hugo von Hofmannsthal, "Ein Brief," *Gesammelte Werke,* 15 vols. [Frankfurt: Fischer, 1946–59] 11: 13 [*Prosa* 2: 13]).

to ostensive imaging, memory, concept-use (predication), and reference, but also by confusing what is distinct among them. For one important upshot of their theorem — derived from Bergson's view of memory as shaping perception — was that it is difficult to preserve any singular experience in memory: "[Those memory images are rare] in which the memory of a singular, literally momentary experience actually remained free of the influence of subsequent similar experiences. Almost always a memory image represents a whole series of impressions." By contrast, Kafka equated involuntary blurring in perception and memory with conceptual and referential confusion, ultimately the inability to write down anything that is remembered in its particularity: "I am incapable of writing down [anything in such a way as to remember it well]. This weakness of mine makes my dull head clear and empty only in order to preserve itself, [inasmuch as] the confusion lets itself be crowded off to the periphery. But I almost prefer this condition to the merely dull and indefinite pressure [of confused thoughts and memories]."[33]

Kafka's writings obviously did not depend on a blurring of memories but, on the contrary, on the focused linguistic reproduction of singular experiences. To Felice Bauer he recalls in great detail the circumstances of their first meeting at the house of the Brods. He did not blur them in memory (despite numerous later visits to the Brods), mainly (presumably) because he had not seen *her* there again: "These are roughly all the outward events of that evening that I still remember — after probably more than 30 other evenings spent meanwhile with the Brod family, which unfortunately may have blurred certain things. I have written them down ... because I have resisted far too long the desire to write down my memories of that evening before they are forgotten." "There was a moment I remember above all others, when you sat at the table .... The changing view of your face, as you slowly turned your head, left an indelible impression on me." For Kafka the greater problem for memory and writing is that, instead of blurring, they initially require an exclusionary, privative apperception: "It is certain that everything I have conceived in advance ... whether word for word or just casually, but in [explicit] words, appears ... [full of gaps] when I try to write it down at my desk, although I have forgotten nothing of the original conception .... Blindly and arbitrarily I snatch handfuls out of the stream so that when I write it down calmly, my acquisition is ... incapable of restoring this fullness." Kafka insists that whatever is remembered and told must first be apperceived through some kind of cognitive attention or privation. In *Amerika* Therese's associative, temporally contiguous storytelling breaks into a description of details that were apperceived clearly at the time and, because of her mother's suicide, produced

[33]Brod and Weltsch, *Anschauung und Begriff* 72. D 1: 301; "Ich bin ganz unfähig, etwas für die Erinnerung Entscheidendes aufzuschreiben .... Mir ist aber dieser Zustand fast lieber als das bloß dumpfe und ungewisse Andrängen" (T 201).

a singular memory trace: "The most trifling circumstance of that morning was still stamped exactly on her memory after more than ten years, and because the sight of her mother on the half-finished house-wall was the last living memory of her." Conversely, Kafka is aware that apperception and memory also depend on the intention and act of writing something down, narrating it: "What is not written down swims before one's eyes and optical accidents determine the [overall comprehension]." At the same time he realizes that, for the kind of writing he desires, he cannot rely on merely physiological input ("that which was seen by our eyes, heard by our ears"),[34] associative selections, and narrowness of consciousness.

Instead, he needs to accommodate increasing cognitive complexity — and that means, as will be shown shortly, increasing syntactic and propositional structure. Important models for such structured complexness are, of course, the texts of favored authors such as Kleist, Dostoyevsky, and Flaubert.[35] Due to his theoretical interests and inclination for painstaking descriptive clarity, however, linguistic and conceptual generalizations become equally important. Perception, description, and good writing depend on each other: "Through too extensive note-taking one loses many notes. It is an eye-shutting. You always have to start seeing afresh. — But if you remain aware of this, taking notes perhaps cannot be so detrimental."[36] Like perception and description, both writing and narrating initially require deliberate concentration, focusing and a selective (privative) consciousness that excludes all that is not attended to: "First write down a thought, then recite it aloud; don't write as you recite, for in that case only the beginning already inwardly pondered will succeed, while what is still to be written will be lost." Even within the narrative itself (as in *Amerika*) inventing characters requires a creatively selecting focus that tends to get blurred when characters proliferate: "Right at the beginning I mastered only two, but if four people are pressing forward, trying to take the floor, and the writer has eyes only for two, the result is a sad ... embarrassment ... because my eyes stray all over the place, they might catch some shadows of these two, but then the two solid characters, being temporarily abandoned, become uncertain, and finally it all collapses." Yet in addition to focus and

---

[34]FE 17–18; F 61. FE 65; "[Einen] Augenblick, den ich vor allen andern genau im Gedächtnis habe .... Diese langsame Kopfwendung und den hiebei natürlich verschiedenartigen Anblick Deines Gesichtes habe ich unvergänglich behalten" (F 127). D 1: 151–52; T 102. A 157; V 130. D 1: 221; T 151. D 1: 26; T 16.

[35]See W. J. Dodd, *Kafka and Dostoyevsky: The Shaping of Influence* (New York: St. Martin's Press, 1992). Hannelore Rodlauer-Wenko, "Die Paralleltagebücher Kafka-Brod und das Modell Flaubert," *Arcadia* 20 (1985): 47–60.

[36]"Durch allzu fleißiges Notizenmachen kommt man um viele Notizen. Es ist ein Augenschließen. Man muß das Sehn immer wieder von vorn anfangen" (Kafka as quoted by Brod - EF 1: 87).

concentration, writing requires, similar to the increase in one's knowledge about the world, more and more propositional (informational) structuring or "space." For instance, the letter to his father must remain incomplete "because the magnitude of the material goes far beyond the scope of my memory and power of reasoning." Several letters to Felice indicate that writing needs to unfold a plenitude of mental contents, to create propositional space: "The difficulties which writing to you creates ... do not consist of an inability to write what I want to say, which are but the simplest things, but there are so many of them that I cannot accommodate them in either time or space." "Sometimes, and I don't know why, everything I want to say to you presses upon me with great intensity, like a crowd of people all trying to squeeze through a narrow door at once." "The images became uncontrollable, everything flew apart until, in my extremity, the notion of a Napoleonic field marshal's black hat came to my rescue, descending on my consciousness and holding it together by force." Conscious focus, noticing, and apperception must broaden into fully realized beliefs. A vivid image from *The Trial* illustrates this: "But under their beards — and this was K.'s real discovery — badges of various sizes and colors gleamed on their coat-collars .... 'So!' cried K., flinging his arms in the air, his sudden enlightenment [required space]."[37] The semantic intricacies of propositional expressions and belief go beyond the explanatory force of psychological theory. Kafka dealt with them in the context of the philosophy of mind and language, which will be surveyed in the fourth chapter.

[37]D 2: 257; T 384. FE 124; F 208. DF 138; H 119. FE 11; F 52. FE 221; F 336. FE 298; F 436. TR 47; P 45.

3: Dualism and Intentionality in the Narrative

THIS CHAPTER SURVEYS PHILOSOPHICAL theorems that were either intensely contended or opposed in the club: Cartesian dualism, Brentanoan intentionality, Meinong's nonentities, and Marty's dual consciousness. Kafka embeds them almost serially in his developing themes and paradigms, struggling with and ironically subverting their conceptual rigidity. He also becomes aware that they do not solve the puzzle of how we come to know about the world. Yet his preoccupation with them bolsters his emerging monoperspectival form and helps him focus on the characters' beliefs — the ways things appear to them — as the main subject of their narratives. The way beliefs must twine together with reference to render an objective world will be discussed in the next chapter.

Cartesian dualism was the most basic philosophical tenet held by the club members. Alfred Kastil especially undertook to explain Brentano's view of mental acts and intentionality along traditional Cartesian lines. Descartes divides reality into two completely distinct and self-contained domains or components: the mind and the physical world. The mind appears complete in itself and immaterial. Thoughts are logically independent of the material world, which their contents purport to represent. The physical world is equally independent from the mind and from its representation of that world. This dualist construction is subject to radical skepticism, because the mind cannot ascertain whether things actually exist outside its thoughts about them. Descartes writes in the *Meditations*: "I never have believed myself to feel anything in waking moments which I cannot also sometimes believe myself to feel when I sleep, and as I do not think that these things which I seem to feel in sleep, proceed from objects outside of me, I do not see any reason why I should have this belief regarding objects which I seem to perceive while awake." In his inaugural lecture as a university lecturer in 1902 and in subsequent courses Kastil defended interactionism, the Cartesian assumption of causal interaction between mind and body, against psychophysical parallelism. Since the immaterial mind and the physical-spatial world are mutually exclusive substances but allow some kind of interaction, according to Descartes, some radical (anti-Cartesian) dualists had mounted theories such as occasionalism and parallelism (which presupposes a predetermined harmony) to avoid accepting the possibility of causal interaction between them. Psychophysical parallelism, the turn-of-the-century version of the latter theory, held that each elementary psychological event corresponds to an elementary physical event. Yet there are no causal links between them because of the incompatibility of physical and mental causation as well as the lawlike conservation of physical energy. As a Cartesian, Kastil argued that without the possibility of causal interaction we could not have the inductive and inferential knowledge of the world that, in fact, we do have.[1] Since these issues were of central interest to him, they were certainly discussed in the club. In 1905 several members presented Bergmann with a signed copy of Busse's well-known book on dualism, which Kastil championed. This work was a comprehensive study of psychophysical interactionism — arguing for the epistemological and ontological necessity of causal linkage between mind and body against various versions of psychophysical parallelism and materialism.[2]

Kafka's "Description of a Struggle" repeatedly echoes Cartesian themes. The narrative is fragmented into three different perspectives, the young man's (the first-person narrator's), the fat man's, and the supplicant's. The first two try to overcome their ontological separation from the physical world by either making their volitions direct causal factors within this world or, inversely, manipulating a phenomenal world within their minds. The young man wills a slope to become steeper and to flatten again, a mountain and the moon to rise. The fat man implores his physical surroundings to give him some room so that he may breathe, and the mountains shift. The supplicant fears that the dualist split actually might occur, that his body would vanish and he might have to "acquire a body." The young man's own body detaches from his mind and grows "beyond [his] field of vision." Several skitlike scenes give pointed examples of interactionism. Whereas sometimes physical actions such as slapping and kicking are intended to cause bodily as well as mental liveliness, the following scene suggests that bodily liveliness is triggered by mental exertion: "Hardly were we outside when I [apparently] began to feel very [lively]. I raised my legs, let my joints crack, shouted a name down the street." Another time he observes his legs rise and run but cannot stop himself from continuing to run. In a bizarre variation on the dualism theme, the narrator of "Wedding Preparations" fantasizes that his body is split into a

---

[1]René Descartes, *The Philosophical Works of Descartes*, trans. Elizabeth Haldane and G. R. T. Ross, 2 vols. (Cambridge UP, 1970) 1: 189. Kastil recalls making this argument in his inaugural lecture (1902) and lecture courses (Alfred Kastil, *Studien zur neueren Erkenntnistheorie*, vol. 1, *Descartes* [Halle: Niemeyer, 1909] 99). In Brod's story "Difficilitäts-Moral" (Brod, *Tod den Toten* 99) the protagonist discusses Descartes's *Meditations* with Dr. Kurt Strasil (the name echoes Kastil's).

[2]Ludwig Busse, *Geist und Körper: Seele und Leib* (Leipzig: Dürr, 1903). Kastil indicated that someone was preparing a monograph that would serve as a historical introduction to Busse's book (*Descartes* 90).

hibernating and an active one and that his mind exists in both of them independently: "I don't even need to go to the country myself, it isn't necessary. I'll send my clothed body ... I assume the shape of a big beetle ... [my body] will manage everything efficiently while I rest."[3]

In "The Metamorphosis," notwithstanding Gregor's immediate acceptance of his transformation into a large insect — "It was no dream" he tells himself, applying Descartes's celebrated analogy between perception and dream — he can also question its actuality: "He looked forward eagerly to seeing this morning's delusions gradually fall away." In any event, his human consciousness remains largely unchanged and self-identical, and he sees his new physique initially as a temporary condition: "One can be temporarily incapacitated, but ... when the incapacity has been got over, one will certainly work with all the more industry." Since Gregor can distinguish between then and now, he is able to discover what is new about his insect body's physiological properties: touch, taste, smell, and pain are drastically changed, while his sight and hearing change much more gradually. For instance, he now is less subject to pain and favors spoiled over fresh food. Gregor probes the range of motor activities he is losing (speaking) or newly capable of (scampering, crawling). After several months his body acquires a new kind of mobility due to the discovery of his changed gravitational property: "He especially enjoyed hanging suspended from the ceiling ... in the almost blissful absorption induced by this suspension it could happen to his own surprise that he let go and fell plump on the floor. Yet he now had his body much better under control than formerly, and even such a big fall did him no harm." His discoveries of and adjustments to his changed physique underscore the interaction — what Descartes called the *union* or *intermingling* — between his mind and body. But this increasing union also results in his turning more and more into an insect-like amorphous brown mass, a shadowy being hidden away in a storage room. Ultimately he realizes that even his sister, the person closest to him, acknowledges the Cartesian split: she divorces him, her brother, from "this creature [that] persecutes us."

The story "A Report to an Academy" also plays on the dualist theme. The changing relation between the ape's mind and body is the reverse of the one depicted in "The Metamorphosis": the ape maintains his animal body while acquiring human consciousness, thereby telescoping millions of years of evolutionary history. He achieves this feat through ever more accelerated learning, by supplanting his previous apelike memories with human ones. Both

[3]K 44; CS 21. K 46; CS 22. K 48; CS 22. K 64; CS 26–27. CS 44; K 118. CS 46; K 128. K 16; CS 11. K 44; CS 21. CS 11; K 14 (for the odd occurrence of *apparently* see chapter 5, note 10). K 56 ("Ich sah, wie sich meine Beine mit ihren breit hervortretenden Kniescheiben hoben, aber ich konnte nicht mehr einhalten"). CS 55–56; E 235–36.

stories illustrate the view that consciousness as the medium of personal identity and self-awareness does not depend on the form of its embodiment, whether it be human, insect- or ape-like.

The story "A Hunger Artist" sketches yet another variation. The hunger artist wastes away his body to achieve a state of immaterial existence or physical nonexistence. He strives for nonembodied (Cartesian) consciousness, so much so, that the verification of his fasting can be realized solely through self-knowledge: "No one could possibly watch the hunger artist continuously, day and night, and so no one could produce first-hand evidence that the fast had really been rigorous and continuous; only the artist himself could know that."[4] In the *Meditations* Descartes showed that the physical state of hunger can be known only as a psychological state (as thought or desire): "But when I inquired, why ... this mysterious pinching of the stomach which I call hunger causes me to desire to eat ... I could give no reason excepting that nature taught me so; for there is certainly no affinity (that I at least can understand) between the craving of the stomach and the desire to eat .... For all these sensations of hunger, thirst, pain, etc. are in truth none other than certain confused modes of thought which are produced by the union and apparent intermingling of mind and body." Kastil records the same distinction between sensory pangs of hunger and the mental desire for food. The hunger artist acts on the primacy of thought and desire over corporeal needs: "I have to fast, I can't help it ... because I could not find the food I liked."[5]

In the letter to his father Kafka had suggested a connection between his interest in dualist constructions and his early awareness of experiential uncertainty: "But since there was nothing at all I was certain of, since I needed to be provided at every instant with a new confirmation of my existence, since nothing was in my own, undoubted, sole possession ... even the things nearest at hand, my own body, became insecure." The writing of "A Hunger Artist" was preceded by a diary entry that exploits the Leibnizian metaphor of the two clocks, which Kastil also used: "The inner [clock] runs crazily on at a devilish or demoniac or in any case inhuman pace, the outer one limps along at its usual speed. What else can happen but that the two worlds drift apart, and they do split apart, or at least clash in a fearful manner." As indicated before, at the turn of the century the two opposing theories of psychophysical parallel-

[4]CS 89; E 56. CS 92; E 59. CS 101; E 66. E 72 ("Sollte ich jetzt weniger Feingefühl haben?"); CS 108. CS 115; E 78–79. CS 134; E 95. E 147–55; CS 250–59. CS 269–70; E 165.

[5]*Philosophical Works of Descartes* 1: 188, 192 (Meditation VI). Hunger is, on the one hand, "a sensory feeling of displeasure and that sensation which serves as its basis," on the other, "a nonsensory, mental (*geistige*) desire for food which is based on these two sensory relations of consciousness" (Kastil, *Descartes* 26). CS 277; E 108.

ism and interactionism were aligned with linguistic theories. According to the Brentano school, language as a physical expression of mental states and the chief means of communication between minds (telementation) is perhaps the most solid proof of interactionism. Accordingly, in *Amerika* Kafka paints physical contiguity — whether literally or metaphorically we cannot know — as a condition of communication between minds. The fact that the uncle is far away not only prevents Mr. Green and Karl Roßmann from speaking to him but also from knowing what he thinks: "We can't see into the uncle's mind, especially at so many miles' distance from New York." An important feature of "In the Penal Colony" can be read as a fatalistic (even masochistic) commentary on language as the evolutionary product of man's duality. The officer tells the explorer who is studying the colony's penal institutions that there would be no point in telling the defendant the verdict, since he will be executed by having the law he violated engraved on his body: "There would be no point of telling him. He'll learn it on his body." "Nothing more happens than the man begins to understand the inscription, he purses his mouth as if he were listening. You have seen how difficult it is to decipher the script with one's eyes; but our man deciphers it with his wounds."[6] With the help of a machine that both wounds and writes on the body, the officer replaces language with a pain-inflicting connection between body and mind and, thus, between two minds. Sensations, even if only of pain, can become, or so the officer believes, a conduit for telementation.

Skepticism and Intentionality

Marty's lecture course on descriptive psychology (which Kafka took in 1902) presented a classification of mental acts that, along with Brentano's publications, provided the framework for much of the research done by the members of the philosophers' club. The types of acts he discussed were ideas, judgments, and the affects of desire and aversion (love and hate). In contrast to Locke or Herbart, for Brentano ideas are not the represented contents but the acts of representing them. Since it is acts that counteract and impede each other, the narrowness of consciousness applies primarily to them, not their contents. Second, the act of judging consists not in a connection or separation of ideas (as for Herbart) but in two basic mental attitudes toward them: acceptance or rejection. The early Brentano emphasized that we always sense, perceive, conceive, imagine, believe, feel, and desire *something*. That is, act-ideas — as well as judgments and desires, since they presuppose ideas — are "intentional": they are about (directed upon) some object. In principle the

[6]DF 178; H 149. D 2: 202; T 345. A 83; V 71. CS 145; E 104. CS 150; E 108.

notion of the mind's consciously active intentionality was a desirable departure from Herbart's theorem of passive associative relations between ideas. The conceptual improvement, however, did not stop the notion from becoming the occasion for endless difficulties. Brentano thought that only the first term of the so-called intentional relation between a thinker (he or she who entertains an act-idea) and the object must exist independently of the relation.[7] An ostensive act-idea, without being subjected to a further existential judgment, in no way entails that its object (the thing presented or thought about) transcendently exists. In contemporary terms, the imagining of a specific thing is merely the having of the respective mental content *that thing*. Only a further judgment might tell us that this content is due to our present perception of the thing or, more generally, acknowledges (refers to) the thing as one that is identified in the world and, as such, exists.

Brentano's concept of intentionality produces a double confusion, assumes different roles for the ostensive act-idea and its concomitant intentional object. The one kind of act-idea is ostensive in that it represents contents; the other does something entirely different, for it refers to things in the world. With respect to objects, in one of its roles *object* is simply a misnomer. It is not an object at all but a mental content — what Brentano called the *inexisting object* because it resides *in* the mind.[8] In its other role, object is the transcendently existing thing which the inexisting object (the representative mental content) points to or stands in for. Brentano chose to call mere contents *inexisting objects* and to make act-ideas appear to "relate" to them, because that way he could account for our imagining or referring to nonexisting entities such as mythological entities (unicorns) or phantasms (ghosts). The blurring of the various functions resulted in another serious drawback. Calling a content of consciousness an *intentional object* strengthened the underlying skepticism of Brentano's epistemology and undercut the act-idea's, and the intentional content's, desired cognitive (perceptual, referential) role in relating mind and external world.

Several of Kafka's stories show a puzzled yet playful concern with an object's possible double role and, due to this conceptual ambiguity, its ontological status — whether it merely "inexists" or perhaps actually exists. In

---

[7]MA 33–78. Brentano, *Deskriptive Psychologie*, ed. Chisholm and Baumgartner, 21. Ideas are acts of presenting-to-oneself. They can be ostensive acts such as imaginings or perceptions of objects; or nonostensive (abstracting) acts such as concepts.

[8]Brentano, *Psychologie vom empirischen Standpunkt,* vol. 1 (Leipzig: Duncker & Humblot, 1874) 115–22. [Only volume 1 appeared of this edition]. We have seen that Marty as well as Brod and Weltsch, all devoted Brentanoans, likewise confused ostensive idea and reference. For a recent view of Brentano's concept of intentionality see John Haldane, "Brentano's Problem," *Grazer philosophische Studien* 35 (1989): 1–33. Intentionality comes into its own with Husserl (see the next chapter).

"Description," someone addresses the sky and the square, challenging them to a game of ontological "chicken," in an attempt to convince his purported interlocutors that they are unreal. In other words, he insists that they are contents of his mind rather than transcendent things: "What is it that makes you all behave as though you were real? Are you trying to make me believe I'm unreal, standing here absurdly on the green pavement?" The notion of the possible content-of-thought character, and thus nonexistence of the sky, succeeds here philosophically because it is just one person (the thinker himself) who doubts the existence of an ontologically well-established entity such as the sky. In "Unhappiness," the ambiguity between the mental representation of a thing and an actual real-world perception of it engenders a contradiction because it is talked about, referred to, by two people. The narrator is surprised by a child who enters his apartment "like a small ghost." He tells his neighbor of this visit, and the following exchange ensues:

"But what if one doesn't believe in ghosts at all?"
"Well, do you think I believe in ghosts? But how can my not believing help me?"
"Quite simply. You don't need to feel afraid if a ghost actually turns up."
. . . .
"Obviously you've never spoken to a ghost. One never gets straight information from them. It's just a hither and thither. These ghosts seem to be more dubious about their existence than we are, and no wonder, considering how frail they are."

Brentano used the term *ghost* to illustrate both the meaning of apparent references to nonexistent entities in statements such as "Ghosts do not exist"[9] and the *ghost*-content of someone's belief in ghosts. Kafka's dialogue explores this dual meaning, weighs *ghost* as both the linguistic reference to a phantasm of popular superstition and the objectlike content of a false belief. However, the ghost's realistic (childlike) appearance and speech also suggest that either meaning may be insufficient to explain a hallucinated (physiologically induced) encounter with a child. The story makes the point that when a ghost visits you, it should not, in truth, be believed to exist and hence, ironically, should cause no fear.

Kafka thought that with "The Judgment" he had achieved his literary breakthrough. I suggest that it also was a breakthrough in the sense that it enabled him to play imaginatively with Brentano's confusing concept of

[9]CS 40; K 106. CS 391; E 19. CS 393–94; E 21–22. Brentano, *Die Lehre vom richtigen Urteil*, ed. Franziska Mayer-Hillebrand (Bern: Francke, 1956) 120. See also Marty, *Schriften* 2.1: xiv.

intentionality, and to do away with it. The friend of his youth, to whom Georg is writing his long letter, could be seen at first to exist merely in Georg's mind. When Georg proceeds to talk to his father about him, the father initially denies the friend's existence. When he changes his mind, acknowledging the friend and offering information about him that is quite different from Georg's, he may be just playing along with what he thinks Georg's fantasy about the friend is in order to manipulate his son's beliefs and actions. Our doubt about the friend's existence appears supported also by the fact that they never identify the friend by his name but only by relational terms such as *Georg's friend*. On the other hand, we realize that something perhaps more tangible is at hand when both, independently from each other, refer to the friend's yellow skin color. The author insisted that the story deliberately left the friend's existence in doubt: "The friend is hardly a real person, perhaps he is more whatever the father and Georg have in common." "The friend is the link between father and son." Years later, a 1921 diary entry concerning not his fiction but his life — "All is imaginary — family, office, friends, the street, all imaginary" — construes more clearly vacuous reference, that is, refers to something that is alleged not to exist in the physical world.[10]

The notion of objects that variably exist inside or outside the mind makes short shrift with our common-sense intuition that knowledge must be awareness of something other than ourselves, something nonmental. Brentano's phenomenalist and ultimately skeptical epistemology does not much care to account for what exists beyond the phenomena available to the mind. For him only mental acts exist in a strict sense, and only the "inner perception" of such acts constitutes certain knowledge. Marty also held that only "the inner awareness ... has the true character of perception, of an immediately evident grasping of an object." Knowledge of external reality, including other minds, is uncertain and hypothetical at best. For him the distinction between perceived sounds and their underlying physical nature (air waves), for Kafka's high-school textbook a scientific commonplace, shows that external entities are, conceivably, mere phenomena. An essay by Bergmann from early 1906 encapsulates this view: "Why do we suppose an external world at all, since our experience is constituted solely of *our* mental states, and we do not immediately ascertain the existence of bodies or the mental states of others? Obviously the assumption of an external world is supported only by a hypothesis .... My mental states are such as if they had been caused partially by bodies and the minds of others. We will never get beyond this 'as if.' And when we speak of a 'you' or a 'he,' this is nothing but an image, an analogy."[11] Kafka

---

[10]CS 77, 87; E 23, 31. CS 267; F 396–97. D 1: 278; T 186. D 2: 197; T 341.

[11]Brentano, *Psychologie vom empirischen Standpunkt* 120–22. MA 123 [APNDX 22]. Bergmann, "Das philosophische Bedürfnis in der modernen Physik, "*Philosophische Wochenschrift* 1 (1906): 337 (APNDX 23).

must have been impressed by his friend's scientifically rationalized view that the existence of other persons is but a hypothesis, an analogy in thought. The theme resounds throughout his work, from "Description of a Struggle" to *The Castle*.

Meinong's Nonentities

Compared to this chapter's other sections, this one offers perhaps the most tenuous reasons for assuming a modeling relationship between philosophy and Kafka's fiction. Yet it throws some light on a highly idiosyncratic "Kafkan" feature, the appearance of entities (things, persons) that do not exist in the everyday world or whose being-so does not accord with its physical laws. In an 1890 article on *Gestalt*-qualities Christian von Ehrenfels — Marty's colleague and later the teacher of Weltsch and Brod — argued that a melody is not perceived as a mere succession of sensory elements but grasped by internal perception as a complex of perceptual elements, as a *Gestalt*. Music, dance, natural motion, color changes (e.g., a sunset), visual objects such as paintings and drawings, and even literary texts are thus perceived. In the winter of 1901–1902 Kafka took Ehrenfels's course on ethics, which to some degree relied on the psychological and ethical theory of value-feelings developed by Ehrenfels's teacher Alexius Meinong.[12] Value-feelings are existence-feelings, concerned with both an object's positive value (how desirable it is) and negative value (how undesirable the case that it not exist). Ehrenfels adopted and modified this value calculus: "[According to Meinong] the intensity of the existence-feelings that accompany our positive or negative existential propositions concerning things determine the things' value .... In our terminology, an existence-feeling is generated by the *most ostensive, vivid and complete representation* of a thing's existence or nonexistence."[13] In his ethics course Ehrenfels was in a position to reflect on Meinong's recent (1899) theory of objects of higher order, which in turn had been suggested by Ehrenfels's *Gestalt* article. These higher-order entities are real or ideal complex entities much like a *Gestalt*. They are more than mere aggregates of elements or

[12]Christian von Ehrenfels, "Über Gestaltqualitäten," *Vierteljahrsschrift für wissenschaftliche Philosophie* 14 (1890): 249–92. Ehrenfels, *System der Werttheorie*, 2 vols. (Leipzig: Reisland, 1897–98) 1: xv; 2: 262. Presumably, Ehrenfels's book served as basis for the lecture course Kafka took with him.

[13]Alexius Meinong, "Über Werthaltung und Wert," *Gesamtausgabe*, ed. Rudolf Haller and Rudolf Kindinger, with Roderick Chisholm, 7 vols. (Graz: Akademische Druck- und Verlagsanstalt, 1969–78) 3: 245–66; 253–54. Ehrenfels, *Werttheorie* 1: 54–62.

relations among parts; they are individuated independently of any mental synthesis (collecting, relating, comparing, etc.). Linguistically speaking, they do not stand for mental acts but for publicly shared meanings or propositional objects.[14] In his 1902 publication *On Assumptions* Meinong repeatedly went back to this distinction between act and meaning, now identifying meanings with entitylike propositions. Bertrand Russell neatly encapsulated Meinong's distinction between the expression of a propositional attitude and the proposition itself: "Words *express* a state of mind, but *indicate (bedeuten)* an object[:] 'the death of Caesar' and 'Caesar died' indicate the same object but express a different state of mind ... the former is an *assumption*, the latter a *judgment*." Contradicting his former teacher Brentano, Meinong saw judgment not as an acceptance or rejection of particulars but as an affirmation or denial of propositions (states of affairs). He characterized propositions as *that-sentences*, *thought-objects*, or *objectives*.[15] Marty and Oskar Kraus were relentlessly critical of the concepts *assumption* and *objective*. Utitz later wrote that Meinong and his school were hated in the club with "intimate enmity" because he had turned philosophical apostate.[16]

In 1904 Meinong published his fully developed theory of entities or, better perhaps, nonentities. He distinguishes between a spatial-temporal entity's existence and the mere being (subsistence) of abstract entities such as squares, numbers, and propositions. The more general term is *subsistence:* existing entities subsist (are subsistents) as well. As before, he emphasizes that cognition and judgment are not directed toward particulars at all but toward positive or negative propositions concerning their being or properties. By taking propositions (his *objectives*) as the objects of judgment, he speculates that it is possible to refer to, and ascribe properties to, entities regardless of whether or not they happen to exist (or subsist). For instance, in the negative existential proposition "Ghosts do not exist," the reference merely seems to be to

[14]The meaning of a word "is not the content, but the object of the representation expressed by the word" (Meinong, "Über Gegenstände höherer Ordnung und deren Verhältnis zur inneren Wahrnehmung," *Gesamtausgabe* 2: 377–471; 385). For a discussion of Meinong's theory see Reinhardt Grossmann, *Meinong* (London: Routledge & Kegan Paul, 1974) 57–111. Also Lindenfeld, *Transformation of Positivism* 115–29.

[15]Bertrand Russell, "Meinong's Theory of Complexes and Assumptions (III)," *Mind* 13 (1904): 512. See also James Heanue, "Editor's Introduction," in Alexius Meinong, *On Assumptions*, ed. and transl. J. Heanue (U of California P, 1983) ix–xlviii. The German term in the singular is *Objektiv* (Meinong, *Über Annahmen, Gesamtausgabe* 4: 428–60).

[16]Marty to Brentano (6 Apr. 1902). See also Marty's criticism of Meinong's *Über Annahmen* (*Gesammelte Schriften* 2.2: 3–56) and Meinong's response (*Gesamtausgabe* 4: 493–506). Utitz, "Erinnerungen an Brentano" 74.

nonexisting entities; actually it is to the fact stated by the proposition *as a whole*:

> There is no doubt that what is supposed to be the object of knowledge need not be [exist] at all ... the being-so of an object is not affected by its nonbeing. The fact is sufficiently important to be explicitly formulated as the principle of the independence of being-so from being .... If the opposition of being and nonbeing is primarily a matter of the proposition and not of the object, then it is, after all, self-evident that neither being nor nonbeing can belong essentially to the object in itself .... The object is by nature indifferent to being, although one of its two existential propositions, stating the object's being or nonbeing, must be factual.[17]

This text insists on an entity's indifference to being or nonbeing — in other words, on the independence of being-so from being. Absence of being does not denote a mere nothing. For Marty, Kastil, and Bergmann this principle of independence was to become a major topic of criticism and polemic.[18] The principle implies that we can cognize nonactual concrete entities (unicorns) as well as impossible abstract entities (round squares), that is, entities that have or can have no being whatsoever. Every concrete term denotes an entity that has at least one essential property, is capable of true predication — even if that entity does not subsist.[19] As Meinong puts it in the same essay, nonexisting or nonsubsistent nonentities (entities so-called) are "outside of being," "beyond being and nonbeing."

Some of Kafka's fiction suggests a fascination with entities beyond being and nonbeing. Although skepticism and its flip side, everyday realistic inferences about the world, remain important throughout his fiction, extramental

[17]Meinong, "Über Gegenstandstheorie," *Gesamtausgabe* 2: 489–94. This slightly altered translation is drawn from Meinong, "The Theory of Objects," *Realism and the Background of Phenomenology*, ed. R. Chisholm (Glencoe, Ill.: Free Press, 1960) 76–117; 81–86.

[18]Marty, *Untersuchungen zur allgemeinen Grammatik* 292–353; 481–89. Kastil, *Descartes* 66. Bergmann, *Untersuchungen zum Problem der Evidenz der inneren Wahrnehmung* (Halle: Niemeyer, 1908) 67 and passim. Bergmann, *Das philosophische Werk Bernard Bolzanos* (Halle: Niemeyer, 1909) 34, 37, 57.

[19]Gottlob Frege and Bertrand Russell opposed this kind of theorem. Bergmann referred to Frege's view that "the existence of a concept (a class) consists in that things can be subsumed under this concept (that the class is not empty)." ("Über den analytischen Charakter des Existenztheorems," *Annalen der Naturphilosophie* 8 [1909] 499). See also Bertrand Russell, "On Denoting," *Mind* 14 (1905): 479–93; Willard V. Orman Quine, "On What There Is," *From a Logical Point of View* (Harvard UP, 1961) 1–19.

nonentities abound. During the winter 1909–10 he added the following brief story to "Description of a Struggle" that was later separately published as "Excursions into the Mountains":

> "I don't know," I cried [without a sound], "I do not know. If nobody comes, then nobody comes. I've done nobody any harm, nobody's done me any harm, but nobody will help me. A pack of nobodies ... I'd love to go on an excursion — why not? — with a pack of nobodies. Into the mountains, of course, where else? How these nobodies jostle each other, all these [arms stretched across or hooked into one another], these numberless feet treading so close! Of course they are all in dress suits. We [walk along so happily], the wind blows through [the gaps made by us and our limbs. In the mountains our throats become free]. It's a wonder that we don't burst into song.

The story idea appears to derive from the grammatical similarity of sentences such as "nobody comes" and "nobody will help me" with sentences such as "somebody comes" and "somebody will help me." *None*, however, means that there is not one single member in a given class of objects; *nobody* means that there is not one single member of the class of human bodies, of persons. The statements "nobody comes" and "nobody will help me" mean that the class of persons who come and the class of persons who will help the narrator are empty. Kafka's story surpasses Meinong's claims about nonentities by showing that even the quantifier *nobody* is not nothing, that it is different from nothing in that, despite its count being zero, it has the property of personhood (being a human body). Hence, Kafka adds with deft poetic license, it has a person's arms, feet, and throat, and, furthermore, since it comes in a pack, a discernible identity. In this way the narrator whose existence we have no reason to doubt is able to mingle physically with nobodies. The dialogue about the sighting of a ghost quoted above similarly insists that ghosts, without their actually existing, have properties: they doubt their own existence, are frail, etc. The independence of an entity's essential nature from its being is implied. In a November 1911 diary entry Kafka recorded "Bachelor's Ill Luck": "It seems so dreadful to stay a bachelor, to become an old man struggling to keep one's dignity while begging for an invitation whenever one wants to spend an evening in company .... That's how it will be, except that in reality, both today and later, one will stand there with a palpable body and a real head, a real forehead, that is, for smiting on with one's hand." The narrator enumerates some of his future properties, describes his future being-so ("that's how it will be") while realizing that this future bachelor-in-old-age will be the result of his current attitude. His future self will be admitting, no less than his present self admits — both embodied in this one body, this palpable head — that the proper response to his bachelorhood is the smiting-on of his forehead.

As suggested earlier, Georg's friend in "The Judgment" conceivably could be nothing more than a mental and linguistic fiction. Yet Georg's obsessive reflections and imaginings about him address the friend's being-so (his characteristics and existential circumstances) in vivid detail. In *The Trial* Josef K. initially deals with his bewilderment about the mysterious court by brushing off the strange events as merely imaginary. For instance, he tells the arresting officer about the unknown law "And it probably exists nowhere but in your own head" and entertains a fantasy of the court as a mere fiction: "While he stayed quietly at home and went about his ordinary vocations he remained superior to all these people and could kick any of them out of his path." And yet the warders, court clerks, judges, and whippers do exist, even if only in some shadowy locations outside the ordinary realm, such as attics or storage rooms. The magistrate whom Joseph K. meets socially does not want to "have his presence made known ... [wants] to be transported again to the darkness where his presence might be forgotten." The priest appears on a pulpit so small that it looks like an empty niche intended for a statue.[20]

In "A Country Doctor" the doctor, called to a patient in the middle of an icy winter night, has no horse to pull his gig. Two "unearthly horses" emerge from the uninhabited pigsty as if in an act of birth. Many years later Kafka interpreted their origin as an emergence out of nothing: "experience proves that something can come out of nothing, that the coachman and his horses can crawl out of the tumble-down pigpen." The doctor later tells himself: "I had to get my team out of the pigsty; if they hadn't chanced to be horses I should have had to travel with swine." In an inversion of Meinong's view, being is conceived as independent from being-so: if the doctor's team had not chanced to be horses, it would have been a different species of animals.[21] Similarly, in "The Departure" someone sets out on an enormous journey without taking any provisions. He argues that the initial absence of provisions guarantees that there will be provisions later, that only nonexisting provisions can save him.[22] The story "The Hunter Gracchus" strikingly utilizes the metaphor of being in a realm beyond being and nonbeing. The dead hunter's death ship is stranded in Riva, and the mayor engages him in the following exchange:

[20]CS 383; E 12. E 22; CS 394. CS 394–95; E 13. TR 6; P 11. TR 59; P 54. TR 104; P 91. P 176; TR 206.

[21]CS 225; E 128. D 2: 212; "Es kann erfahrungsgemäß aus Nichts etwas kommen, aus dem verfallenen Schweinestall der Kutscher mit den Pferden kriechen" (T 352). CS 223; E 126. According to Meinong, the converse of the principle of independence, that of being from being-so, does not hold (Karel Lambert, *Meinong and the Principle of Independence* [Cambridge UP, 1983] 27).

[22]The pertinent passage is left out of the English version (CS 449): "Ich brauche keinen [Eßvorrat], die Reise ist so lang, daß ich verhungern muß, wenn ich auf dem Weg nichts bekomme. Kein Eßvorrat kann mich retten" (E 321).

"Are you dead?" "Yes," said the Hunter, "as you see." ... "But you are alive too," said the Burgomaster. "In a certain sense," said the Hunter, "in a certain sense I am alive too. My death ship lost its way ... I only know this, that I remained on earth and that ever since my ship has sailed earthly waters." ... "And you have no part in the other world?" asked the Burgomaster, knitting his brow. "I am forever," replied the Hunter, "on the great stair that leads up to it."

The hunter may still belong to this world in the sense of not having been able, for the last fifteen centuries, to depart from it. But he does not belong to it in the sense of fully being there ("nobody knows of me"). And neither does he belong to nonbeing, the world of the dead. In this sense the story may be an allusion to Meinong's theory, but possible alternate sources are easily available. It is likely that Kafka knew Perez's story "Three Gifts," in which a dead man's soul remains homeless, suspended "between heaven and earth" because at his death his good deeds and his sins are found to balance each other exactly.[23] Kafka also continued to be intrigued with Albert Ehrenstein's satire about an "extra-territorial" (extraterrestrial) alien and knew Brod's story "The First Hour after Death," in which someone from a different world dies into, and is encountered in, the everyday human world.[24] In fact, all of these motifs may have expressed the concept that death is something more than nonbeing, that it constitutes an ontological limbo.

Dual Consciousness

Marty devoted a great deal of commentary to the awareness of one's own mental acts — he called it secondary or dual awareness — which, he hoped, avoided the self-defeating regression of introspective "self-observation." He sees introspection, understood as a concurrent separate act, not only as regressive but also as depriving itself of observing what it intends to observe: it neutralizes affects (such as anger), divides acts of "highest mental concentration" such as mathematical calculations. To avoid these pitfalls Marty con-

[23]CS 228; E 287. BK 248; CS 231. CS 230; E 288. Jizchok Lejb Perez, "Drei Geschenke," J. L. Perez, Scholem-Alejchem and Scholem Asch, *Ostjüdische Erzähler*, ed. Alexander Eliasberg (Weimar: Kiepenheuer, 1917) 80; cf. F 713; FE 512. Meinong later called nonentities *homeless* (Meinong, *Gesamtausgabe* 5: 220).

[24]Albert Ehrenstein, "Ansichten eines Exterritorialen," *Die Fackel* 323 (1911): 1–8; cf. B 322; L 279; also Hannelore Rodlauer, "Kafka und Wien. Ein Briefkommentar," *Anzeiger der philosophisch-historischen Klasse der österreichischen Akademie der Wissenschaften* 122 (1985): 216–17. Max Brod, "Die erste Stunde nach dem Tode," *Die weißen Blätter* 3 (1916): 223–56.

ceives consciousness as consisting of dual intentional relations that can be discerned but not separated in thinking. The duality consists in that the conscious act of primary cognition is accompanied by a secondary awareness of it. Each cognitive act does not relate just to its presented, perceived, or adjudged object but also to itself as an act of presenting, perceiving, or judging. Secondary awareness thus is an important aspect of the intentionality of all acts; it yields certain knowledge because in it perception and the perceived are parts of the same mental reality. Perhaps inspired by Marty, Kafka appears to emphasize some kind of secondary consciousness. Instances of self-reflexive awareness of one's focusing, fantasizing, deliberating, remembering, naming, etc. are strewn throughout the early work. In "The Sudden Walk" narrative consciousness is directed upon judgmental and volitional acts rather than their contents:

> When it looks as if you had made up your mind finally to stay at home for the evening ... [but] in spite of all that you have started up in a sudden fit of restlessness ... [have banged the] door more or less hastily according to the degree of displeasure you think you have left behind you ... when as a result of this decisive action you feel concentrated within yourself all the potentialities of decisive action, when you recognize with more than usual significance that your strength is greater than your need ... [then you] grow to your true stature.

Kafka never refers to the notion of secondary awareness, and thus it is impossible to say whether he would, like Marty, distinguish it from introspection, which is a major topic for him: "There are doubtless several reasons for the wild tempo of the inner process; the most obvious one is introspection, which will suffer no idea to sink tranquilly to rest but must pursue each one into consciousness, only itself to become an idea, in turn to be pursued by renewed introspection." This description of the regression of introspective acts appears surprisingly technical, comparable to this (non-Brentanoan) philosophical description: "We are racing along on our ideas and feelings .... Each thought *about* our ideas is a new idea. When we believe to have captured one moment, we already are the booty of the next one. When an idea acknowledges something, it requires another idea to acknowledge the acknowledgment. Nothing can free us from this infinite regress ... we never reach the highest constant self which could generate definitive knowledge. We cannot pull ourselves up by our bootstraps."[25]

---

[25]MA 53. MA 106–7 (APNDX 24). MA 123–24 (APNDX 25). CS 397; "[Wenn man] Ärger zu hinterlassen glaubt ... alle Entschlußfähigkeit in sich gesammelt fühlt" etc. (E 11). D 2: 202; T 345. Theodor Ziehen, *Psychophysiologische Erkenntnistheorie* (Jena: Fischer, 1907) 3.

Once Kafka's narrative point of view has become figural (the character's), the conceivable secondary awareness of the character's thoughts forgoes independent expression and merges with the narrative record of these thoughts. Several of Kafka's diary reflections imply that introspection is a perhaps unavoidable human condition but detrimental to writing: "Hatred of active introspection ...: Yesterday I was so, and for this reason; today I am so, and for this reason .... To put up with oneself calmly ... not to chase one's tail like a dog." "This inescapable duty to observe oneself: if someone else is observing me, naturally I have to observe myself too; if none observes me, I have to observe myself all the closer." "How would it be if one were to choke to death on oneself? If the pressure of introspection were to diminish, or close off entirely, the opening through which one flows forth into the world." In an incisive comment, Kafka observes that obeying the laws of writing in the act of writing may be the most effective circumvention of introspection: "The strange, mysterious, perhaps dangerous, perhaps saving comfort that there is in writing: it is a leap out of murderers' row [introspection-of-act, introspection-of-act]. This occurs by a higher type of observation, a higher, not keener type, and the higher it is and the less within reach of the 'row,' the more independent it becomes, the more obedient to its own laws of motion." Kafka makes an even more sweeping statement about the kind of conscious experience required for good writing: "How pathetically scanty my self-knowledge is compared with, say, my knowledge of my room .... Why? There is no such thing as observation of the inner world, as there is of the outer world. At least descriptive psychology is probably, taken as a whole, a form of anthropomorphism, a nibbling at our own limits. The inner world can only be experienced, not described."[26] Edmund Husserl insisted that secondary awareness is not needed for cognition, that conscious activity is naturally directed at the external world; the quoted text expresses just such a stance, invoking a Husserlian opposition between experiences taking place within our consciousness and our knowledge of the external world. The following chapter explores this complex semantic issue.

[26]D 1: 318; T 212. D 2: 200; T 342–43. D 2: 223; T 359. D 2: 212; "Das Hinausspringen aus der Totschlägerreihe Tat-Beobachtung, Tat-Beobachtung, indem eine höhere Art der Beobachtung geschaffen wird" (T 52; the reading is corrected according to TKA 1: 892). BN 14–15; H 53.

4: Reference and Belief Within Fiction

CERTAIN FEATURES OF EDMUND Husserl's early phenomenology, an important topic of discussion in the philosophers' club, are reflected in Kafka's distinctive style. Husserl plays a pivotal role in transforming the nineteenth-century psychological conception of knowledge into the modern linguistic one. His knowledge paradigm is sketched in the first section of this chapter. The remainder of the chapter discusses concepts from the turn-of-the-century philosophy of mind and language — reference, propositional content, and belief — that apparently were not treated broadly in the club. Kafka was familiar with them nonetheless, affording them sophisticated treatments in his fiction. In *The Trial* and *The Castle*, for instance, the cognitive, logical, and linguistic procedures that generate and justify the K.s' beliefs about their surrounding world are the main elements of an increasingly complex narrative structuring.[1] Of all the psychological and philosophical models that have left discernible traces in Kafka's narratives, phenomenological interpretation, reference, and belief are those most conducive to fostering modernist innovations in the narrative form.

Bergmann claimed that his book on the evidential truth of secondary (inner) awareness, an attempted Brentanoan refutation of Husserl's *Philosophical Investigations* (1900–1901), was representative of the kind of topics discussed in the club.[2] He was aroused polemically by Husserl's dismissal of secondary consciousness as irrelevant for cognition and by his innovative, and

---

[1]Therefore, the textual meanings in these novels are not to be derived primarily from semiotic codes ("narrative grammars") such as have been postulated for the novel in general. See Michael Riffaterre's recent statement of this postulate: *Fictional Truth* (Baltimore: Johns Hopkins UP, 1990).

[2]Wagenbach, *Franz Kafka* 112, 215 (note 409). Hugo Bergmann, *Untersuchungen zum Problem der Evidenz der inneren Wahrnehmung* (quoted as *Evidenz*). Bergmann later acknowledged that this book, based on his doctoral thesis of 1905, had accepted uncritically Brentano's and Marty's dismissal of Husserl. Kastil praised it in his review (*Zeitschrift für Psychologie* 53 [1909]: 390–92), and so did Kraus in his preface to Brentano, *Psychologie vom empirischen Standpunkt*, ed. O. Kraus, 2 vols. (Leipzig: Meiner, 1924–25) 1: lxiii–lxxvi.

by then fairly influential, view of intentionality. Husserl credits Brentano with
having introduced the latter notion to the theory of mind. But he completely
redefines it, by giving it a meaning-conferring role in the constitution of
knowledge. Brentano considered all mental states intentional acts in the sense
that they are directed upon phenomena (objects) — primary or secondary
phenomena, depending on which of the two types of consciousness is involved. The primary objects of mental acts — of ideas (presentings-to-one-
self), judgments, or affects — he called *physical phenomena*. These acts
themselves he called *psychical phenomena*, since they are perceived by inner
consciousness. In the early 1890s, a few years after his study with Brentano,[3]
Husserl gave serious consideration to what the predominant physiological
psychologies of his day were saying about the importance of sensations for
cognition. Hering's and Mach's phenomenalism favored appearing objects
over actual ones. Wundt's emphasized apperception as a scanning of and
focusing on perceptions of atomistic sensory impingements. Husserl concluded
that Brentano's ascription of intentionality to all ostensive representations is
false, that, in fact, elementary experiences of sensory qualities are noninten-
tional. As a Kantian, he also understood that the physiological emphasis on
sensory noticings and the narrowness of consciousness (the inhibition of the
greater part of one's sensory input) cannot account for the cognition of a
coherent physical world.

In response, he distinguishes between our preintentional sensations and our
intentional being-appeared-to by the respective object. Two distinct mental
activities, sensory and conscious-intentional, contribute to our knowledge of
the sense-perceptible world. Sensations are experienced (perceived, imagined,
reproduced) as qualities, such as seen colors, heard tones, felt hardness. These
provide "analogues" in cognition for the properties of the objects themselves.
That is to say, preintentional qualities serve as mediating "representations,"
signify a want to be interpreted, seek fulfillment in the intentional (perceptual
or conceptual) knowledge of the object itself. Parsed in non-Brentanoan
terminology, ostensive representations point beyond their phenomenal content,
become object-directed, meaning-conferring acts.[4] By reserving the concept
intentional for those acts that represent aspects of the things themselves,
Husserl insists on distinguishing between what is *in* consciousness (sensory

---

[3]During the years 1885–86 (Husserl, "Reminiscences of Franz Brentano," *The
Philosophy of Brentano*, ed. Linda McAlister [London: Duckworth, 1976] 47–55).
Marty's and Brentano's letters contain many cutting remarks about Husserl's having
left the fold.

[4]See Husserl's early explorations of physiological perception and intention (*Aufsätze
und Rezensionen 1890–1910* [Husserliana, vol. 22], ed. Bernhard Rang [The Hague:
Nijhoff, 1979] 275–99, 406–19). See also Karl Schuhmann, "Husserls doppelter
Vorstellungsbegriff: Die Texte von 1893," *Brentano Studien* 3 (1990–91): 119–36.

impingements, sensed qualities) and what consciousness externally grasps, the perceived aspects of things and, thus, the things themselves: "The perceptual presentation simply arises from the fact that the experienced complex of sensations gets informed by a certain act-character, a conceiving, an intending; to the extent that this happens, the perceived *object* appears, while the complex itself is as little perceived as is the act in which the perceived object is as such constituted."[5] In other words, the *Logical Investigations* replaces atomistic with phenomenological apperception:

> For us apperception is the surplus that exists within experience itself, within its ideational [descriptive] content as opposed to the raw sensory material; it is the act-character which as it were ensouls our senses and enables us to perceive this or that object, i.e. see this tree, hear this ringing, smell this scent of blossoms etc. The *sensations* and likewise the acts that "apprehend" and "apperceive" them are *experienced,* but they *do not appear as objects*; they are not seen, heard, perceived by any "sense." The *objects* on the other hand appear, are perceived, but they are not *experienced*.

In discussing the example of pain Husserl shows that sensations are not intentional in the phenomenological sense: "[Our sensations] function as representative contents of perceptual acts ... they receive an objectual 'interpretation' or 'uptake.' They themselves thus are not acts, but acts are constituted through them, that is, wherever intentional act-characters of the perceptual uptake-kind lay hold of them." Consciousness consists in the conceivings of objects other than itself, it is not simultaneously aware of the mental states that contribute to these conceivings. If we were to perceive our sensations, we would be prevented from perceiving aspects of the very object we want to perceive through these sensations: "If an external object (the house) is perceived, presenting sensations are experienced in *this* perception, but they are not perceived. When we are deluded regarding the existence of the house, we are not deluded regarding the existence of the experienced sensory content, since we do not pass judgment on it at all, do not perceive it in this perception.

---

[5] Edmund Husserl, *Logische Untersuchungen*, 2 vols. (Halle: Niemeyer, 1900–1901) 2: 75 [Untersuchung I, § 23]. Translations are based freely (without indicating the changes) on the English translation of the second edition of *Logische Untersuchungen* (1913–21): *Logical Investigations*, transl. J. N. Findlay, 2 vols. (New York: Humanities Press, 1970) [= LI 310]. Joint references to both Husserl and Bergmann (*Evidenz* 57) indicate that Bergmann quotes this text as negative foil for his own (Brentanoan) position. Husserl's term *erlebte Empfindungscomplexion* stresses that the "complex of sensations" is *experienced in* consciousness. *Empfindungscomplex* was first used by Ernst Mach in his *Die Analyse der Empfindungen* (Jena: Fischer, 1886) 20.

When we afterwards take note of these contents ... then we certainly perceive them but not *through* them the external object."[6]

Husserl remained close enough to Brentano to accept that the distinction between a sensed quality and the respective property of the fully conceived thing does not necessarily entail that this thing "transcendently" exists. Therefore, the important distinction he is making in this quotation holds true even for hallucinations, illusions, and dreams, where cognition is contrived, where one senses (reproduces) qualities and perceives the corresponding properties of the thing without its existing. In another important passage he attacks the notion *physical phenomenon* (such as a color), which for Brentano can be either an experienced phenomenal quality or a property of the perceived thing itself. Husserl attempts to clarify this confusion:

> The seen color — i.e. the color attributed to the appearing object of visual perception as its property — does not occur (if it exists at all) within the perceiver's experience. Yet within this experiencing state, i.e. the object's appearance, a real part corresponds to that seen color. What corresponds to it is the perceiver's *color-sensing*, that qualitatively determined subjective color-aspect which in his perception — in an intrinsic part of it ("the appearance of the object's color-property") — receives an objectifying "interpretation." These two, the color-sensing and the object's color-property, are often confounded .... The object's appearance (the experience) is not the appearing, purportedly transcendent thing; within the connecting stream of consciousness we experience the appearings; the things appear to us as existing within the phenomenal world. The appearings themselves do not appear, they are experienced.[7]

For Husserl, sensations (seeing a color, hearing a tone) are sensory events — they are felt, lived, experienced — but they themselves do not appear to us. Rather, they help us perceive the respective color or tone properties of the (possibly transcendent) object. In other words, the qualitative determinations of the object itself can never be conscious in the sense of being an experiential part of consciousness. Only a complex of sensations can be such a part. However, any such complex must be interpreted phenomenologically if it is

---

[6]Husserl, *Logische Untersuchungen* 2: 363 (V, § 14) [LI 567] [Bergmann, *Evidenz* 57]; 2: 370 (V, § 15) [LI 573] [Bergmann, *Evidenz* 61]. 2: 709 ("Beilage" [Appendix]) [LI 864] [Bergmann, *Evidenz* 60–61]; this appendix consists of a thorough refutation of the concept of secondary consciousness.

[7]Husserl, *Logische Untersuchungen* 2: 327–28 (V, § 2) [LI 2: 537–38]. Marty likewise confuses quality and property: "verschiedene Gegenstände [können] uns im Bewußtsein gegenwärtig sein, z. B. ein Ton, eine Farbe" (MA 69).

to help us intend or perceive the qualitative properties of the objects themselves. Husserl directs his phenomenological construction of intentionality
expressly against Brentano,[8] and thus Bergmann considers it Husserl's most
grievous error. He is offended by, and repeatedly returns to, the notion that
sensation initially is supposed to be without an object, to require an additional
act of intention or interpretation.[9] "[Husserl] does not tell us how what initially is merely 'experienced' and has no direction upon something objectual
suddenly obtains this direction .... How can something be interpreted ... that
is not perceived?" "[He] holds ... the psychical phenomena for originally
without object and tries, through artificial theories, to show that the object-
direction of consciousness which is part and parcel of the mental is the result"
of a further act. Both sensory impression and ostensive perceptual representation must be "*intrinsically* a singular presentation," "an ostensive, straightforward act [not requiring] interpretation."[10] Unmediated object-direction is
inherent in consciousness. If Bergmann, as he indeed indicated, presented this
spirited polemic to the club, he must have given Husserl's full-blooded concept of intentionality large play.

Husserl's recasting of intentionality as interpretation allows the insight that
the *same* complex of sensations can be perceived as *different* objects: "Whatever the origin of the presented (experienced) contents in consciousness, it is
possible that it contains the same sensory contents and yet yields different
interpretations, that, in other words, based on the same contents, different
objects are perceived." The following example illustrates how close the
concept of the intentional interpretation of sensations is to that of linguistic
signification — words serving as signs for meanings. We can see drawings on
a page as either arabesques or letters depending on which objects we happen
to apprehend: "Let us imagine, for instance, that certain figures or arabesques
have affected us aesthetically, and that we then suddenly apprehend that we
are dealing with symbols or verbal signs. In what does this difference consist?" The example resembles two passages from "In the Penal Colony" in

---

[8]See the second chapter of the fifth Investigation (*Logische Untersuchungen* 2:
344–74) [LI 552–76]. Brentano learned about Husserl's argument from Utitz (Brentano to Bergmann, 17 Sept. 1906, "Briefe Franz Brentanos an Hugo Bergmann,"
ed. Bergmann, 85–86).

[9]Bergmann, *Evidenz* 57, 69. He expressly equates sensation and act (64), sensation
and perception (6, note 1). His unwillingness to ascribe different roles to sensation
and perception-through-interpretation is surprising since he agreed with Helmholtz's
observation that in perception we exclude certain sensory data from awareness
(Bergmann, rev. of *Hermann von Helmholtz' psychologische Anschauungen*, by
Friedrich Conrat, *Philosophische Wochenschrift* 2 [1906]: 251–52) [APNDX 26].

[10]Bergmann, *Evidenz* 62, 22, 55, 58. "Die Anschauung hat den Vorzug, mittels
eines *einfachen* Inhaltes einen einzigen Gegenstand vorzustellen" (Bergmann, "Das
philosophische Werk Bernard Bolzanos," *Deutsche Arbeit* 8 [1908–09]: 85).

which two drawings yield alternate objects. The explorer makes out arbitrary
or ornamental lines, the officer reads off words:

> [All the explorer] could see was a labyrinth of lines crossing and
> recrossing each other .... "Read it," said the officer. "I can't," said
> the explorer. "Yet it is clear enough," said the officer. "It's very
> ingenious," said the explorer evasively, "but I can't make it out." ...
> "I told you before that I can't make out these scripts." "Try taking a
> close look at it," said the officer and ... outlined the script with his
> little finger ... in order to help the explorer to follow the script ....
> Now the officer began to spell it, letter by letter, and then read out the
> words.[11]

Since phenomenological interpretations of the same sensory qualities can yield
different objects, they cannot guarantee reference by themselves. Husserl is
not quite consistent here; he allows for the referential success of intentions in
cases where different sensory qualities yield aspects that belong to *one and the
same* object. With every turning of a perceived box the sensory input — and,
thus, one's perspectival experiences or adumbrations of the box, its aspects —
will change, but one continues to perceive (and thus refers to) the same box:
"I see a thing, e.g. this box, I do not see my sensations. I always see *one and
the same* box, however *it* may be turned and tilted. I have always the *same*
'content of consciousness' — if I care to call the perceived *object* a content of
consciousness. Each turn yields a *new* 'content of consciousness,' if, in a
much more appropriate sense, I call the *experienced* contents that. Very
different contents are therefore experienced, yet the same object is perceived."
Any given perception (like any conceptual representation) of an object is
perspectival, an aspect-perception. Yet that does not prevent it from being
interpreted referentially, as latching on to the object itself:

> The object shows itself from various sides ... it appears perspectivally
> foreshortened and adumbrated only to appear "just as it is" from

[11]Husserl, *Logische Untersuchungen* 2: 360–61 (V, § 14) [LI 565]. 2: 362 (V, § 14)
[LI 566]. Bergmann refers to this example (*Evidenz* 52, 56–57]. CS 148–49, 161;
E 107, E 117–18 (the explorer's phrase "Es ist sehr kunstvoll" could be a reflection
of Husserl's distinction between the arabesque's aesthetic effect and its signifying
(linguistic) meaning. Husserl's view of signs and language as requiring (just like
perception) interpretation overcomes Nietzsche's objection to any representational
link between sensory impingements and language or metaphor (Friedrich Nietzsche,
"Über Wahrheit und Lüge im außermoralischen Sinn," *Werke in drei Bänden*, ed.
Karl Schlechta [Munich: Hanser, 1960] 3: 312). The objection is based on an
outdated, atomistic mirroring model of perception and, consequently, language.

another side. All perceiving and imagining is, on our view, a web of partial intentions, fused together in the unity of a single total intention. The correlate of the latter is the *thing,* while the correlates of these partial intentions are the *objectual parts and moments.* Only in this way can we understand how consciousness reaches out beyond what it actually experiences. It can (so to speak) mean beyond itself, and this meaning can be fulfilled.[12]

Husserl's examples of the arabesque and the box show that the qualitative perceptual content and the object of a perceptual experience are logically independent from each other: the same content can denote different objects, and one and the same object can be denoted by different contents or aspects. As the next section will show, this important distinction goes a long way toward overcoming the naive mirroring concept of nineteenth-century physiological epistemology that bedeviled Brentano and Marty and, as a consequence, Brod and Weltsch.

Given Kafka's evident interest in explanations of sensory reception, one of his observations quoted at the end of the last chapter ("The inner world can only be experienced, not described") may very well imply that *sensa* (which are "inner") are not the immediate objects of our knowledge. They must be interpreted to yield objective aspects, and only through webs of such partial (perspectival, aspect-directed) intentions do we grasp the object itself. In "The Judgment" Georg's dismissive ruminations about his friend ("What could one write to such a man") cannot yield an adequate understanding of his friend's existence. Additional information provided by his father ("Of course I know your friend") contributes to a more complete insight: "His friend in St. Petersburg, whom his father suddenly knew too well, touched his imagination as never before. Lost in the vastness of Russia he saw him." Kafka's observation that "The friend's changing shape may be a change in perspective in the relationship between father and son" also would imply that the friend — if indeed he existed — could not be known by them but through each one's individual changing perspective.[13]

Husserl's conception of knowledge reverberates in other Kafka works, as well. The insect of "The Metamorphosis" is gradually revealed through a process of phenomenological discovery. Gregor's new *Gestalt* is not instantly accessible to him but is presented through initially blurred, then only partial perceptions. The fact that one morning in bed he finds "himself" transformed into this vermin gives him, beyond the sensory-perspectival or phenomenal,

[12]Husserl, *Logische Untersuchungen* 2: 360 (V, § 14) [LI 565] [reference to this passage by Bergmann, *Evidenz* 52]. 2: 513 (VI, § 11) [LI 701] [Bergmann, *Evidenz* 52].

[13]BN 14–15; H 53. CS 77; E 23. CS 85; E 29. CS 85; E 30. FE 267; F 397.

no clues about his body — the lower part of which "he had not yet seen and of which he could form no clear conception." Subsequently, Gregor's awareness expands through unceasing aspect-directed perceptions of his physiological properties. He augments this knowledge through the other characters' reactions to his appearance. Thus, he sees the chief clerk press his hand against his open mouth, slowly back away, and later stare at him with pouting lips over one twitching shoulder. He also can surmise that his mother sees him as a brown blot. What he really is saying is that she sees a brown-blot phenomenon and intends it to be Gregor: "[His mother] caught sight of the huge brown [blot] on the flowered wallpaper, and before she really [apprehended] that what she saw was Gregor, screamed in a loud, coarse voice." The short story "The Cares of a Family Man" can be read as a parodic toying with phenomenological interpretation. A narrator describes a strange wooden living thing that calls itself Odradek; since the creature is unusually nimble and can never be laid hold of, he conceives it through its separate parts. Odradek at first glance looks to him like a star-shaped spool, covered with knotted and tangled pieces of thread. On closer look it consists of a star and a crossbar with a small rod joined to it. Once its various aspects are thus assembled in the narrator's understanding, the thing looks somehow complete: "the whole thing looks senseless enough, but in its own way perfectly finished." In *The Castle,* upon arrival at night K. sees nothing of the castle. Since the castle hill is veiled in darkness, he stares into a seeming emptiness. Walking toward the castle on the following morning and assessing it from afar, he entertains two distinct thoughts: the castle looks like a clearly delineated and impressive whole yet is, from this distance, nothing more than an appearance; he knows the object (the referent) to be a castle, but it looks much more like a small town.

> Now he could see the Castle above him, clearly defined in the glittering air, its outline made still more definite by the thin layer of snow ... everything soared light and free into the air, or at least so it appeared from below. On the whole this distant prospect of the Castle satisfied K.'s expectations. It was ... a rumbling pile consisting of innumerable small buildings closely packed together and of one or two stories; if K. had not known that it was a castle he might have taken it for a little town.

As he gets closer, details appear that make the buildings look much more dilapidated than he first thought them to be. The castle's appearance changes from that of a small to that of a wretched-looking town. The tower is attached to nothing more than a residential dwelling: "With his eyes fixed on the Castle, K. went on farther, thinking of nothing else at all. But on approaching it he was disappointed in the Castle; it was after all only a wretched-looking town, a huddle of village houses."[14] The observer's different mental contents, yielding successive castle-aspects, are caused, of course, by his changing physical position in relation to the object. Since he knows that he is moving toward it ("With his eyes fixed on the castle, K. went on"), he is able to fix on it, through its changing appearances, as one and the same. The following section will address the puzzle — which Husserl did not completely resolve — of how reference is possible despite the subjectivity of the phenomenal aspects by which objects appear to us. It also will reveal Kafka's insightful sophistication in dealing with the puzzle.

Linguistic Reference

As indicated earlier, for Marty intrapsychic ostension determines reference. He also does not clearly distinguish between the referential and the conceptual function of certain terms. Usually both proper name and "definite description" (*the house*) name — refer to, designate — singular things. By contrast, so-called common nouns (sortal or general terms) designate concepts proper and thus serve in predicate expressions. Curiously, Marty holds that common nouns also designate the members of the specified class: for instance, the common noun *house* refers to all houses, *what is white* to all white things. Therefore, he calls not only proper names and definite descriptions but also common nouns *names*. An episode from "Description of a Struggle" suggests Kafka's familiarity with Marty's usage. A first-person narrator (the fat man) attributes to his interlocutor (the supplicant) a sort of semantic incompetence ("a sea sickness on solid land"), that is, the use of *name* for proper names, definite descriptions, and common nouns alike. Since the supplicant does not know how to identify the object by the respective common noun (*poplar*) or its "true name" (its definite description *the poplar*), he calls it by a proper name so completely arbitrary (*Tower of Babel*) that he almost instantly forgets it. He will soon have to replace it with an equally arbitrary name:

> [It is the nature of this seasickness that you have forgotten the true and proper name] of things, and that ... you're just pelting them with any old names ... hardly have you run away from them when you've forgotten the names you gave them. The poplar in the fields, which you've called the "Tower of Babel" because you [didn't know or]

[14]CS 92–93; E 59. E 65–67; CS 100–102. CS 119; E 82. CS 428; E 139. C 11–12; S 12–13.

didn't want to know it was a poplar, sways again without a name, soon
you have to call it "Noah in his cups."[15]

Phenomenalist theory was meant to overcome an earlier naive realism; it was
noncommittal or ambiguous with regard to truth and reference because phenomenal contents are incapable of being false. The self cannot be mistaken
about sensory and other experienced qualities; they are exactly as they are
seen, felt, reproduced, etc. In other words, qualities are subjective, independent of any object they might inhere in or be attributable to.[16] To a degree
Husserl agreed with this position, seeing the mental content of a perceptual
experience as independent from its object. He was well aware of illusions and
hallucinations, perceptual contents failing to latch on to purported sense-
perceptible objects. This awareness led him to his phenomenological approach, the attempt to overcome both phenomenalism and the view, shared by
many late-nineteenth-century philosophers, of singular reference as intrapsychic (intraindividual) ostension.

A pair of passages from Kafka's *Amerika*, discussed before in another
context, illustrate the two points. Veridical perception is by no means guaranteed by what is in appearance; some kind of independently establishable causal
relation to the perceived object is required for it. From the ocean liner on
which he has made the crossing, Karl observes in great detail the large ships
in New York harbor. Setting out again from New York, he turns around to
look at the harbor from a distance. The passage makes clear that memory
traces of the ships he previously had perceived not only induce him to direct
his attention more sharply but also to apperceive an actual ship in the distance
now and then. In other words, memory traces of past perceptions shape his
present representational contents and result in his seeing ships. Yet Karl
admits to himself that these sightings are a mirage ("now and then ... did one
fancy that one saw a ship"), thus dismissing the appearance's mistaken referential import.

Around the turn of the century two important theories of reference, by
Gottlob Frege and Bertrand Russell, strove to overcome the confused view of
reference by intraindividual ostension. Their solution is that we cannot identify
objects through ostensive ideas but will do so through the linguistic employment of, above all, definite descriptions, ascriptions of properties to purported
objects. Frege's influential discovery (1892) was that referential (singular)

---

[15]CS 33; K 88. For Marty's peculiar view of common nouns see Gottfried Gabriel,
"Why a Proper Name has Meaning: Marty and Landgrebe vs. Kripke," *Mind,
Meaning and Metaphysics*, ed. Mulligan, 70.

[16]For an excellent discussion of these issues see the third chapter of Colin McGinn's
The Character of Mind (Oxford UP, 1982). Curiously, it makes no mention of
Husserl's pioneering contribution.

terms express an objective, shareable meaning — a conceptually specifying mode of presentation — through which they succeed in identifying things in the world. Even a proper name (*Aristotle*) must carry with it some description of its bearer, must show *who* he was.[17] Although I would not want to claim any direct links between Kafka and Frege's reference theory, the former shows astonishing insights into the intricacies of this central semantic problem. "The Metamorphosis" establishes repeated reference to a man not through the narrator's changing ostensive ideas but an adopted defining description of him. Gregor first catches sight of the family's new lodgers one evening when they are seated at the dinner table while his door remains open. The one seated between the other two acts as their spokesman. The defining (indexical, contextual) description by which Gregor refers to him (*the man in the middle*) is based entirely on how Gregor describes and identifies the man (the referent) on this particular occasion. For the remainder of the story, however, Gregor keeps identifying him through the same description, regardless of whether or not his position in relation to the other two lodgers still satisfies it.[18] Kafka is confident that the reader will adopt Gregor's chosen description in maintaining a referential fix on this specific man.

Perceptual identifications are fallible; they may designate objects other than those actually given to us in these perceptions. In *The Trial,* at the scene of his arrest Josef K. recognizes the three employees in his bank only after the inspector reveals their identity. In *Amerika* the Head Porter mistakes Karl for another lift-boy who allegedly carouses nightly in the nearby town: "So I've mistaken you for someone else, have I? .... In all my thirty years' service I've never mistaken anyone yet, as hundreds of waiters who have been here in my time could tell you, and is it likely that I would make a beginning with you, you wretched boy? With that smooth face of yours that nobody could mistake?" An entry from Kafka's 1915 diary soberly deals with reference to something seemingly nonexisting. A few months into the First World War, during a depressed spell, he reads a newspaper report about Sweden's intention to remain neutral despite threats of the "Triple Entente" (France, Great Britain, and Russia). He observes that only now is he able to understand what the report means. Three days earlier he would have felt that a "Stockholm ghost" was speaking, that its words were "creatures of air" that one could

---

[17]A 112; V 93. About turn-of-the-century theories of reference see Leonard Linsky, *Referring* (London: Routledge & Kegan Paul, 1967); David W. Smith and Ronald McIntyre, *Husserl and Intentionality* (Dordrecht: Reidel, 1982) 176–219. Frege's theory of propositional judgment and reference was directed mainly against the physiological phenomenalism of Wundt and Mach (Hans D. Sluga, *Gottlob Frege* [London: Routledge & Kegan Paul, 1980] 31, 38, 104).

[18]"The man in the middle" (CS 128); "der, welcher in der Mitte saß" (E 90). "The middle lodger" (CS 131, 137); "der mittlere der Herren "(E 93, 97).

never succeed in touching with one's fingers. In other words, the reported events would have had no referential significance for him, the referring term *competent authority* (the Swedish government) would have designated nothing more than a ghost. In contrast to his puzzled reference to a ghost in the story "Unhappiness," here *ghost* designates something (the Swedish government) that, had he heard about it three days ago, would have appeared not to exist at all. Nonetheless, after he overcomes his depressed mood, he acknowledges that his belief would have been a false one, that the Swedish government would have existed just the same. A "Hunter Gracchus" fragment, shorter than the one previously discussed, emphasizes that a term is only properly referential if it designates an actual item in the world. The "green Hunter Gracchus" is told by the narrator that no one has time to think of him or find out about him. Only on his deathbed might someone let the hunter pass "through his idle thoughts." The reason is "that you are not the talk of the town, however many [things are talked about,] you are not among them, the world goes its way and you go on your journey, but until today I have never noticed that your paths have crossed." There is no causal, referential, or linguistic contact between him and other people; he is not one of the items the world contains.[19]

In "The Great Wall of China" (also from early 1917) the narrator is well aware that one must accept the fallibility of one's beliefs ("doubt of one's own knowledge"). His village is thousands of miles south of the imperial capital. Initially counting himself as one of the villagers, he says "we think only about the Emperor. But not about the present one; or rather we would think about the present one if we knew who he was or knew anything definite about him ... [our people] do not know what Emperor is reigning .... Long-dead emperors are set on the throne in our villages, and one that only lives on in song recently had a proclamation of his read out." When an imperial official visits and admonishes them in the name of the ruling Emperor, they think that the official is "speaking of a dead man as if he were alive." They pretend that they do not notice his mistake, but after his departure they pledge obedience to "our present ruler," some nonexistent emperor resurrected from a decayed urn. The narrator's satirical exaggeration about their ruler's illusory origin makes it clear that the person designated by the villagers (*our present ruler*) is not identical with the real-life emperor, the referent of the narrator's own earlier referring term *the present [Emperor]* and, presumably, the official's *the ruling Emperor*. Although Kafka apparently did not intend it that way, his story's various emperor-descriptions are in tune with Frege's insight that attributions of beliefs to others render referring terms within these belief-contexts undecidable and nonextensional (nonreferential). A speaker who attributes a belief to someone else cannot be sure about the identity, or the

[19]A 180; V 149. D 2: 109; T 284. CS 233; BK 250.

existence, of the believer's referents, no matter how unambiguously descriptive or well established his referring terms are. In the sentence "Peter believes that the German capital lies on the Spree" we do not know whether the description *German capital* refers to Berlin, Bonn, some other city, or no existing city at all. The denotation is Peter's, not that of the speaker of the sentence who, therefore, cannot legitimately substitute Berlin for it. The same semantic rule applies to the narrator's tale. Although he counts himself among the villagers and thus speaks in the first-person plural, he also makes it clear that he does not share the villagers' beliefs and thus cannot know for sure to whom their use of *our present ruler* refers. He eventually concludes that the villagers' referring terms are not referential at all, do not guarantee the referent's existence: "If from such appearances anyone should draw the conclusion that in reality we have no Emperor, he would not be far from the truth."[20]

In *The Castle* the problem of reference becomes a central theme. When K. meets his two new assistants, Arthur and Jeremiah, he cannot tell them apart; they are epistemic twins: "'You're a difficult problem,' said K., comparing them, as he had already done several times; 'how am I to know one of you from the other? The only difference between you is your names ... I can only see you with my own eyes, and with them I can't distinguish you. So I will treat you as if you were one man and call you both Arthur; that's the name of one of you — yours, isn't it?' he asked one of them. 'No,' said the man, 'I'm Jeremiah.'" K.'s attempt to identify one of the two perceptually and to match him with the name *Arthur* fails. He cannot identify either of them, distinguish between them, or properly use their respective names. The correct use of a proper name requires the perceptual, and thus referential, distinctness of its bearer. The mayor tells K. that through his easy contact with the lower-level authorities he has not gained any real access to the castle: "You haven't once up to now come into real contact with our authorities. All those contacts of yours have been illusory, but because of your ignorance of the circumstances you take them to be real." K. receives letters from Klamm, a top-level official, and has seen him once in the officials' inn through a peephole. But Klamm's identity remains doubtful to K. as well as to the villagers. Olga tells K. that her brother Barnabas, Klamm's courier, doubts that the official whom he meets face to face, and whom they call Klamm at the castle office, really is Klamm: "He says, he's assigned to Klamm, who gives him his instructions in person .... Only think, directly assigned to Klamm, speaking with him face to face! But is it really so? Well, suppose it is so, then why does Barnabas doubt that the official who is referred to as Klamm is really Klamm?" Olga

---

[20]CS 242; "Zweifel am eigenen Wissen" (E 295). CS 243–45; E 295–97. Gottlob Frege, "On Sense and Meaning" (1892), *Translations from the Philosophical Writings of Gottlob Frege*, ed. Peter Geach and Max Black (Totowa, N. J.: Rowman & Littlefield, 1952) 56–78. CS 246; E 298.

further explains that the villagers know Klamm through various sightings, and reports about his appearance, and rumors. Their descriptions of Klamm differ from each other in drastic ways, even contradict each other, depending on the occasion of sighting and the observer's mood. They villagers are at such a loss to explain these discrepancies that they attribute them to Klamm's constantly changing appearance:

> We do not often speak about Klamm, whom I've never seen ... still, his appearance is well known in the village, some people have seen him, everybody has heard of him and out of glimpses and rumors and through various distorting factors an image of Klamm has been constructed which is certainly true in fundamentals. But only in fundamentals. In detail it fluctuates, and yet perhaps not so much as Klamm's real appearance. For he's reported as having one appearance when he comes into the village and another on leaving it ... when he's alone he's different from when he's talking to people, and — what is comprehensible after all that — he's almost another person up in the Castle.

Admittedly, descriptions are often indexically (contextually) determined, they may differ from each other to various degrees, depending on the particular observer-describer, his or her occasion of use, and the concepts under which the object is presented to him or her. The villagers' constantly changing descriptions are, however, perhaps too different from each other to be true of any single person; they make it doubtful whether there exists any one person whose name is Klamm. Olga reinforces these doubts by returning to her brother's account of the man he knows as Klamm. Finding his descriptions inexplicably conflicting, she concludes that Barnabas never had any contact with someone who might be Klamm:

> Barnabas is familiar with all those accounts of Klamm's appearance ... he has collected and compared a great many, perhaps too many, he even saw Klamm once through a carriage window in the village, or believed he saw him, and so was sufficiently prepared to recognize him again, and yet — how can you explain this? — when he entered an office in the Castle and had one of several officials pointed out to him as Klamm, he didn't recognize him, and for a long time afterwards couldn't accustom himself to the idea that it was Klamm .... He speaks to Klamm, but is it Klamm? Isn't it rather someone who's a little like Klamm? A secretary perhaps, at the most, who resembles Klamm a little and takes pains to increase the resemblance ... a man like Klamm who is so much sought after and so rarely seen, is apt to take different shapes in people's imagination. For instance Klamm has a village secretary here called Momus .... A stoutly built young man, isn't he?

And so evidently not in the least like Klamm. And yet you'll find
people in the village who swear that Momus is Klamm, he and no
other.[21]

Thus, paradoxically, the more detailed the descriptions gathered by the villagers become, the less determinate becomes their knowledge of Klamm. Kafka
manages to illustrate the complex notions of perceptual and descriptive identification while pushing them to their rational limits.

Expressing Propositions and Beliefs

Brentano's theory of judgment provides the insight that one is aware of
one's mental acts not by ascribing existence or predicates to them but by
immediately acknowledging or denying them. Since only these (opposing)
stances toward one's own acts constitute certain knowledge, they are the basis
for our knowledge of the world. Thus, existential judgments about primary
objects — such as "I know that 'A' exists" or "I know that 'A' does not exist"
— reduce to the known acknowledgment or denial of them ("I accept 'A'", "I
reject 'A'"). The positive particular judgment "Some men are wise" and the
negative particular judgment "Some men are not wise" of traditional logic
reduce, respectively, first to the positive existential judgments "Wise men
exist" and "Unwise men exist" and then to "I accept a wise man" and "I
accept an unwise man." The universal judgment of traditional logic, "All men
are mortal," is reparsed as a negative existential judgment, "Immortal men do
not exist" (or "No immortal man exists"), and then as "I reject immortal
men."[22] In short, for Brentano judgments concerning the existence and properties of (as well as relations between) things become reduced to accepting or
rejecting the things themselves — whatever simple or composite singular terms
stand for.

Through the work of Bernard Bolzano, Frege, Meinong, Stumpf, Husserl,
and Marty the members of the philosophers' club, especially Bergmann,
became aware of an emerging philosophical consensus[23] (in which Brentano

[21]C 24–25; S 23. C 93; S 72. S 39, 168 ("ich selbst habe ihn gesehen"); C 47, 229.
C 229; S 168. C 230–31; S 169. C 232–37; S 170–74.

[22]Brentano, *Psychologie vom empirischen Standpunkt* (1874) 186–88; 283–89; 277.

[23]Edgar Morscher, "Von Bolzano zu Meinong: Zur Geschichte des logischen Realismus," *Jenseits von Sein und Nichtsein: Beiträge zur Meinong-Forschung*, ed.
Rudolf Haller (Graz: Akademische Druck- und Verlagsanstalt, 1972) 69–102.
Morscher, "Propositions and States of Affairs in Austrian Philosophy before Wittgenstein," *From Bolzano to Wittgenstein: The Tradition of Austrian Philosophy*, ed.

did not share) that judgments are psychological attitudes not toward things but toward meanings expressed by either existential statements or sentences of the subject-predicate form. In this consensual view of judgment, initiated by Gottfried Wilhelm von Leibniz and taken up by Bolzano,[24] meanings are defined as *thoughts* (Frege), *objectives* (Meinong), *states of affairs* (Stumpf), *judgment-contents* (Marty), or, as they will be referred to here, *propositions* (Locke, Russell). Propositions are (1) abstract or ideal in that they are not objects in space and time, (2) mind-independent by being neither ostensive ideas nor psychological acts of judging, and (3) language-independent, distinct from spoken or written sentences.[25] Furthermore, propositions are either true or false; they are truth-bearers: being true they correspond to facts (states of affairs that obtain), being false they state what is contrary to fact (refer to states of affairs that fail to obtain). The individual can relate to things causally and intentionally (through perception) but relates to propositions merely intentionally, by making them the contents of his or her states (thought, belief, doubt, desire, etc.). The statement "I believe that p" — consisting of an attitude ascription ("I believe") and a that-clause ("that p") — expresses an intentional relation between myself and the proposition "p" or, put differently, expresses a mental state with "p" as its content. This relation (my having this belief) consists in both my holding the proposition to be true and my understanding of what conditions make the proposition true or false.

Marty did not adopt the full-fledged theory of truth-bearing (true *or* false) propositions. He accepted only one kind of mind-independent, ideal (though temporal) entity: the judgment-content of a true existential judgment (the fact of a thing's existence). An existential judgment does not have a mind-independent content if it is false (if no such thing exists).[26] In other words, Marty claimed a middle ground between the propositional school and his teacher's position. Brentano came to reject all ideal entities and propositions (even Marty's "existence facts") as complete fictions. For him, judgments were intentional (yet real) relations to the particular things with which they were

J. C. Nyiri (Vienna: Hölder-Pichler-Tempsky, 1986) 75–85. Bergmann, *Das philosophische Werk Bolzanos*.

[24]These two influenced Frege's emphasis on propositions or thoughts over concepts (E.-H. Kluge, *The Metaphysics of Gottlob Frege* [The Hague: Nijhoff, 1980] 231–90).

[25]See Dallas Willard, *Logic and the Objectivity of Knowledge: A Study in Husserl's Early Philosophy* (Athens: Ohio UP, 1984) 176–86. Ernst Tugendhat, *Vorlesungen zur Einführung in die sprachanalytische Philosophie* (Frankfurt: Suhrkamp, 1976) 62–65, 98–102.

[26]Marty, *Grundlegung der allgemeinen Grammatik* 288–362, 391–431. See Edgar Morscher, "Judgement-Contents," *Mind, Meaning and Metaphysics*, ed. Mulligan, 181–96.

directly concerned. In the summer of 1906 Bergmann was staying with Brentano and was drawn into the long-standing argument between him and Marty
over this issue. Bergmann ultimately embraced the latter's position, conceiving the true existential judgment not as a thing's unmediated acknowledgment
but as a relation to or correspondence with the thing's existence. He repeatedly defended this supposition of a mind-independent, propositional meaning
of true existential judgment.[27]

The issues of factualness, truth, verification, and knowledge pervade
Kafka's work from the early perception-based descriptions to the complex
belief structures woven through his mature fiction. He had a keen eye for the
fallibility of perceptual belief, as illustrated by a passage from "Children on
a Country Road" (written during 1909–10). The narrator observes flocks of
birds quickly rising against the sky and then suddenly gets the impression that
he himself is falling: "Then birds flew up as if in showers, I followed them
with my eyes and saw how high they soared in one breath, till I felt not they
were rising but that I was falling." Descriptions arising from perceptual
content do not necessarily result in veridical beliefs. With regard to the structure of belief in general,[28] Kafka clearly distinguishes propositional attitudes
("knows that") from contents (expressed by the clause following the "that").
In a diary entry he remarks that psychological ascriptions — phrases containing words such as *indescribable*, *sad*, and *beautiful* — contribute little to
making the respective propositional contents comprehensible to the listener.
Statements in writings by others are more intelligible to us than our own
statements since they are mostly not introduced by attitude expressions. Put
differently, free-standing propositional statements latch on to the world in a
more direct fashion than those qualified through propositional attitudes:

> Our own experience inclines us to think that nothing in the world is
> further removed from an experience (sorrow over the death of a
> friend, for instance) than its description. But what is right for us is not
> right for the other person. If our letters cannot match our own feelings
> ... [if] expressions like "indescribable," "inexpressible,"or "so sad,"
> or "so beautiful," followed by a rapidly collapsing "that"-clause, must
> perpetually come to our assistance, then as if in compensation we have
> been given the ability to comprehend what another person has written

---

[27]See Brentanos letter to Marty of 2 Sept. 1906 (Brentano, *Die Abkehr vom Nichtrealen*, ed. Franziska Mayer-Hillebrand [Bern: Francke, 1966] 172–77. Bergmann, *Das
philosophische Werk Bolzanos* 10–27. Bergmann, "Das philosophische Werk Bolzanos" 82.

[28]CS 379; E 7. For a good contemporary overview see Michael Devitt and Kim
Sterelny, *Language and Reality: An Introduction to the Philosophy of Language*
(Oxford: Blackwell, 1987).

with [the calm exactitude which we lack, at least in the same degree,] when we confront our own letter-writing. Our ignorance of those feelings ... becomes [comprehension] the moment we are compelled to [stick to this letter,] to believe only what it says, and thus to find it perfectly expressed.

Kafka's frequent nominalizing of attitude ascriptions — the *assumption that* ("I am not going to [make the assumption] that it is kept from me") or the *idea that* ("You must just try to get rid of the idea that this is Gregor") — indicate that such attitudes are justifiably called *propositional:* they are mental states not having singular representations but propositions as their contents. His work displays a wide range of expressions of such contents. A single attitude marker may introduce several propositions, yet the *that*, preferably, should be repeated when the subject term of the content expression changes — for instance, from the self-referential *I* to the reference term *people:* "I have [no] defense to offer [that I stand] on this platform, [hold] on to this strap, [let] myself be carried along by this tram, [that people] give way to the tram or walk quietly along." The preposition *without* and the past participle of a verb express a counterfactual proposition: "I feel a little meditative, without having met anything on the stairs worth meditating about." "Someone must have been telling lies about Joseph K., for without having done anything wrong he was arrested one fine morning." Content statements can be nominalized through terms such as *circumstance* or *fact*: "Perhaps my long body displeased him by making him feel too small. And this [circumstance] tormented me"; "At first K. thought very little of the offer made him, but the fact that an offer had been made seemed to him not without significance." Gregor's family pronominalizes the proposition that Gregor cannot understand them through the pronoun *that*: "'If he could understand us,' said her father, half questioningly; Grete, still sobbing, vehemently waved a hand to show how unthinkable that was. 'If he could understand us,' repeated the old man, shutting his eyes [to yield completely to] his daughter's conviction [of the impossibility of that]."[29] Grete's belief is that it is inconceivable, or rather, impossible that Gregor could understand them. Her gesture excludes other beliefs and, in effect, other possibilities. By shutting his eyes, her father assents to what she believes, shuts out the proposition that Gregor understands them — just as conscious awareness actively impedes what it does not attend to.

Paradoxically, Kafka's character-narrators sometimes entertain propositions while engaging in the denial of the mental attitudes that introduce them: "And without [thinking of the fact] that he was still unaware what powers of

---

[29]D 1: 174; T 117. CS 82; E 27. CS 134; E 95. CS 388; E 16. CS 387; E 15. TR 1; P 7. CS 16; K 26. C 118; S 89. CS 133–34; E 94.

movements he possessed, without even [thinking of the fact] that his words ... [had] again been unintelligible, he let go the wing of the door." Sometimes they show an awareness of their beliefs' fallibility, the fact that one can believe (hold true) a proposition even if it is false. For instance, in a passage from "Description" quoted earlier the narrator first simply imagines, then actually believes that a girl in a white dress loves him, and he contemplates how this love affects him. He does not accept the belief's falseness until he tries and fails to remember his reasons for acquiring it in the first place: "I imagined that I was loved by a girl in a beautiful white dress ... the love of the white-clad girl put me into a sad rapture ... of the dear girl I only knew that she had worn a white dress, but I could not remember what reasons I had for believing that the girl loved me."[30]

In *Amerika* the stoker answers Karl's statement "I think my [trunk] can't be lost yet" with the proverbial saying "Faith makes blessed." He plays on the word's double meaning as faith and belief: "Believing makes blessed" would mean that a belief about factual matters is as tenuous as a religious faith. He further suggests that Karl's belief about his trunk is either false, or, if true, should lead to an action different from the one Karl is intending: "Either the [trunk] is stolen and then there is no help for it, or the man left it standing where it was, and then we'll find it all the more easily when the ship is empty." Karl suspects that the stoker's otherwise convincing statement that the trunk can be found more easily after all the passengers have disembarked holds something hidden that makes it false: "it seemed to him that the idea, otherwise plausible, that his things would be easier to find when the ship was empty must have a catch in it somewhere." Later in the novel, before his dismissal from the Hotel Occidental, Karl suspects that the Head Waiter will misconstrue his, Karl's, version of what had happened: "He knew that all he could say would appear quite different [from how he had meant it] and that whether a good or a bad construction was to be put on his actions depended alone on the spirit in which he was judged." Taking the Head Waiter's lying (though, for the Head Porter, "unimpeachable") assumptions about Karl's behavior at face value, the Manageress constructs an elaborate web of false propositions about him — alleged facts she accuses him of having hidden from her: "No, Karl, no, no! We won't listen to any more of this. When things are right they look right, and I must confess that your actions don't .... Perhaps you merely acted without thinking, but perhaps too you aren't the boy I thought you were .... No one must know how or where you got drink for that man, who couldn't have been one of your former friends .... Therefore it must

---

[30]CS 102; E 68. "[Es fiel mir ein,] daß ich geliebt würde von einem Mädchen in einem schönen weißen Kleid ... ich konnte mich gar nicht mehr erinnern, welche Gründe ich gehabt hatte, an die Liebe des Mädchens zu glauben" (K 36-38). The passage does not appear in CS.

have been an acquaintance you just picked up one night in some drinking den in the town. How could you hide all these things from me, Karl?" True belief (knowledge) is belief in a true proposition that corresponds to a state of affairs in the world. After Gregor's death, the three lodgers realize that their situation in the Samsa household has changed — specifically, that Mr. Samsa means exactly what he is telling them: that they must leave the apartment immediately. The idea of propositional correspondence or "fit" is expressed by a metaphor: one of the lodgers understands the request, the changed situation in terms of a rearrangement of his mind's "furniture": "He stood his ground at first quietly, looking at the floor as if [the things in his head arranged themselves into] a new pattern."[31]

Kafka's minimalist yet syntactically complex story "Up in the Gallery" illuminates the nature of beliefs, their correspondence (or lack thereof) to factual states of affairs, with great effect. It consists of two paragraphs each of which is a long, grammatically and logically complex sentence. The first is a counterfactual conditional whose antecedent and consequent clauses could be loosely paraphrased in this way: if the occurrences in a circus arena involving an equestrienne were inhumane in the specified way — if she were forced by a ruthless ringmaster to perform for months on end without interruption, etc. — "then, perhaps, a young visitor to the gallery might race down the long stairs through all the circles, rush into the ring, and yell: Stop! against the fanfares of the orchestra." Counterfactual constructions do not exclude the possibility that the imagined circumstances could exist, but they express the sentence user's (here, the narrator's) belief that the circumstances related in the antecedent clause are contrary to fact.[32] By stating that the young visitor perhaps would have acted to stop the events in the arena, the sentence's consequent clause also entails that, if the antecedent, and thus the entire construction, expressed facts, the visitor would try to stop the inhumane proceedings because he believed them to be factual. In other words, by means of the conditional sentence construction the narrator declares that someone's beliefs about the world (along with other belief-based attitudes such as desires, hopes, fears) may dispose him or her to act in certain ways.

The story's second sentence is a causal construction in the indicative (factual) mood: "But since that is not so; a lovely lady, pink and white, floats in between the curtains ... the ringmaster, deferentially catching her eye, comes toward her breathing animal devotion; tenderly lifts her up on the

---

[31] A 5; "Glauben macht selig" (V 11). A 6; V 11. A 188–89; V 156. A 190–91; V 157–58. CS 137; E 98.

[32] CS 401–2; E 129. The user of the counterfactual construction expresses "in the form of words he uses, his belief that the antecedent is false" (John L. Mackie, *Truth, Probability and Paradox: Studies in Philosophical Logic* [Oxford: Clarendon, 1973] 71).

dapple-gray ... finds her artistic skill almost beyond belief ... before the great somersault lifts up his arms and implores the orchestra to be silent; finally lifts the little one down from her trembling horse, kisses her on both cheeks, and finds that all the ovation she gets from the audience is barely sufficient; while she herself ... invites the whole circus to share her triumph — since that is so, the visitor to the gallery lays his face on the rail before him and, sinking into the closing march as into a heavy dream, weeps without knowing it." The introductory phrase, "since that is not so," allows the subordinating conjunction *since* (which is not repeated but elliptically presupposed) to govern a series of twelve paratactic sentences. This single *since* assembles the sentences into the long dependent clause within the larger causal construction. Subordination to that *since* also allows the elimination of the anaphoric pronoun in the subject position of eleven of these sentences and the moving of each finite verb (in the German text) to the end of the clause. The stylistic effect is a dynamic, crescendolike rush to descriptive and narrative closure. The indexical adverb *so* denies the factual being-so of the happenings described in the first paragraph's antecedent and consequent; in other words, it affirms their counterfactual (false) status. It also makes that paragraph's equestrienne, ringmaster, and visitor the imaginary doubles of the second paragraph's actual individuals.

The summing-up phrase following the paratactic clauses, "since that is so," asserts that their account is to be taken as factual. They provide overwhelming evidence that the equestrienne is in command of her art and that the ringmaster treats her in a completely empathetic, solicitous, and even celebratory fashion. Because the events in the arena affirm the respect for art and for humanity in general to such a degree, they do not dispose the young visitor to intercede and put a stop to them. Instead of such an action he tearfully sinks into a heavy dream. The interplay between the story's counterfactual and factual construction shows that one's beliefs about the happenings in a circus arena (metaphorically, the world at large) are evidenced, identified, by one's dispositions to act in certain ways. As the counterfactual shows, the visitor would act differently — he would perhaps stop the performance or, in any case, not sink into a tearful dream — if the contents of his beliefs were different from what (in the second paragraph) they actually are. Of course, the visitor's tearful reaction at the end of the factual account is emotionally and thus semantically inscrutable. It performs an ironic somersault with regard to the rationally assumable identity between one's beliefs and dispositions to act. The reader suspects that the visitor's response may express his belief that the art- and life-affirming impetus of the proceedings in the arena is due to the circus entertainers' skill at deceiving their audience concerning the equestrienne's well-being. Yet it gives no certain clues as to his actual beliefs or rationale for acting in this way.

5: The Development of Narrative Structure

KAFKA'S EARLY FOCUS ON physiological precision is partly responsible for his initial difficulties in achieving coherence of plot, consistent perspectives, and closure. His response to these failings is an ever-increasing complexity in cognitive, propositional, and syntactical structuring. The most widely discussed stylistic outcome of this process is the nearly exclusive third-person self-narration by a singular consciousness. This figural perspective will be reviewed here in the light of contemporary criticism and then probed in interpretations of two works of his literary breakthrough period, "The Judgment" and "The Metamorphosis." The remainder of the chapter will focus on the figural narrator's beliefs and motivations as the most intriguing formal feature of *The Trial*. Here the ambiguity of the self-narrating paradigm gains its full symbolic force. K.'s wavering between veridical and delusional belief, between rational and irrational motivation, becomes intertwined with the mysterious, ontologically ambiguous status of the court system.

"Description of a Struggle," told in the first person, minimizes the temporal and experiential gap between the self that experiences and the self that narrates. The focus is on the narrator's mental experiences — perhaps one of the reasons why Kafka, despite substantial revisions in 1909–10, never finished the story. In its pursuit of heightened self-awareness it employs two types of psychological attitude ascribers. Through the first the narrator tracks his perceptions, beliefs, inferences, and conjectures. At the beginning he takes a walk after a party with a casual acquaintance, then dismisses him from the tale until just before the end: "I listened to the sounds of our steps and could not understand why I was incapable of keeping step with my acquaintance. It agitated me a little bit ... I realized that my acquaintance had begun to hum a melody; it was low but I could hear it. I thought that this was insulting to me ... I imagined that I was taking a walk by myself .... I wondered if it would not be a good idea to turn down a side street since I was not obliged to go on this walk with him."[1] Through a more conspicuous type of linguistic marker

---

[1]This translation is fashioned from the first version (K 16), with help from the second version's printed English translation (CS 11–12; K 17). [K] prints the later version synoptically alongside the original. Jost Schillemeit ("Kafkas *Beschreibung*

the narrator self-ascribes a series of imaginary and hallucinatory experiences — such as his being "loved by a girl in a white dress" or the events in the story's middle section involving the fat man.[2] These self-ascriptions progressively splinter the narrative perspective, with the fat man relating his encounter with yet another figure (the supplicant), who has his own story to tell. The short stories in Kafka's first book, *Meditation* or *Reflection* (1912), are minutely observed vignettes of thinking, gesture, and feeling. They are narrated in the first person (with the exception of an occasional impersonal *one*) and predominantly in the present tense. With the rarest of exceptions ("I asked myself [then]"),[3] they do not separate the experiencing and the narrating self. And despite the use of self-reflexive attitude expressions, they identify no personal protagonist-narrator beyond a mere speaker's function. The collapsing of the experiencing and narrating first-person perspectives in both "Description" and the early short stories lays the groundwork for Kafka's preferred third-person figural perspective.

The eighteenth- and nineteenth-century novelistic tradition places great emphasis on a personal (authorial) speaker-narrator. This traditional narrator has two kinds of access to the minds of his or her figures. The narrator's thought- or attitude-report sets off the figure's mental attitudes from the narrated events and actions with the help of such propositional attitude ascribers as discussed earlier ("She thought [believed; knew] that"). Through these verbs the narrator attributes to the figures attitudes toward the content of their thoughts and, at the same time, makes these contents known. On the other hand, the narrator (really, the author) can employ the narrative convention of "free indirect speech" ("free indirect style"), known since Flaubert, presenting the figures' thought contents — without the embedding ascriptions — as free-standing propositions. "Wedding Preparations," the first of Kafka's many third-person narratives, is believed to offer his earliest instances of free indirect speech. To be more precise, however, in his hands this stylistic device for revealing (yet not grammatically ascribing) a character's thoughts becomes

eines Kampfes," Der junge Kafka, ed. Gerhard Kurz [Frankfurt: Suhrkamp, 1984] 102–32) observes that the second version, by stressing dialogue, overcomes the first version's monologic presentation of a predominantly inner world.

[2] K 36. The middlesection is marked as "diversions" (CS 20, 460; "Belustigungen" - K 44, 126), arguably referring to hallucinations — or shown as imaginary: "the following idea occurred to me" (CS 25); "als ich diesen Einfall bekam" (K 58).

[3] Kafka, *Betrachtung* (E 7–22). These stories have justly been called *Nervenidylle* in a 1913 review which Kafka knew and liked (*Franz Kafka: Kritik und Rezeption zu seinen Lebzeiten 1912–1924*, ed. Jürgen Born [Frankfurt: Fischer, 1979] 42). Hermann Bahr's well-known blanket description *nerves* for decadent literature (*Die Überwindung des Naturalismus. Zweite Reihe von "Zur Kritik der Moderne"* [Dresden: Pierson, 1891] 150) does not have the same physiological ring as *Nervenidylle*. CS 389; E 16.

integrated into an overall monoperspectival design. The events, witnessed within the character's conscious horizon, are continuous nonascribed (self-ascribed) figural third-person thought. What is narrated is delimited entirely by what the chief character Raban perceives, knows ("A barefoot boy came running up — Raban did not see from where"), infers, or, occasionally, conjectures ("there was surely mud flying up into the spokes"). Kafka thus fashions his preferred, radically reductive, single-minded perspective: "Raban laid his curved hands palm-down on his knees .... He did not understand anything of what the traveler was talking about." Both sentences are best read as Raban's self-narrated thought: the propositional content expressed — Raban's putting his hands on his knees, his lack of understanding — is available to him through his own perceptions, thoughts, and instantaneous narration. Kafka's figural monoperspectivism is viewed as one of his most important stylistic accomplishments and has been a central topic of Kafka research since the late 1950s.[4] The previous chapters have shown that this narrative stance grows out of the author's curiosity and doubts about the possibility of objective knowledge and description.

Third-person Self-narration

The novelistic convention sees an experiencer-narrator's continuous self-reference in the first person as a commonplace linguistic phenomenon. In the past tense the narrator ascribes past utterances to his past experiencing self; in the present tense the witnessing and conversing "I" occurrently self-narrates, including his own and the other characters' direct speech.[5] The received view is that in third-person figural narratives, even in radically figural prose such as Kafka's, the character-narrators or (as they are often called) *reflectors* ultimately do not do the narrating themselves. Only free indirect speech allows third-person self-reference. "A reflector-character never narrates in the sense of verbalizing his perceptions, thoughts and feelings, since he does not attempt to communicate [them] to the reader." In figural narration "the mediacy of presentation is characteristically obscured by the reader's illusion that he is

---

[4]CS 67; E 245. CS 69; E 247. CS 64; E 243. See Roy Pascal, *Kafka's Narrators: A Study of His Stories and Sketches* (Cambridge UP, 1982) 18–19, 56–57. Also Peter Beicken, in *Kafka-Handbuch* 2: 38–44; Klaus Ramm, in *Kafka-Handbuch* 2: 101–4. Kafka's monoperspectivism is by no means airtight (Winfried Kudszus, "Changing Perspectives in *The Trial* and *The Castle*." In *The Kafka Debate: New Perspectives for Our Time*, ed. Angel Flores [New York: Gordian, 1977] 385–95).

[5]Early examples in Kafka are E 10–11, 21–22; CS 395–97, 393–94 ("I said"). E 17; CS 383–84.

witnessing the action directly," the "narrator develops the ability to camou-flage himself ... by assuming the mode of perception ... of the fictional charac-ters."[6] In her comprehensive study of fictive representations of consciousness, Dorrit Cohn also does not accept the concept of third-person self-narration, even in Kafka's thorough blend of free indirect speech and figural narration: "the continued employment of third-person references indicates, no matter how unobtrusively, the continued presence of a narrator." This assumption ignores the fact that Kafka voids the distinction between free indirect speech and the overall figural narration that shapes "the entire fictional world as an uninterrupted *vision avec.*" Kafka's third-person self-narration — which is no more than an extension of the third-person self-reference in free indirect speech — produces an exclusive figural awareness, original third-person self-reference, and subsequent anaphoric self-reference without a separate, identifi-able narratorial voice. In other words, these works are narrated in the gram-matical third person yet from a virtually subjective first-person perspective on the phenomena within the character-narrator's mindscape. The protagonist structures and instantly narrates his own perceptions concerning himself and others, his speeches and those of others, his beliefs, inferences, and conjec-tures. Thus, a third-person thinker's self-narrated thought is in principle no different from a first-person narrator's. The following are self-ascriptions of attitudes by Raban and Georg Bendemann that vouch no independent narrating voice: questions ("[Peevishly] he asked a neighbor"), beliefs ("Raban be-lieved"; "thought"), realizations ("Georg said to himself"), and utterances.[7]

The Castle provides striking illustrations of the logic of third-person self-narration. Its revision from the original first-person to the later third-person version required no other changes than replacing the first-person by the third-person pronoun (or *K.*). Cohn maintains that the original version was a "po-tential third-person novel miscast in first-person form," while admitting that in both versions the narrators "remain effaced, 'transparent,' the attention is rivetted on the protagonist (K. in the [later] version, the experiencing 'I' in the [original]) and only through him on the surrounding world." Yet Kafka's easy revision illustrates that for him third-person narration does not presuppose or imply a narrator other than the protagonist K. himself. The Castellan's son calls the castle on the phone and reports K.'s unannounced presence in the

[6]Frank K. Stanzel, "Teller-Characters and Reflector-Characters in Narrative Theo-ry," *Poetics Today* 2.2 (1981): 7. Why then, one might ask, should there be first-person narrators "who do not communicate with the reader but only, as it were, with their own selves" (7)? F. K. Stanzel, *A Theory of Narrative* (Cambridge UP, 1984) 146–47 and 198.

[7]Dorrit Cohn, *Transparent Minds: Narrative Modes for Presenting Consciousness in Fiction* (Princeton UP, 1978) 111–12. However, does an "absent" (170) narrator narrate? CS 54; E 235. CS 53–55; E 233–34. CS 81; E 26. CS 81–87; E 26–29.

village. In the original version K. relates this incident in the first person: "The young man, announcing himself as Schwarzer, reported that he had found me, a disreputable-looking man in his thirties." In the later version's "The young man ... reported that he had found K.," K. cannot be Schwarzer's reference to K. but must be K.'s reference to himself, since he has not introduced himself to Schwarzer by name. The original naming role of the initial K. here is replaced by its mere function as an anaphora, referring it back through a chain of like antecedents (K. and he) to the naming K. of the opening sentence. There are other instances of collapsing initial and pronoun. In the original version K. narrates his first encounter with Frieda this way: "As soon as her eye caught me, it seemed to me that her look had decided things concerning me, things which I had not known to exist, but which her look assured me did exist." The revision reads: "As soon as her eye [caught K.], it seemed to him that her look [had decided things concerning K., things] which he had not known to exist, but which her look assured him did exist." Within the that-clause the self-narrating K. refers anaphorically to himself ("concerning K.") by using the initial. This reference appears to violate the standard linguistic practice to such a degree that the Muirs' English translation substitutes a reflexive pronoun for K: "it seemed to him that her look decided something concerning himself." The reason for Kafka's phrasing cannot be an avoidance of reflexive pronouns, since he frequently uses them ("while K. fought for something vitally near to him, for himself").[8] Rather, the K. functions anaphorically, like the personal pronoun, and the entire text becomes unmarked figural self-narration. Nothing is lost in the transposition: the third person is no obstacle to construing the novel in this way.

It may be granted that the first-person version of *The Castle* is occasionally inconsistent in a customary sense: "apparently I was unwilling, tired as I was, to leave the street." Kafka forgets "that the self cannot 'appear' to the self, but only to others .... As soon as we transpose these sentences to the third person ... they regain a familiar fictional logic .... Now the lone K. has someone to appear to: the implied narrator who, since he sees him as an object, can legitimately speculate on the meaning of K.'s 'strange' gestures."[9] There are two objections to such an interpretation, however. First, it is not clear why a figure should "appear" to a well-informed narrator. Second, for Kafka the *apparently* appears to make sense in the first person, and thus does not necessarily entail an independent narrator when changed to the third. In the past Kafka occasionally contrived to have the body appear to its knowing self:

---

[8]Dorrit Cohn, "K. Enters *The Castle*," *Euphorion* 62 (1968): 30. Cohn, "The Encirclement of Narrative," *Poetics Today* 2.2 (1981): 174. SKA 1: 11; 2: 124. C 6; S 9. SKA 2: 178. C 47; S 38. C 74; S 58.

[9]SKA 1: 21; 2: 136. Cf. the third-person version (C 15; S 15 "offenbar ... zögerte er, die Straße zu verlassen"). Cohn, "K. Enters *The Castle*" 36.

"Hardly were we outside when I [apparently] began to [act with great liveliness]." The fact that K.'s past life and nonconscious thoughts largely remain hidden from the reader[10] — as is true of most Kafka heroes — does not by itself defeat K.'s self-narrating stance. More problematic, perhaps, for assuming self-narration is that K. sometimes withholds "the truth about his own inner being, [feigns] ignorance of his own conscious motives"[11] — as in accepting his host's false claim, and he himself alleging, that the two assistants sent by the castle are his old assistants. Two explanations are available here. For some idiosyncratic reason K. "occurrently" may not think of the fact that these men are not his old assistants — in other words, this fact may be momentarily not within his conscious awareness — and, thus, he would be in no position to narrate the truth of this matter. More plausibly, K. has decided to play along with his host's pretense that these are his old assistants and chooses to narrate only his overt actions and speech.[12] Kafka fashions the character's cognitions, inferences, and memories, as well as instances of the self's opaqueness (forgettings, paralipses) into elements of third-person figural self-narration.

Recent poststructuralist readings claim that a tale's reduction to the figure's perspective destroys the singular narrative consciousness. For Josef Vogl, for instance, *The Castle* effects a blending of, or a sliding transition between, character and narrator, first-person and third-person perspective, experiencer and observer stance. The third-person pronoun (or *K.*) refers to no one but the character; it merely "repeats" the stance of the experiencing self. Against this plausible view he makes the facile claim that this blending, sliding, or repeating destroys the experiencing, narrating subjectivity. The sliding transitions cause the nonidentity of the experiencing self with itself, and thus of the narrative perspective.[13] Such readings obscure the semantic and linguistic insights offered by this single-minded self-narrating perspective. Allegedly, because it reveals little or nothing beyond the character-narrator's perceptions, illusions, or surmisings — his representational mindscape — it subjects the reader to a similar subjectivism in understanding the text. Yet, in

---

[10]CS 11; K 14. See Eric Miller, "Without a Key: The Narrative Structure of *Das Schloß*," *Germanic Review* 66 (1991): 135–36.

[11]Cohn, "K. enters *The Castle*" 35. This objection is directed at the novel's first-person version but applies as well to the revision if in fact it is self-narrated.

[12]The narrator's deliberate suppression of important information is known as *paralipsis* (Gérard Genette, *Narrative Discourse Revisited* [Ithaca: Cornell UP, 1988] 74, 124).

[13]Josef Vogl, *Ort der Gewalt: Kafka's literarische Ethik* (Munich: Fink, 1990) 75–79. Avital Ronell likewise sees "the protagonist's identity" shattered ("Doing Kafka in *The Castle*," *Kafka and the Contemporary Critical Performance*, ed. Alan Udoff [Bloomington: Indiana UP, 1987] 219).

effect, it reinforces the reader's awareness of the perspectival and fallible nature of all belief, of the potential gap between what is believed and what is factual. More than perhaps any other narrative stance, third-person self-narration presents a permanent stumbling block to unequivocal interpretation. In this sense it may be true that "from inside a figural consciousness that grasps the world immediately, not critically — for which the world is sheer evidence, givenness, just being-there — it is impossible to undertake a critique either of this consciousness or of the world."[14] Yet due to their conceptual, syntactical, and semantic complexity, these texts defeat the subjectivity of their singular perspective and probe the possibilities of objective knowledge.

"The Judgment" as Continuous Self-Narration

"The Judgment" portrays the struggle between the father and the son of a Jewish-German middle-class family in turn-of-the-century central Europe through the exclusive perspective of the son, Georg.[15] Georg has just finished a letter to a friend of his youth who years ago emigrated to Russia. He looks out on the riverbank and the hills with their weak green. The unobtrusive colors in his visual field allow him to focus on the friend's voluntary exile and failed life, which he briefly summarizes. Thereafter, his deliberative train of thought concerning the friend runs on for over three pages, patterning present and past (reproduced) thoughts in such a syntactically complex fashion that it does not fully determine, for the reader, each thought's original occasion within the sequence of events in Georg's past and present mental life. For instance, his recollection that the friend told him that he (the friend) has resigned himself to permanent bachelorhood triggers the third paragraph's deliberations — presumably occurring during the writing of the letter he just finished ("What [would one want to] write to such a man") — about whether to advise him to return to his native city as a failed emigré, or to forego this advice and leave him permanently where and "just as he was." Georg recalls that he opted for the latter, thus presupposing, as far as he was concerned, finality for his friend's exile and bachelorhood. The next three paragraphs make it clear, however, that such deliberations repeatedly occurred within Georg's thinking on these matters for the purpose of writing other letters to

[14]Stanley Corngold, "The Author Survives on the Margin of His Breaks: Kafka's Narrative Perspective," *The Fate of the Self: German Writers and French Theory* (New York: Columbia UP, 1986) 169.

[15]E 23–32; CS 77–88. All examples Pascal (*Kafka's Narrators* 21–32) offers from the story as evidence for an independent narrator's stance — allowing for a double perspective or dual voice — can be construed as Georg's thought and narration.

his friend. For instance, he had made scrupulous determinations not to inform the friend fully about events in his native city so as not to cause him envy and unhappiness: "For such reasons ... one could not send him any real news." "So Georg confined himself to giving his friend unimportant items of gossip." He especially withheld news about his own business success in the last few years. In ruminating about these past efforts to protect the friend's feelings, however, he is airing the counterfactual proposition that he is telling the friend now, belatedly, of his own success ("if he [had it done] now retrospectively that certainly would look peculiar"). The indexical *now* refers to a moment at which the proposition is being thought and expressed as a counterfactual, and such a moment must be *after* Georg has finished and sealed the letter. Toward the end of his long train of thought Georg recalls that he had been at pains not to tell his friend about his engagement ("Yet Georg preferred to write about things like these rather than to confess that he himself had got engaged"). At his fiancée's prompting, however, he became convinced that "it could not really involve him in trouble were he to send the news to his friend." He then no longer wished to trim the facts of his life down in size ("I can't cut myself to another pattern that might make a more suitable friend for him") but rather wanted his friend to know about the changes that had occurred in their native city and his own life.[16] It was then that he decided to abandon his empathetic pretense and deception and to announce his engagement. Retracing the thought process that generated this decision, his mind returns to the moment at which he was setting out to conclude his letter: "And in fact he did inform his friend, in the long letter he had been writing that Sunday morning, about his engagement, with these words: 'I have saved my best news to the end.'" The *in fact* indicates both that Georg amends his previous deceit and turns his originally nonsequential ruminations — which contained interspersed bits of an ongoing sequential narration — into a straightforward self-narrating account from here on.

The reader discerns in these complex thoughts not only a narratorial mastery but also a cognitive-valuative "narrowness" or "solipsism" that grants the friend no independent thought or will, restricts him phenomenally to Georg's consciousness.[17] Given the importance of eye contact for Kafka,

---

[16]CS 79; "hätte er es jetzt nachträglich getan, es hätte wirklich einen merkwürdigen Anschein gehabt" (E 25). In 1920 Kafka expresses his awareness of how limited one's apprehension of others is: "No man, even if he be infallible, can see [in the other] more than that fraction for which the strength [and kind of his gaze suffice]. He has, like everybody, but in its extreme form, the longing to limit himself to [how the other's strength of gaze is capable of seeing him]" (GW 271–72); "Seine Blick-kraft und Blickart" (BK 220).

[17]See John Ellis, "The Bizarre Texture of *The Judgment*," *The Problem of "The Judgment": Eleven Approaches to Kafka's Story*, ed. Angel Flores (New York: Gordian, 1977) 76–79. J. P. Stern, "Guilt and the Feeling of Guilt," *The Problem*

Georg's behavior after sealing the letter suggests that no communication between him and the friend has taken or will take place: "With this letter in his hand Georg had been sitting a long time at the writing table, his face turned toward the window." Kafka wrote the story two days after he had sent his first letter to his future fiancée Felice Bauer, sensing already that marriage to her would conflict with his literary vocation. Thus, the friend's inscrutable figure could symbolize the author's undiminished desire for bachelorhood, a life devoted to writing.[18] The friend's hostile emergence in the father's camp indicates that this conflict bears directly on the author's difficult relation with his father: "The friend is the link between father and son, he is their strongest common bond .... [The development of the story shows how out of what both have in common, the father ascends and sets] himself up as Georg's antagonist ... Georg can only feel it as something foreign." "The story may be a journey around father and son, and the friend's changing shape may be a change in perspective in the relationship between father and son."[19]

Kafka believed that his father would welcome his marriage, that it would help him escape his father's condemnation.[20] The story reverses this relationship. Georg's father censors his son's engagement, which, he alleges, has resulted in the subjugation and betrayal of the bachelor friend. Besides these suggested meanings, the friend's figure is also a device to direct Georg's, and thus the reader's, awareness within the story. Georg's reflections on the friend's dilemma (occasioned by his just-completed letter writing) permit him to attend to the changes in his own life. When the narrative's focus first moves from Georg's monologic thought to his interaction with his father, a somewhat

---

of "The Judgment" 129.

[18]Ronald Gray, "Through Dream to Self-Awareness," The Problem of "The Judgment" 67–71. Anthony Northey, Kafka's Relatives: Their Lives and His Writing (New Haven: Yale UP, 1991) 97–99. About the significance of eye contact in Kafka see Binder, Kafka in neuer Sicht 163–93.

[19]D 1: 278–79; the German text ("[Die Geschichte zeigt,] wie aus dem Gemeinsamen, dem Freund, der Vater hervorsteigt" - T 186) shows the psychological root of the image Kafka employs: hervorsteigen recalls Herbart and Wundt (see Wundt, Physiologische Psychologie 2: 292). FE 267; F 397. The story contains echoes of Gregers Werle's relationship to his father and his friend Hjalmar Ekdal in Ibsen's The Wild Duck.

[20]Georg's father "is still a giant of a man" (CS 81; E 26); Kafka called his own father "huge, a giant in every respect" (DF 154; H 131). Kafka later was at pains to establish some referential link between Georg and himself (T 186; D 1: 279. F 394; FE 265). Hartmut Binder emphasizes that any interruption in Kafka's correspondence with Felice resulted in his dread of the father's curse (Kafka Kommentar zu sämtlichen Erzählungen [Munich: Winkler, 1975] 131). Only in 1917 did Kafka irreversibly opt against his desire for marriage to Felice, choosing the literary vocation instead.

reciprocal, dialogic dimension is gained. Georg's gaze must now direct itself at his father's cognitive behavior toward him and his own toward his father — and, furthermore, to his father's linguistic attitudes (intonations of speech, facial expressions, and gestures[21]). The expandings (awareness, remembrances) and narrowings (fatigue, memory loss) of both their consciousnesses now become the *foci* of Georg's self-narration. For instance, upon entering his father's room Georg momentarily perceives him without apperceiving him ("[Georg] had been vacantly following the old man's movements"). He tells him that at long last he is letting the friend know about his engagement. The father's phrase "you have changed your mind" and Georg's affirmation[22] are underscored by the father's corresponding physical action: he puts the newspaper on the windowsill, his glasses on top of the paper, and his hand on top of the glasses. Phrases as well as actions suggest that changing one's beliefs and intentions can be compared to the putting of one thought on top of another, covering up, impeding, replacing it.

The father uses terms derived directly from the psychological theories discussed earlier. He plays on the image of stirring up ideas, raising them into consciousness ("I don't want to stir up matters that [don't belong] here"). He explains that his attention, memory, and informational register are diminishing due to old age and grief: "There's many a thing in the business I'm not aware of ... — I'm not equal to things any longer, my memory is failing, I haven't an eye for so many things any longer." He compares Georg's bringing the matter concerning the letter before him to the stopping of a train of thought ("But since we are stopping at this matter, at this letter"). He questions whether Georg really has this friend in St. Petersburg. Georg takes this question as a sign of the father's decline, suggesting that it may be due to forgetfulness ("Just think back a bit ... you're bound to remember"). The ensuing struggle between them, and the friend's alleged role in it, depicts metaphorically a fight of ideas for ascension into and survival in consciousness: "You wanted to cover me up ... but I'm far from being covered up yet. And even if this is the last strength I have, it's enough for you, too much for you ... [you have] stuck your father into bed so that he can't move. But he can move, or can't he? .... And now that you thought you'd got [your friend] down, so far down that you could set your bottom on him and sit on him and he wouldn't move, then my fine son makes up his mind to get married." The struggle's outcome

---

[21]They are shaped by Kafka's encounter with the Yiddish theater (Evelyn Torton Beck, *Kafka and the Yiddish Theater* [Madison: U of Wisconsin P, 1971] 70–121).

[22]CS 81; E 27. CS 82; "Jetzt hast du es dir wieder anders überlegt"; "jetzt habe ich es mir wieder überlegt" (E 27). *Überlegen* literally means putting one thing on top of another. It may hint at the father's later crucial question whether he has been "well covered up" (CS 84; E 29) and his eventual superiority (*Überlegenheit*) over the son.

reverses the biological and psychological state of affairs that existed at the beginning: while the father accumulates strength and apperceptive powers ("a father doesn't need to be taught how to see through his son"), Georg becomes absent-minded, forgetful, and disoriented: "Georg, almost distracted, ran toward the bed to take everything in ... he had firmly made up his mind to watch closely every last movement so that he should not be surprised ... recalled this long-forgotten resolve and forgot it again, like a man drawing a short thread through the eye of a needle." In response, his thoughts about his father take on a solipsistic quality: "Now he'll lean forward ... what if he topples and smashes himself!" runs hissing through his head — as if the father's smashing-up somehow could be caused in Georg's brain. But the father now has gained the upper hand, and his version of what is factual wins the battle: "Georg made a grimace of disbelief. His father only nodded, confirming the truth of his words." He knows that he has smashed up Georg's solipsism: "So now you know what else there was in the world besides your-self."[23]

The story transports the naturalist (as well as decadent) motifs of biological evolution and degeneration to the arena of cognitive competence[24] and the finally emerging question of Georg's guilt. The father claims to have exposed his son's cognitive self-centeredness, his disloyalty toward the father, his deceased mother, and the friend, and condemns him to death. Georg kills himself because, we assume, he has internalized the father's alleged moral (and legal) authority and accepts the imputation of guilt to himself. The story's ending reveals that guilt, this negative value that both of them assign to Georg, is not derived from an objective (universal) view of justice. It originates in the subjective perspectives of these two men and represents their spurious idea of what merits capital punishment. In coming works, especially *The Trial* and "In the Penal Colony," will Kafka endeavor to expose this idea of guilt as an ethical and existential contradiction. In the meantime, however, the author permits the character, and himself, a way out of the guilt-generating dilemma. In contrast to the delays in his cognitive, social, and emotional maturity that purportedly warrant his death, Georg's self-narration (the structuring of the story itself) does not become subject to the father's judgment. The author

---

[23]CS 82; E 27. "Since we are talking about it" (CS 82) should be translated as "since we are stopping at this matter" (E 27). CS 83; E 28. CS 84–85. CS 85; E 30. CS 87; E 32.

[24]Silvio Vietta's and Hans-Georg Kemper's view that the story is an expressionist transposition of realist motifs (*Expressionismus* [Munich: Fink, 1975] 286–305) cannot capture its central cognitional features.

himself wins survival[25] from the paradoxical split within Georg among his experience of losing the battle of wits, his acceptance of the death verdict, and his task of self-narration, which keeps track of his gradual self-destruction up to the end.

Self-narration and Guilt in "The Metamorphosis"

At the outset of "The Metamorphosis" the chief character's body is changed into a large insect. The opening phrase, "he found himself transformed," suggests that this is an instance (and expression) of knowledge of a special sort, that is, self-knowledge.[26] It is Gregor himself, instead of some independent narrator, who properly can cognize and know that it is Gregor's body that has been transformed. From his subjective perspective he acknowledges that a transformation has occurred and, despite the grammatical third person, tells the event himself. The sentence, "Gregor was wildly curious to know what [his sister] would bring him instead, and made various speculations about it" seems to suggest an independent narrator's voice. The word *actually*, however, in the sentence "Yet what she actually did next ... he could never have guessed at" makes sense only if it describes an outcome that is different from the guesses previously fixed on by Gregor himself, not some omniscient narrator. Thus, both sentences should be seen as narrated by the character. It is not necessary to accept a break of perspective for the seeming authorially conceived ending. The widening gap between Gregor's self-narrating mind and changing physique makes it plausible that after his physical death his narrating consciousness remains.[27]

The story emphasizes the vast discrepancy between Gregor's old and new body and the stark contrast between the latter and his mind — which has preserved its human quality and emotions. The transformation's symbolic meaning draws on what has failed to change, the continuous psychophysical

[25]"Conclusion for my case from *The Judgment*. I am indirectly in [Felice's] debt for the story. But Georg goes to pieces because of his fiancée" (D 1: 296; T 198). For Kafka the writing of this story represented his birth as author. See Gerhard Neumann, *Franz Kafka: Das Urteil. Text, Materialien, Kommentar* (Munich: Hanser, 1981) 46, 73, 81, 102.

[26]It is a contemporary philosophical insight that ascriptions of bodily postures and movements as well as intentions to oneself are not based on observation but on this special kind of knowledge. See for instance G. E. M. Anscombe, "The First Person," *The Collected Papers*, 2 vols. (Minneapolis: U of Minnesota P, 1981) 2: 21–36.

[27]CS 107; E 72. Pascal (*Kafka's Narrators* 32–40) implausibly attributes the entire story to a full-fledged narrator other than Gregor.

union between Gregor's mind and body, and thus how, due to this union, the verminous body ultimately must reflect on the mind it embodies. In a letter to Brod from 1904 Kafka construes a simile (comparing himself to a mole) and immediately turns it into a metaphor (attributing some mole properties to himself): "We burrow through ourselves like a mole and emerge blackened and velvet-haired from our [buried sand] vaults, our poor little red feet stretched out for tender pity." In another letter he compares himself to sliced meat and then sees himself feeding one of these pieces to a dog: "I lie stretched out on the floor, sliced up like a roast, and with my hand I am slowly pushing a slice of meat toward a dog in the corner." These examples are sometimes cited to illustrate how easily Kafka could see his body metaphorically transformed into an animal or "animal stuff" — as if the story's transformation could be grasped best in analogy to Kafka's attribution of his nightmarish daydream imagery (alienation, dismemberment) to his actual self. On closer look, some of the vermin's features are shaped by the memory image of something Kafka had observed on a trip through Switzerland. He and Brod had noticed a type of boat with iron arching ribs across its open hull, forming a domelike awning frame that could be covered by canvas. Brod described these boats as "big freight-boats with arching ribs" and added a pen-and-ink drawing. Kafka noted the "awning frame on the boats" and a "man framed by the arching ribs of his boat, bent over the oars." Kafka uses these and other features of boats to describe the insect's belly, back, and gravitational properties: "He was lying on his hard, as it were armor-plated, back and when he lifted his head a little he could see his domelike brown belly divided into stiff arched segments on top of which the bed quilt could hardly keep in position .... However violently he forced himself toward his right side he always rolled onto his back again." "He set himself to rocking his whole body at once in a regular rhythm, with the idea of swinging it out of bed ... he needed only to hitch himself across by rocking to and fro ... he could barely keep his equilibrium when he rocked himself strongly." The description is transferred to the vermin with such completeness that Gregor's head functions like a boat's rudder: "despite its breadth and mass the bulk of his body at last followed the movement of his head." And even after he has swung himself onto his feet ("his legs had firm ground under them"), he is swaying like a boat ("rocking with suppressed [movement]." This astonishing, underhanded attribution of properties of a specifically perceived inanimate object, that is, of emotionally neutral properties, to the insect suggests that the meaning of this central metaphor is not exhausted by the insect's nightmarish or grotesque qualities.[28]

---

[28]L 17; B 29. L 95; B 114–15. "Große Lastboote mit Reifen" (Brod, "Reise Lugano - Mailand - Paris," EF 1: 88). Given Brod's and Kafka's admiration for Flaubert's personal writings, it is noteworthy that, in Como, Flaubert had noticed boats with

The transformation usually has been seen to represent human grotesque-
ness (irreversible alienation and disfigurement) or moral offensiveness. The
first quality is thought to result from Gregor's obsessive work habits and
emotional self-denial, the second to express condemnation by his kin for his
rebelliousness toward the father or for excluding himself from family and
community.[29] A hidden, only gradually discernible subplot suggests, however, that the transformation represents, more than anything else, Gregor's self-
degrading attitude of having allowed his family to treat him with utter selfishness. Five years ago he became the sole breadwinner for his able-bodied
parents and sister. Unbeknownst to him, they took advantage of him by
squirreling away some of his hard-earned money and thus prolonging his
servitude to his father's creditor.[30] Even after he becomes aware of this situation, Gregor does not condemn them for their long-standing exploitation of
him. He is full of filial piety and morbid familial pride and attributes shame
and guilt solely to himself for leaving them in the lurch. They, in turn, reject
and neglect him not so much for his repulsive shape but for his present inability to sustain their upper middle-class life-style. His by now irreversible distance from and inability to communicate with them affords him an awareness
of the wrong they did him, yet he remains subservient to their wishes. His
mother expresses her selfish hope that Gregor will be returned to his previous
role: "Doesn't it look as if we were showing him, by taking away his furniture, that we have given up hope of his ever getting better and are just leaving
him coldly to himself? I think it would be best to keep his room exactly as it
has always been, so that when he comes back to us he will find everything unchanged and able all the more easily to forget what has happened in between."
Their ingratitude and his present parasitical role allow them to extend no
moral obligation toward him, only the barest duty in seeing to the vermin's
needs: "The serious injury done to Gregor ... seemed to have made even his

wooden awning frames ("kleine Nachen mit Holzbögen, die das Zelt tragen").
Gustave Flaubert, "Tagebuch des jungen Flaubert," *Pan* 1 (1910–11): 181–88; 181.
"Gerüst für Tuchbespannung auf den Booten"; "Schwarzer Mann im Boot in der
Umrahmung der Reifen stehend, über die Ruder gebeugt" (Kafka, "Reise Lugano -
Mailand - Paris - Erlenbach," EF 1: 152, 154; also: T 380–81; D 2: 252–53). CS
89; E 56. CS 94; E 60. CS 93; E 59. CS 102; E 68.

[29]See Peter U. Beicken, *Franz Kafka: Eine kritische Einführung in die Forschung*
(Frankfurt: Athenaion, 1974) 261–72. Also Karlheinz Fingerhut, "Die Phase des
Durchbruchs," *Kafka-Handbuch* 2: 296–302. Hartmut Binder, "Entfaltung einer
Metapher: *Die Verwandlung*," *Kafka: Der Schaffensprozeß* (Frankfurt: Suhrkamp,
1983) 149, 171, 180.

[30]E 62, 66, 67, 74–76; CS 96, 101, 102 ("they had convinced themselves ... that
Gregor was settled for life in this firm"), 110–12. Beicken argues this point (*Franz
Kafka* 267–68); recently so does Ulf Abraham (*Franz Kafka: Die Verwandlung*
[Frankfurt: Diesterweg, 1993] 47–51).

father recollect that Gregor was a member of the family, despite his present unfortunate and repulsive shape, and ought not to be treated as an enemy, that, on the contrary, family duty required the suppression of disgust and the exercise of patience." Thus the transformation can be seen to express what the family's scheming and Gregor's negation of his personal rights have made of him. This view would square with the fact that the insect's thinglike properties illustrated above — which make it less grotesque or beastly than some of its other characteristics do — are unsuited to symbolize a condemnation or to encumber Gregor morally for anything but a self-inflicted alienation from his right to self-enhancement. The gradual liberation of his self, made possible by the transformation, may help to explain why his physical needs (such as hunger) subside and are replaced by spiritual desires. Observing the lodgers' supper and listening to his sister's violin playing afford him two discoveries:

> [The lodgers] ate their food in almost complete silence ... he could al-
> ways distinguish the sound of their masticating teeth, as if this were a
> sign to Gregor that one needed teeth in order to eat .... "I am hungry
> enough," said Gregor sadly to himself, "but not for that kind of food.
> How these lodgers are stuffing themselves, and here am I dying of
> starvation!" .... Was he an animal, that music had such an effect upon
> him? He felt as if the way were opening before him to the unknown
> nourishment he craved.

In a previously unthinkable act of self-liberation he crawls out in front of the lodgers to hear the music and sends them into open rebellion against their hosts. Previously he would have done nothing to cause his family further financial hardship. Coming on the heels of "The Judgment," this story further evolves Kafka's views on guilt and justice. Gregor becomes aware of his past economic and emotional enslavement; his beliefs, desires, and dispositions to act attain a sense of personal freedom and of an objective morality. The author's ironical reserve toward Gregor's plight acknowledges the spurious nature of the guilt the transformation alleges.[31]

---

[31]CS 116; E 80. CS 122; E 85. CS 129–31; E 90–92. When he read the story to Brod, they both lost themselves in laughter (F 320; FE 209).

Contradictory Belief in "The Trial"

The *Trial* consists of figural self-narration;[32] the disclaimer of criminal guilt within the opening statement ("without having done anything wrong") is K.'s, not an independent narrator's. Only in this way can the novel set out and sustain its central ambiguity: is the court internal or external to Joseph K.'s mind? Due to the self-narrating stance, his occasional cognitive incompetence and his swings between attention and inattentiveness and veridical and delusional belief pose special interpretative problems. In one respect his attention is fixed on the ways the court's actions (arrest, hearing, conviction, execution) defeat his reasonable expectations about such proceedings. Yet at the same time he is preoccupied with unusual happenings of a harmless kind that appear to signal the meaning of his arrest and trial.[33] If indeed these were intentionally misleading clues of some kind, they would imply a somewhat teasing narratorial consciousness independent of K.'s. These happenings plausibly can be read, however, as coincidental, "occurrent" phenomenological contents of Josef K.'s self-narrating consciousness. His attention to them signifies, more than anything, confused judgment, the failure to distinguish between what is and what is not important to assessing the legal damage and possible remedies vis-à-vis the unknown court. For instance, he worries about the warder's unofficial-looking pleated black suit but later is told that the warder and his suit are completely immaterial to his case. The inspector arranges the objects on Miss Bürstner's night table in certain ways and pays close attention to them, but his actions signify nothing except that they divert K.'s attention from pressing the inspector on the reasons for the arrest. The old woman's observing K. with importunity is gratuitous, devoid of the behaviorist rationale other instances of observing K. have, yet it upsets and distracts him. Sometimes the objects of K.'s attention are hidden allusions to the author's personal life. He notices a white blouse dangling from a windowlatch in Mrs. Bürstner's room, as well as its later absence, and then mentions it to Miss Bürstner. The blouse resembles the one Felice was wearing when Kafka first met her and which, being an important part of his first impression of her, soon creates a memory recorded in his diary and letters. The possibility of such autobiographical traces is hinted at in the novel itself (in an unfinished part) by K.'s considering a past impression of Miss Bürstner as "indelible." Felice's memo-

[32]Against Winfried Kudszus' well-informed objections ("Erzählperspektive und Erzählgeschehen in Kafka's *Prozeß*," *Deutsche Vierteljahrsschrift für Literatur- und Geistesgeschichte* 44 [1970]: 306–17).

[33]See Peter Hutchinson, "Red Herring or Clues?" *The Kafka Debate*, ed. Flores, 206–15. For some curious speculations about religious-allegorical clues in the novel see *Verteidigung der Schrift: Kafkas "Prozeß,"* ed. Frank Schirrmacher (Frankfurt: Suhrkamp, 1987).

rable blouse does not enter the phenomenological field of the stories written at the time of Kafka's first meeting with her but appears two years later in the work occasioned by the breakup of their relationship. The blouse's prominence in the novel may signal K.'s unconscious sexual obsession with Miss Bürstner but, just as plausibly, his lack of attention to the urgency of an effective legal defense. K. himself records that his lack of discriminating cognition is putting him at risk. He is told that three of the men present at his arrest are his employees, and that the inspector has brought them along to render K.'s return to the bank as unobtrusive as possible. A little later, continuing to be distracted by his misidentification of these men, he overlooks the inspector's departure. This discovery triggers his decision to pay more attention henceforth: "The Inspector had usurped his attention so that he did not recognize the three clerks, and the clerks in turn had made him oblivious of the Inspector. That did not show much presence of mind." Progressively he becomes tired and unfocused, overlooks potential dangers, and loses the vigilance his defense requires.[34]

Other irrelevant noticings do not result from phenomenological displacements but suggest a deficient logical faculty. K. interprets a look the warder Franz gives him as inexplicable, yet significant. He conceives the examining magistrate's eyebrows as bushy, black, and big but as otherwise inconspicuous. Inconsistent attitudes further impair his defense. In the court offices he is afraid of attracting the officials' attention because the only explanation of his presence that he deems acceptable (to discover the date of his next interrogation) he is not willing to declare openly. He seeks out a lawyer for professional help but considers the discussion between him, his uncle, and the court's chief clerk a jabbering of old men. If he were more rational, he would engage the officials about the trial's rationale and legitimacy. He is painfully aware of his lawyer's habit of chatting about irrelevant generalities to distract his attention from his defense. But K. himself is worse than his lawyer in this regard. His belated insight, just before his execution, into his habit of snatching at the world "with twenty hands" indicates that he has become aware of his lack of determined concentration, and that he must accept some responsibility for his conviction. A model for him of cold-blooded attentiveness and efficient attitude should be the court itself. Its policy of remaining inconspicuous appears motivated by a desire to carry out its functions without disrupting the everyday world. Thus, K. is arrested but permitted to continue his work

---

[34]P 7, 15–16; TR 1, 11–12. P 14; TR 10–11. P 7–17, 51 (the student's observing both the usher's wife and K.), 73 (Miss Montag's and the captain's observing K.); TR 1–13, 55, 82. P 14, 23, 28; TR 10, 21, 27. About Felice's blouse see Hartmut Binder, *Kafka Kommentar zu den Romanen, Rezensionen, Aphorismen und zum Brief an den Vater*, 2nd ed. (Munich: Winkler, 1982) 200–201. P 209; TR 248. P 18; TR 15. TR 16; P 19. P 108, 149, 119; TR 126, 174 ("too tired and distracted to think"), 138 ("alertness of his faculties").

at the bank. The house in which the interrogation takes place and the entrance to the offices look undistinguished. The chief clerk, who is visiting with the lawyer, does not want to be noticed; he wants to slip back into the darkness where his presence might be forgotten. At the same time, the court aims to lull the accused into a false sense of security and strikes back aggressively whenever an accused draws attention to himself.[35] The flogging of Franz and Willem, Block's being browbeaten into doglike submission by the lawyer, and K.'s own swiftly sinking fortunes illustrate the court's aggressive attention to its own success.

K. does have the ability to acknowledge new evidence and to correct his beliefs. He thinks that some of the men at his first hearing somehow oppose the court, and he intends to represent "their point of view." A bit later he discovers that they are no different from the rest of those attending the hearing. K. believes that he completely dominates the meeting, only to register the disruption caused by the washerwoman's shrieking. Yet he is also capable of denying factual evidence to preserve patently false beliefs that please him. Little prevents his beliefs from becoming wishful and delusional. For instance, when the law student takes the washerwoman away from K. against his wishes, he acknowledges his first defeat by the court but believes that if he "stayed quietly at home ... he remained superior to all these people and could kick any of them out of his path." He fancies that if he had been more present-minded and avoided the scene of his arrest by having breakfast in the landlady's kitchen, he would have nipped the whole thing in the bud. Most damaging to his defense, however, is his inexplicable ability to hold contradictory beliefs. He entertains the idea that by erasing every trace of his arrest (Mrs. Grubach's restoring her household to good order), the fact of it could be obliterated. He does not recognize the court and dismisses the arrest as "some wild prank" but then acknowledges that there is a "great organization" — from a judicial hierarchy all the way down to its hangmen — that accuses innocent people of guilt. He wants to make the flogging of the warders disappear or stop by having the bank clerk clean out the lumberroom. We expect a person's beliefs to make up a logically coherent, intelligible network. Their occasional irrationality in K. raises questions not only about his logical abilities but also about the veracity of his account. K.'s encounter with another accused throws some light on how the ability to hold any belief at all is impaired by the court's irrational power over those it puts on trial. The apparently well-educated man does not know how to reply to K.'s simple questions:

---

[35]P 11; TR 6. P 30; TR 40. P 60; TR 66. P 93; TR 107. P 158; TR 184. P 192; TR 225. P 108 ("den Angeklagten einzuschläfern und hilflos zu erhalten"); TR 126. P 104; TR 121.

He gazed at the others as if it were their duty to help him, as if no one could expect him to answer should help not be forthcoming ... [he began] by intending to make an exact reply to the question, but did not know how to go on ... "I handed in several affidavits concerning my case and I am waiting for the results." "You seem to put yourself to a great deal of trouble .... Do you consider such things necessary, then?" "I can't exactly say," replied the man, once more deprived of all assurance ... [he] appeared to be on the point of repeating his first answer all over again for fear of making a new mistake, but under K.'s impatient eye he merely said: "Anyhow, I have handed in my affidavits." "Perhaps you don't believe that I am under arrest?" asked K. "Oh, yes, certainly," said the man, stepping somewhat aside, but there was no belief in his answer, merely apprehension. "So you don't really believe me?" asked K. and, provoked by the man's humility, he seized him by the arm as if to compel him to believe.[36]

This text suggests that the unexpected, inconsistent, and legally impenetrable reasonings and actions of the mysterious court undermine an accused's ability to cognize, infer, believe, and act rationally. Although K.'s apparent failure of reason and nerve raises questions about the consistency of his tale, it does ease somewhat the ontological and symbolic ambiguity of the court's role in the novel. It has often been read as an externalization of the character's (and, of course, the author's) self-imposed inner tribunal (*superego*), his boundless guilt. This popular reading is in flat contradiction, of course, to a jurisprudential (criminal law) interpretation, which will be explored in the next chapter. The former reading — which insists on K.'s self-attribution of guilt in the form of a hallucinatory legal persecution — squares well with the court's presuming him guilty from the start, a presumption that will admit no evidence to the contrary. It does not square at all, however, with K.'s undeniable attempts to escape or circumvent court and trial, because he assumes them to be an objective, alien, life-threatening reality.

[36]TR 40; "[er war] überzeugt, in ihrem Sinne zu sprechen" (P 39). P 43; TR 45. TR 58–59; P 54. P 22; TR 20. P 20; TR 17. P 43; TR 45. P 79; TR 90. TR 64–65; P 58–59.

6: Constitutional and Criminal Law

KAFKA'S WORKS REVEAL HIS interest in the complex interrelationships of constitutional, civil, administrative, and criminal law with the history of law and with moral thought. "The Judgment" and "The Metamorphosis" do not refer to any statutory laws; they explore interpersonal ethics and the dynamics of power within the family. *Amerika* moves beyond the circle of the family but restricts the use of law to disputes between employer and employee that in Austria, for the most part, were not actionable in civil courts but seen as matters of discipline and contractual duties.[1] By contrast, *The Trial*, "In the Penal Colony," *The Castle*, and several shorter stories of the middle and late periods offer specific examples from the history of law and jurisprudence. In *The Trial*, for instance, the conceptual models run the gamut from procedural, civil, and criminal to constitutional and natural law. As the last chapter will show, *The Castle* contemplates the origins of societal laws in the so-called divine law of the Judaic-Christian tradition.

One of Kafka's principal law teachers was Heinrich Singer, a professor of canon law with broad constitutional law interests. An important research area of his was the early-nineteenth-century Catholic *Koordinations* theory, which conceived of church and state as coordinated (coequal) sovereign powers.[2] Singer acknowledged the theory's contribution in shaping a Roman Catholic cultural and political movement that was able to curb the post-Napoleonic

---

[1] Josef Ulbrich, *Das österreichische Staatsrecht* [*Handbuch des öffentlichen Rechts der Gegenwart*, ed. Georg Jellinek and Robert Piloty, vol. 4, pt. 1, sect. 1, pt. 1] (Tübingen: Mohr, 1904) 224. V 32; A 33. V 150; A 181. "The Judgment" offers an analogy to ancient and especially Roman law, to a father's absolute legal right over his son.

[2] Heinrich Singer, "Zur Frage des staatlichen Oberaufsichtsrechtes," *Deutsche Zeitschrift für Kirchenrecht*, 3rd series, 5 (1895): 60–166; 161. During his second year at the university Kafka took eleven weekly hours with Singer. For a list of Kafka's university courses see Wagenbach, *Franz Kafka* 243–44. Singer refers to Marty as "ein befreundeter Professor der Philosophischen Fakultät" (Heinrich Singer, *Einige Worte über die Vergangenheit und Zukunft der Czernowitzer Universität* [Warnsdorf: Stracke, 1917] 19).

states' absolutist control over their citizens. But he also insisted that coordination amounted to a contradictory legal principle that could never legitimize the rule of law. It would turn the relation between state and church into an out-and-out political struggle, almost like a war between nations. To ensure freedom of conscience for all and peace between the religions, the state had to achieve sovereignty based on individual rights and morally sanctioned laws. Although a devout Catholic, Singer was critical of Austria-Hungary's concordat (1855) with the Vatican. To avoid a political conflict, the concordat had surrendered some of the empire's legislative sovereignty to the church, which was able to determine its own relation to the empire as well as to control many institutional issues that traditionally had been in its domain. For instance, it retained the jurisdiction over all marital matters as well as the supervision of the elementary school system. Kafka was well aware of the legal and constitutional sovereignty that modern states had won. In a suppressed passage from *The Trial*, Josef K. tells one of his executioners: "What if I transferred the trial into the domain where the writ of the state law runs? The outcome might very well be that I would have to defend you two gentlemen against the state!" K. envisions himself in the role of a defense counsel on behalf of two henchmen of an illegal court system that aspires to compete with the state's criminal jurisdiction. When the lawyer Huld shows himself informed about K.'s case even before he has met him, and K. is briefly tempted to say to him: "But you're attached to the Court in the Palace of Justice, not the one in the attics," it implies that the court system is somehow coequal with or rivaling the state's court system. Just as Singer saw coordination as a product of jurisprudential (canonical or natural law) speculation, K. sees the court system related to a "mysterious jurisprudence." Singer was well aware that the political success of the theory would have resulted in a "caricature of the Middle Ages."[3]

Kafka also took classes with Josef Ulbrich, professor of Austrian public and constitutional law and coeditor of the most comprehensive dictionary in this field. Ulbrich emphasized, for instance, that in Austria the constitutional division of executive, legislative, and judicial power remained incomplete and that the judiciary exercised its function in the emperor's name: "We have to keep in mind that the Emperor holds the entire power of the State, including the judiciary power which is really only a ... special function of the power of the State." To implement the rule of law through the administration of justice, the emperor installs independent courts as a "special kind of state authority." Ulbrich dwells here on the fact that only with the introduction of the constitution (1867) did the lowest courts cease to be combined with the local adminis-

---

[3]TR 263; P 222; TR 103; P 90. TR 56; P 51. Singer, "Oberaufsichtsrecht" 156, 152. According to Brod, Singer was a Jew who had converted to Catholicism (see Brod, *Streitbares Leben* 198–99). In Austria it was unheard of for a professor of canon law to be of Jewish descent.

trations. In *The Trial* there exists a "highest Judge," in apparent analogy to the emperor's judicial role; the court system is constantly referred to as an administrative body, and clerks and most judges conduct themselves like petty officials. At his arrest Josef K. tells himself: "K. lived in a country with a legal constitution, there was universal peace, all the laws were in force; who dared seize him in his own dwelling?" He shows awareness of constitutionally guaranteed individual rights such as the protection against illegal seizure of person and property. The term *legal constitution*, however, denotes something beyond these rights for Kafka, whose specialty in his job as jurist for the Governmental Workers' Accident Insurance Agency was public administrative law. Because the Austrian constitution did not establish the complete separation of powers (the various administrative branches, for instance, were thought to make "legal" decisions), it tried to make up for this constitutional deficiency by protecting citizens' rights through public-administrative policies and a central court of administrative justice.[4] Austrian public law made efforts to make group rights (entitlements such as accident insurance in the workplace) into constitutional rights similar to the individual rights recognized by civil and constitutional law. Decisions of governmental agencies that infringed on a citizen's rights could be challenged in the Administrative Court in Vienna. It was a quashing (*Kassations-*) court, able only to uphold or quash legally binding administrative decisions of lower agencies based on the constitutional rights in question. If it "destroyed" (quashed) a decision, the case went back to the originating agency for a new decision. The court's sole function of final (upholding or voiding) judicial review is echoed in *The Trial* by the court painter's description of the nonexisting "definite acquittal": "For the Judges of the lowest grade ... haven't the power to grant a final acquittal, that power is reserved for the highest Court of all, which is quite inaccessible to you, me, and to all of us .... In definite acquittal the documents relating to the case are said to be completely annulled, they simply vanish from sight, not only the charge but also the records of the case and even the acquittal are destroyed, everything is destroyed."[5]

Kafka's fiction and personal writings (diaries, letters, aphorisms) circle around the relations of societal norms and laws to the concepts of ethics and justice. All indications are that he owed part of this interest to Oskar Kraus, the intellectually most distinguished member of the philosophers' club. Kraus had been university lecturer of philosophy since 1902, specializing in the history of law and ethics. In the 1890s, as a doctor of jurisprudence he had

[4]Ulbrich, *Das österreichische Staatsrecht* 222–24. TR 46; P 44. Karl Freiherr von Lemayer, "Die Verwaltungsgerichtsbarkeit und der Verwaltungsgerichtshof," *Österreichisches Staatswörterbuch*, ed. Ernst Mischler and Josef Ulbrich, 2nd. ed., 4 vols. (Vienna: Hölder, 1905–1909) 4: 23–46.

[5]Von Lemayer, "Die Verwaltungsgerichtsbarkeit" 33 [APNDX 27]. TR 158; P 136.

taken Franz Brentano's side in a legal dispute with an influential Prague law
faculty member over Brentano's right to have married (1880) after he had left
the priesthood. Because Kraus was also known to champion Brentano's ethical
and legal theories, the law school initially discouraged its students (who were
required to take at least one course in the philosophy department) from taking
Kraus's courses. Gradually, however, Kraus became highly respected among
the law faculty due to a series of well-placed articles as well as several lectures before the Prague German Jurists' Association. As an introductory
speaker for a sponsored lecture, he commented about the role of legal philosophy in the Prague University law school curriculum.[6] Kraus held a middle
position between legal positivism and a partly Aristotelian, partly utilitarian
natural-law theory. Positivism, the almost unchallenged legal theory of the
time, recognized no other law than the existing (positive) statutory law. Inas-
much as Kraus accepted this theory, he was pleased to find support for it in
Aristotle and Bentham, who both insisted that judicial decisions must predict-
ably be derived from literal applications of the law in order to safeguard the
social-legal order and to curb judicial arbitrariness and abuse. Kafka was well
aware of these requirements. The narrator of his story "Advocates" expresses
a belief in the sanctity of the positive (civil and criminal) law and the need for
strict adherence to it: "A court, one assumes, passes judgment according to
the law. If one were to assume that this was being done unfairly or frivolous-
ly, then life would be not possible; one must have confidence that the court
allows the majesty of the law its full scope, for this is its sole duty. Within the
law everything is accusation, advocacy, and verdict; any interference by an
individual here would be a crime." The same theory, applied to administrative
procedure, is expressed in *The Castle*: "[The officials'] rigid obedience to and
execution of their duty [is] the greatest consideration that the applicants can
really wish for."[7] As an antidote to his moderate positivism, however, Kraus
also held that positive law is to be seen always as derivative and relative, that
is, *defeasible*.[8] It must be constantly measured against an absolute natural law
or norm, be this a highest practical good (Aristotle, Bentham), universal moral
duty (Kant), or self-evident ethical valuations aiming at a highest good (Brentano). What proves positive (e.g. civil) law's derivative nature is that it is
often defective, outdated, or incomplete. In an article, which he also read
before the German Jurists' Association in 1904, Kraus maintained that both

[6]Kraus to Brentano, 22 Oct. 1902. Kraus to Brentano, 26 Oct. 1905.

[7]Oskar Kraus, "Rechtsphilosophie und Jurisprudenz," *Zeitschrift für die gesamte
Strafrechtswissenschaft* 23 (1903): 763–94. CS 450; E 322. C 338; S 247.

[8]H. L. A. Hart introduced this term into ethics and jurisprudence to describe rules
that can be defeated by supervening conditions and considerations ("The Ascription
of Responsibility and Rights," *Logic and Language*, ed. Anthony Flew [Oxford:
Blackwell, 1960] 145–66).

jurisprudence and practical adjudication must seek a balance between literal adherence to codified civil law and the constant consideration of distributive justice and natural-law principles.[9] Especially where the law leaves gaps (fails to cover particular cases), the judge must fill these gaps with respect to the ethical consideration of fairness and justice:

> The judge receives not only the duty of obedience to the law but the most important rules for his conduct on the whole not from the positive law but from ethics. I am thinking here not only of those cases in which the law itself instructs the judge to proceed according to the principles of fairness and equity; but especially also those in which the judge is in duty bound to fill in the gaps of the existing law ... where the law leaves us in the lurch, we must base our decision on what is naturally just, what is just and fair in view of all the circumstances.[10]

Kraus agreed with a comment in a leading journal ascribing to him the position of mediator between legal positivism and what a 1906 publication called *Free Law*.[11] This latter theory criticized positivism, especially in its extreme form of legal conceptualism — the assumption (derived from the nineteenth-century reception of Roman law) that specific judicial applications must follow deductively, and in no other way, from the most general concepts of a given law. Free Law promoted instead the judge's free interpretation (even reconstruction) of a law within its social context. It acknowledged gaps in the existing law and devised interpretative strategies for dealing with them — such as allowing analogies to cases that are covered by other provisions of the law, applying restrictive or expansive interpretations, and taking into account the law's (the lawmaker's) original intent. The Free Law theory's insistence that civil law is not a logically coherent conceptual system but is riddled with gaps aimed to reveal the fact that positivism and conceptualism only rationalize what really is the judge's intrinsically decisional function. Since judges always

[9]Kraus, "Rechtsphilosophie und Jurisprudenz" 763–78. Kraus, "Die leitenden Grundsätze der Gesetzesinterpretation," *Zeitschrift für das Privat- und Öffentliche Recht der Gegenwart* 32 (1905): 628–29.

[10]Oskar Kraus, "Rechtsphilosophie und Jurisprudenz" 778–79 [APNDX 28]. The term *gaps* in reference to the court appears in *The Trial* (P 101; TR 117), *gaps in the law* (*Gesetzeslücken*) in "Investigations of a Dog" (E 349; CS 309–10).

[11]Kraus to Brentano, 2 Aug. 1909. Gnaeus Flavius [Hermann Kantorowicz], "Der Kampf um die Rechtswissenschaft" (1906), H. Kantorowicz, *Rechtswissenschaft und Soziologie*, ed. Thomas Würtenberger (Karlsruhe: Müller, 1962) 13–49. See Gustav Radbruch's positive appreciation: rev. of *Der Kampf um die Rechtswissenschaft*, by Gnaeus Flavius, *Zeitschrift für die gesamte Strafrechtswissenschaft* 27 (1907): 241–43.

interpret the law, the theory asked them to "create" it from the perspective of social responsibility and distributive justice.[12] An article in a Social Democratic party journal endorsed the Free Law position as the legal profession's acknowledgment that, given the rigid conceptualism of civil adjudication, much recent social legislation (e.g., the workers' accident insurance law) was inconsistent with the traditional (Roman Law) principle of unfettered private ownership and thus nothing more than a legal hodgepodge, a parliamentary compromise. On the other hand, the Austrian attorney general Franz Klein condemned Free Law as undermining the legislative role of parliament and the rule of law.[13]

The leading officials of the Governmental Workers' Accident Insurance Agency, Kafka among them, avoided the political debate over Free Law but clearly favored judicial activism in attempting to expand the application of the insurance law. The agency enforced the collection of premiums by putting administrative and public pressure on employers. Kafka interpreted mandatory participation and coverage for excluded types of work as broadly as possible. He wanted not only to protect workers in those occupations that the present law did not cover but also to redistribute the burden of insurance costs among the various branches of industry, that is, more equitably than required by law. In a skillful argument, published in the agency's annual report for 1907, Kafka directly opposed the Administrative Court's far-reaching binding interpretation (1908) of the workers' accident insurance law and its amendment that arbitrarily restricted mandatory coverage to selected types of work in industry and construction. He noted that these restrictions made it easier for certain enterprises to claim fewer insured workers and to defraud their competitors and the agency. He called the court's interpretation formalistic (tainted by conceptualism), unauthentic, an "insufficient interpretation of an insufficient law," and

[12]See Dietmar Moench, *Die methodologischen Bestrebungen der Freirechtsbewegung auf dem Wege zur Methodenlehre der Gegenwart* (Frankfurt: Athenäum, 1971). Moench references but otherwise ignores Kraus's contribution to the Free Law theory. The practice appeared sanctioned by Section 1 of the Swiss Civil Code which Eugen Ehrlich, one of the founders of the Free Law movement, was the first to draw on ("Freie Rechtsfindung und freie Rechtswissenschaft" [1903], Eugen Ehrlich, *Recht und Leben*, ed. Manfred Rehbinder [Berlin: Duncker & Humblot, 1967] 191). Ehrlich taught at the University of Czernowitz, where Marty and Singer had started their academic careers.

[13]Richard Engländer, "Die Renaissance des Naturrechts," *Der Kampf* 1 (1907–1908): 547–52. Franz Klein, "Freie Rechtsfindung," *Das Recht* 10 (1906): 916–19; also in the Viennese daily *Neue Freie Presse* (22 July 1906) and in *Allgemeine österreichische Gerichtszeitung* (57.34 [1906]). Compare Klein's "Heute gilt der Grundsatz: Der Richter habe nach dem Gesetze oder in tunlichster Anlehnung an das Gesetz zu urteilen" (917) and Kafka's "Advocates": "das Gericht spricht sein Urteil nach dem Gesetz, sollte man annehmen" (E 322; cf. note 7).

he appealed to the law's legislative history and original intent, the principles of "just distribution," as well as social or "practical expediency." He stated the agency's legal position in an in-house address: "whatever mandated and useful reforms are possible within the existing laws, they will be carried out".[14] His "The Problem of Our Laws" (1920) portrays a society in which the laws are known to and applied by only a small clique of aristocrats. He may have based it on the ancient Roman judicial system, in which jurists and patricians kept the code of legal procedure secret. Around 450 B.C. Gnaeus Flavius, a judicial clerk, publicized it and, as a result, became popular with the masses.[15] In the story, the fact that the laws are applied by such a small group is not seen as in itself detrimental to the people, since in any case only the initial interpretations and applications of a law are relatively "free" (an allusion to Free Law), while later ones are more and more restricted by precedent ("though there is still a possible freedom of interpretation left, it has now become very restricted"). The greatest obstacle to judicial change is the possibility that the alleged law does not exist, or that it consists in the simple positivist rule that whatever the nobility decides is the law. Unfortunately, this mere possibility discourages the fight against the nobility because without it one might have no law at all.

Criminal Investigation and Procedure

Kafka studied criminal procedure and law with Hans Groß, author of two widely used books on criminal investigation and criminal psychology. Groß's writings on investigative methods (which he wanted to be construed as scientifically as possible), his emphasis on the unreliability of human perception, memory, and, consequently, eyewitness testimony, and the scientistlike role of the investigating judge are echoed as well as mocked in *The Trial*. Inspired by experimental psychology, Groß taught that a trial must be based on both

[14]Kafka, "Die Arbeiterunfallversicherung und die Unternehmer," Franz Kafka, *Amtliche Schriften*, ed. Klaus Hermsdorf (Berlin: Akademie-Verlag, 1984) 163–74; 166. Kafka, "Umfang der Versicherungspflicht der Baugewerbe und der baulichen Nebengewerbe," *Amtliche Schriften* 95–120; 105, 120. "Was innerhalb der heutigen Gesetze an verlangten und nützlichen Reformen möglich ist, es wird geschehn" (Kafka, "Rede zur Amtseinsetzung des Direktors," *Amtliche Schriften* 122). A legislative amendment doing away with the arbitrary restrictions that Kafka opposed became effective in 1912 (*Soziale Praxis* 21 [1911–12], column 1272).

[15]CS 437–38; E 314–15. See Rudolph von Jhering, *Geist des römischen Rechts auf den verschiedenen Stufen seiner Entwicklung*, 3rd and 4th ed., 3 vols. [vol. 2 in 2 pts.] (Leipzig: Breitkopf & Härtel, 1875–80) 2.2: 390–420. Kantorowicz used the pseudonym *Gnaeus Flavius* when he spearheaded Free Law (see note 11).

the scientific investigation of relevant facts and the critical evaluation of testimony, that is, on the fallibility and testing of the accuracy of perception. In his seminar on criminal law during the winter semester 1904–1905 (in which Kafka was enrolled), Groß gave his students assignments that tested the reliability of people's perceptions and memory. In one such assignment, students found that a number of people who used the Karls Bridge every day had never noticed the statues for which it is famous. Groß's insistence on the close connection between the psychology of noticing and criminal investigation echoes in K.'s repeated failures of noticing comprehension: he does not recognize the three young men from his bank, cannot identify the men attending his first hearing as court officials or the attics as court offices, and never gets a fix on the court's crushing, pervasive power although everyone else takes it for granted.[16]

Another topic of discussion in Groß's criminal-law seminar was the establishment of evidence through psychological questioning. Two of his students, Max Wertheimer (the later *Gestalt* theorist) and Julius Klein, showed that when suspects or witnesses are asked to respond associatively to a series of words — some of which refer to specific objects (a painting, for example) at the scene of the presumed crime — they inadvertently betray their knowledge of these objects. Groß hoped that this investigative technique could answer the question of guilt and innocence with near-scientific accuracy: "Under certain conditions one could solve the question of guilt and innocence through *evidence diagnostics* with some, often with great certainty." During the winter semester 1904–1905, he invited Wertheimer to give a lecture and had one of his students, Alfred Groß (a freshly graduated doctor juris), as well as Wertheimer conduct several association experiments with and before students of his criminal law seminar (Kafka among them). Hans Groß said about this seminar that "it contained a gratifyingly great number of young people who are taking up the modern, theoretical-criminalist investigations with enthusiasm and understanding."[17]

---

[16]Hans Groß, "Zur Frage des Wahrnehmungsproblems," *Allgemeine österreichische Gerichtszeitung* 56 (1905): 51–54 (11 Feb. 1905); 59–60 (18 Feb. 1905). TR 15 ("They were subordinate employees of the Bank .... How could he have failed to notice that?"); P 18. Hans Groß is usually regarded a positivist and a criminal law disciplinarian. Ernst Fuchs, another pioneer of Free Law, however, considered the hands-on, empirical approach of Groß a model for the reform of criminal law *(Schreibjustiz und Richterkönigtum* [Leipzig: Teutonia, 1907] 35, 47, 66).

[17]Groß, "Zur Frage des Wahrnehmungsproblems" 60. The psychological procedure was called *Tatbestandsdiagnostik.* Groß, "Zur psychologischen Tatbestandsdiagnostik," *Archiv für Kriminalanthropologie und Kriminalistik* 19 (1905): 49. During his clerkship at the Prague county court in late 1906 and the first half of 1907 Kafka experienced trial law as it was actually practiced.

Alfred Groß also reported that in early 1905 he and his teacher success-fully conducted such an association experiment in front of numerous leading judges, prosecutors, and police officials as well as students (Kafka conceivably among them).[18] Oskar Kraus, who had been present at the experiment, criti-cized it publicly[19] and triggered a protracted polemical exchange[20] between Max Lederer (a former Marty student and judge in Prague) and Alfred Groß, who declared the new method nearly infallible: "It is understood that our method requires that the person to be investigated is willing to express his reactions. But I don't believe that the innocent person will refuse to cooperate because he has nothing to fear from the investigation, on the contrary, might escape an undeserved detention pending-investigation. If he refuses, he might have to blame himself for the consequences. If today an innocent person tells the examining judge: 'I am innocent, don't bother to ask me any questions because I won't answer a single one,' he probably will wind up in the clink."[21] Groß's whole thesis rested on the Wundtian assumption that associ-ations in the form of words or gestures are involuntary expressions of one's mental life. In accordance with Marty's and Kraus's anti-Wundtian linguistics, Lederer insisted that associations induced by verbal stimuli are private mental events and, as such, do not find involuntary expression in gesture and word. A suspect will not betray himself readily; he can disguise his true associations by deliberately altering his responses. Lederer tested the method in a "circle

[18]Alfred Groß, "Zur psychologischen Tatbestandsdiagnostik als kriminalistisches Hilfsmittel," *Allgemeine österreichische Gerichtszeitung* 56 (1905): 133–34. "Die Assoziationsmethode im Strafprozeß," *Zeitschrift für die gesamte Strafrechtswissen-schaft* 26 (1906): 19–40. Alfred Groß and Professor Hans Groß apparently were not related.

[19]"A procedure which creates a new source of suffering especially for the innocent defendant" (Kraus, "Psychologische Tatbestandsdiagnostik," *Monatsschrift für Kriminalpsychologie und Strafrechtsreform* 2 [1905-1906]: 61). The first public criticism from within the philosophers' club was Kastil's: "Ich kann's nicht glauben" (Rev. of *Psychologische Tatbestandsdiagnostik* by Max Wertheimer and Julius Klein, *Deutsche Arbeit* 3 [1903-1904]: 789).

[20]Max Lederer, "Zur Frage der psychologischen Tatbestandsdiagnostik," *Zeitschrift für die gesamte Strafrechtswissenschaft* 26 (1906): 488–506. Lederer, "Die Verwen-dung der psychologischen Tatsbestandsdiagnostik in der Strafrechtspraxis," *Monats-schrift für Kriminalpsychologie und Strafrechtsreform* 3 (1906-1907): 163–72. Alfred Groß, "Die Assoziationsmethode im Strafprozeß," *Zeitschrift für die gesamte Strafrechtswissenschaft* 26 (1906): 19–40; 27 (1907): 175–212.

[21]Alfred Groß, "Zur psychologischen Tatbestandsdiagnostik," *Monatsschrift für Kriminalpsychologie und Strafrechtsreform* 2 (1905-1906): 184.

of philosophy students"[22] and reported in his articles the results of several association experiments, all of which implicated (and in a real trial would have convicted) an innocent person. He argued that this much-touted diagnostic questioning should not be used in criminal proceedings since it could easily entrap the accused. In fact, evidence produced by this method was never admitted in a court of law.[23]

The simulations of evidence-diagnostic criminal investigations before large groups, and the discussions following them, had an impact on the legal procedures portrayed in *The Trial*. The wrongdoing Josef K. is charged with — the section of the statute he presumably violated — is never spelled out. The officials never tell him anything or ask him questions concerning this all-important issue. Instead they form impressions about him based on his reaction to and his arguing against the arrest. They write reports about him and rely on observations of his behavior. Since there is no formal charge, the hearings are fake but also suggest that the court continues to take Josef K. unawares. It uses inscrutable criteria and tricks to prove, or rather fabricate, his guilt: "You've all come rushing here to listen and nose out what you can about me, making a pretense of party divisions, and half of you applauded merely to lead me on, you wanted some practice in fooling an innocent man." "And in the end, out of nothing at all, [the court conjures up] an enormous fabric of guilt." Ironically, at the same time that Hans Groß conducted and encouraged associative experiments in front of audiences, he also was apt to emphasize that a successful inquiry, and especially the testing of an eyewitness's perceptual reliability, can never be realized in the courtroom but only in the investigating judge's quiet office: "The courtroom with its unwieldy apparatus of the whole court ... the loitering witnesses, the attending public and the time pressures are absolutely unsuited to a scrupulous, calm and difficult work ... as would required by any scientific test; such test can be conducted only in the quiet office where only witness, examining judge and stenographer are present .... The examiner's sole duty is to discover the truth.[24]

On the way to his first hearing, Josef K. assumes that it will be held in the investigating judge's examining office; but to his surprise he enters a room

[22]Most likely, the philosophers' club. Lederer, "Zur Frage der Tatbestandsdiagnostik" 503. Even the club's nonlawyers were aware of the polemic. Cf. Bergmann: "The new method — which in my opinion Lederer rightfully is fighting against — to prove the criminal's guilt by investigating his associations" (Rev. of *Psychophysik*, by Constantin Gutberlet, *Philosophische Wochenschrift* 3 [1906]: 119).

[23]Ernst Lohsing, *Österreichisches Strafprozeßrecht: In systematischer Darstellung* (Graz and Vienna: Moser, 1912) 332.

[24]P 16-18; TR 13–15. P 52; TR 56. P 99; TR 115. TR 47; P 45. TR 149; P 128. Hans Groß, "Über Zeugenprüfung," *Monatsschrift für Kriminalpsychologie und Strafrechtsreform* 3 (1906–1907): 578.

holding a crowd of the most diverse people. The judge first states that because of K.'s late arrival he has the procedural right not to hear him that day but then decides to waive this right. K. addresses the assembly, which is seemingly divided into two opposing parties, attempting to influence it in his favor. These occurrences contradict the spirit of scientific investigation Groß was fond of describing; they appear more in the line of the associative experiments Kafka had witnessed. Perhaps they also are modeled on the early Roman criminal trial, which enabled the accused to address the assembled citizens and try to win them over to his side: "I have no wish to shine as an orator .... The Examining Magistrate, no doubt, is much the better speaker, it is part of his vocation."[25] In addition, the episode contains two vivid theatrical images. The room of inquiry is surrounded by a gallery just below the ceiling, packed with people in a bent posture because of insufficient headroom. This scenario is reminiscent of the top gallery of a theater described in a novel by Brod. Josef K. then discovers that the judge has given a secret signal, apparently a request to the crowd either to clap or to hiss. The incident is based on the common practice of actors — which Kafka had experienced firsthand in a Paris theater — who employed paid applauders.[26] The investigation's mocking public format, be it political, rhetorical, or theatrical, undermines its supposed purpose, the truthful assessment of the facts and a chance for the accused to defend himself. At the same time it intriguingly makes the hearing appear to be not a preliminary investigation but the trial itself. This conceivable scenario is the earliest indication that, since all those in attendance turn out to be court officials, the public is not admitted to trials.

The function and sequence of the procedures involving Josef K. are to a large degree systematic distortions of the *Austrian Code of Criminal Procedure* (1873), with which Kafka was familiar. For instance, the court painter points out that "of course" the law requires that the innocent be acquitted but that the court's actual practice is the opposite. This mirror-image design of the fictional court helped Kafka to plot the narrative's triallike progression in advance. In contrast to his other works, he wrote *The Trial* with a preconceived plan in mind, completing the first and last chapter before writing the intervening text.[27] The novel's portrayal of criminal procedure is steeped in historical analogies. In the German-speaking countries the reception of Roman

[25]Rudolph von Jhering, *Geist des römischen Rechts* 2.1: 10–11. TR 42; P 41.

[26]"Ja oben sind wir gesessen ... und haben uns mit der flachen Hand an der Decke festgehalten" ["Yes, we sat at the top ... and steadied ourselves by touching the ceiling with our flat hand"] (Max Brod, *Jüdinnen* [Leipzig: Wolff, 1915] 227). P 37; TR 44. EF 1: 51, 180 (T 399–400; D 2: 277), 276.

[27]TR 153; P 132. Malcolm Pasley, "Die Handschrift redet," *Franz Kafka: Der Proceß*, Marbacher Magazin, vol. 52, ed. M. Pasley and Ulrich Ott (Marbach: Deutsche Schillergesellschaft, 1990) 10–11. Also Pasley, PKA 2: 111.

and canonical procedure (around 1500) replaced the indigenous adversarial with an inquisitorial, that is, a written and secret, criminal procedure, requiring no accuser. In Austria the proceedings, according to the *Constitutio Criminalis Theresiana,* the penal code issued by the Empress Maria Theresia in 1768, were written and secret in all stages; the informer and the grounds for suspicion remained secret, and no defense counsel was admitted except for the submission of a written appeal. Even after the abolition of torture in 1788, the main goal of the criminal inquisition and trial was to secure the accused person's confession. The pressures for a confession and the complete absence of a public, oral, and adversarial trial before a judge are, of course, prominent elements of K.'s trial. The court appears to take his guilt for granted and to condemn him before the trial gets underway. The nature of the accusation and the trial afford him no possibility of acquittal.[28]

The *Code of Criminal Procedure* in effect during Kafka's time had done away with most of the Theresian code's inquisitorial practices. It granted the accused the constitutional right to an adversarial and public trial: "The proceedings before the trial judge both in the civil and the criminal court are oral and public." Three principles, (a) substantive truth, (b) substantive defense and (c) procedural defense, are central to these proceedings. As for (a), even a confession does not relieve the court of the obligation to fully investigate the evidence and to obtain independent corroboration.[29] As for (b), the defendant is not the object of but a party to the adversarial proceedings; he has the right to defend himself. Thus, Section 199 of the code requires that the examining judge inform him of the nature of his alleged crime and demand from him a detailed statement about the facts relevant to the charges. The accused then must be provided the opportunity to clear himself completely on all grounds of suspicion and accusations.[30] During the trial the court must give careful consideration to the evidence and statements presented in his defense. As for (c), at all stages of the trial the accused has the right to be represented by counsel and to have access to all relevant documents. Josef K.'s trial does away with many of the code's provisions, thereby denying him the most basic rights. Whether this situation is a throwback to the older code or an inversion of the existing one, the court system's perversion of justice remains the same.

[28]P 94 ("man muß das Geständnis machen"); TR 108. This paragraph follows Ernst Lohsing, *Österreichisches Strafprozeßrecht,* 3rd ed. (Vienna: Österreichische Staatsdruckerei, 1932) 8–18.

[29]Lohsing, *Österreichisches Strafprozeßrecht* (1912) 35–37.

[30]Ulbrich, quoting the Austrian *Constitution* on judicial power (*Das österreichische Staatsrecht* 227). Lohsing, *Österreichisches Strafprozeßrecht* (1912) 35–41; 194–95, 361. *Österreichische Strafprozeßordnung,* ed. Leo Geller, 4th ed. (Vienna: Perles, 1894) 154. Cf. "In the Penal Colony": "But he must have had some chance of defending himself" (CS 145; E 104).

K.'s attorney explains that from its inception the court system has established "the secret court": "The proceedings were not public; they could certainly, if the Court considered it necessary, become public, but the Law did not prescribe that they must be made public. Naturally, therefore, the legal records of the case, and above all the actual charge-sheets, were inaccessible to the accused and his counsel." "The proceedings were not only kept secret from the general public, but from the accused as well. Of course only so far as this was possible, but it had proved possible to a very great extent. For even the accused had no access to the Court records." Secrecy applies even to the judges: "The final decisions of the Court are never recorded, even the Judges can't get hold of them." K. is denied the right to substantive defense, the right to defend himself. At his arrest he is not given the "reason for his arrest" as required by the code's Section 209 but instead is reprimanded for protesting his innocence ("don't make such an outcry about your feeling innocent").[31]

His right to procedural defense, to retain counsel, is undermined in two ways. First, the criminal procedure does not really admit defense lawyers: "The defense was not actually countenanced by the Law, but only tolerated, and there were differences of opinion even on that point ... none of the counsels for the Defense was recognized by the Court, all who appeared before the Court as counsels being in reality merely in the position of pettifogging lawyers." Kafka may have derived the idea of an illegitimate court system closeted away in attics from the image of pettifoggers, who originally were thought to have their offices in attics: "The lawyer's room was in the very top attic."[32] Second, because of the trial's secret and completely encapsulated stages, the judges seek out the defense attorneys privately, and the attorneys, because of their unofficial status, in turn seek out the judges. This practice makes a mockery of the judges' impartiality and independence; it allows them to use the lawyers against their clients' interests because "certain turns in the various cases" could advance the judges' careers: "Could they possibly employ the lawyer to bring about such turns in the case, turns which were bound, of course, to be unfavorable to the accused?" *The Trial* turns the lawyer into an enemy who creates obstacles for the client and transforms him into the lawyer's dog. This practice violates the lawyer's obligation to his client and the law: "It is the lawyer's duty to represent his client in accordance with the

[31]TR 118; "das geheime Gericht" (P 102). TR 115; P 99. TR 116; P 100. TR 154; P 133. TR 12; "Grund seiner Verhaftung" (P 16). TR 12; P 16.

[32]TR 115–16; P 100. *Winkeladvokat* (pettifogger) is derived from the attic location of the lawyer's office (Rudolph von Jhering, *Der Zweck im Recht*, 2 vols., 4th ed. [Leipzig: Breitkopf & Härtel, 1904] 1: 118). Kafka apparently got this etymology from von Jhering (so also Lida Kirchberger, *Franz Kafka's Use of the Law in Fiction* [New York: Lang, 1986] 79–82).

law and to defend his rights against anybody with diligence, loyalty, and conscientiousness."[33]

There are features of the trial that blatantly revoke specific sections of the code. During his encounters with the officials who arrest and interrogate him K. looks in vain for a chair he could use, and he is told that it is not customary for the accused to sit down. This is a direct reference to the code's Section 198: "During his interrogation every accused has the right to sit down." The examining judge's remark to K., that "today you have flung away with your own hand all the advantages which an interrogation invariably confers on an accused man," refers to the code's instruction to the examiner (Section 203) that he remind the accused "that through obstruction of the inquiry he could deprive himself of the grounds for defense."[34] It is not clear in this instance whether K. in fact has the right to prove his innocence — the judge's remark could be meant merely to deceive and disorient him further — or whether his conduct was so procedurally incompetent as to deprive him of this advantage. Of course, the ambiguity is only apparent, since K. is ignorant of the charges against him and thus cannot in any way defend himself.

The novel makes another remarkable reference to matters of criminal procedure, this one having to do with a public debate then going on in Austria and Germany about the merits of conditional conviction or sentencing. Introduced by Oskar Kraus, the widely known criminologist Franz von Liszt in 1903 lectured on the topic before the Prague German Jurists' Association; in 1904 the first Czech Jurists' Convention in Prague resolved to recommend the introduction of conditional conviction.[35] In 1907 Max Lederer gave a report in the philosophers' club about the court systems he had studied on a trip through the United States, especially the institution of probation — which offers the convicted person a conditional suspension of sentence based on his future conduct. In two articles Lederer showed himself impressed with the fact that under some U.S. state laws a successful probation does not earn a suspension of the sentence but the voiding of the (presumably conditional) conviction itself.[36]

[33]P 102–3; TR 118–19. TR 125; P 108. P 164, 109, 166; TR 192, 127, 193. *Die Advokatenordnung*, commentary by Hanns Christl, *Österreichische Gesetzkunde*, ed. Max Ehrenreich (Vienna: Patriotische Volksbuchhandlung, 1912) 3: 785–830; 794.

[34]P 8, 15; TR 3, 11. TR 48; P 45. *Strafprozeßordnung*, ed. Geller, 153, 155. Lohsing, *Strafprozeßrecht* 361.

[35]Kraus to Brentano, 20 Nov., 1903. *Allgemeine österreichische Gerichtszeitung* 55 (1904): 195.

[36]Utitz to Brentano, 1 May 1907 (see APNDX 5). Max Lederer, "Das *probation system* in den Vereinigten Staaten von Nordamerika," *Allgemeine österreichische Gerichtszeitung* 59 (1908): 99 (APNDX 29). Lederer, "Das *probation system* in Nord-Amerika," *Zeitschrift für die gesamte Strafrechtswissenschaft* 28 (1908): 426.

In this discussion within the legal profession, procedural options even more radical than conditional sentencing or conviction were considered, such as conditional suspension of the criminal trial or conditional acquittal with a threat of resumption of trial.[37] The voiding of a conviction — or, in the case of a conditional acquittal, its permanent conversion — would depend on a successful probation. In addition to the novel's numerous other reversals of criminal procedure, *The Trial* includes a mocking inversion of the notion of conditional acquittal. The court painter Titorelli discusses with K. the possibility of obtaining a temporary acquittal or a temporary "withdrawal of the indictment." This kind of acquittal is called *ostensible* because it lets the accused go free but keeps the indictment in circulation so that it can be reactivated, regardless of the accused's recent conduct. It thus prevents a permanent acquittal: as soon as some judge happens to pay renewed attention to the indictment, he will order another arrest. In substituting random judicial action for the accused's probation, the novel again suggests Josef K.'s unmitigated guilt, inescapable conviction, and punishment. When it comes to his trial's actual outcome, the proceedings "gradually merge into the verdict." Even if this guilty verdict is not decided at once, for the defendant it comes unexpectedly at any moment.[38]

Criminal Law, Criminal Guilt

Law may refer to a general ethical norm, to unwritten natural or societal norms, to written rules (such as the Ten Commandments), or to a specialized system of rules (e.g., civil or procedural law) that demand or prohibit specific individual conduct. A criminal statute lists and specifies those acts that, willfully committed or omitted, constitute punishable crimes and specifies the punishment for each. A basic principle of criminal law dictates that there can be no punishment — nor any crime or its entailment, criminal guilt (willfulness, knowledge of consequences) — without there being a publicized statute specifying them as such: "The types of conduct threatened by punishment are not prohibited by generally stated norms but the criminal statue itself."[39] In

---

[37]See Karl Warhanek, "Strafe, bedingte Verurteilung und bedingte Entlassung," *Allgemeine österreichische Gerichtszeitung* 62 (1911): 199.

[38]TR 158; "für den Augenblick der Anklage entzogen" (P 136). P 139; TR 161. TR 211; P 180). P 168; TR 196. These options strongly suggest that Kafka heard Lederer's report in the club.

[39]Oskar Kraus, "Das Dogma von der Ursächlichkeit der Unterlassung," *Juristische Vierteljahrsschrift* 30 (1898): 70. See also Karl Janka, *Das österreichische Strafrecht* 3rd ed., revised by Friedrich Rulf (Prague and Vienna: Tempsky, 1894) 44–45, 73.

an ambiguous exchange in an unfinished chapter of *The Trial* the defendant is told that ignoring a summons to appear before the court is not punishable (constitutes no violation), yet the court has ways of enforcing it:

> Nevertheless, conscious of his own rights, he asked through the telephone what would happen if he failed to put in an appearance. "We shall know where to find you," was the answer. "And I shall be punished for not having come of my own accord?" asked K., and smiled in anticipation of the reply. "No," was the answer. "Splendid," said K., "then what motive could I have for complying with [today's] summons?" "It is not usual to bring the powers of the Court upon one's head," said the voice.

Austrian law specified proceedings for nonappearance, initiated by a public summons containing "the request to the defendant ... to appear before the court in default whereof legal proceedings would be taken against him as a lawbreaker."[40] According to Kraus, criminal law is the one legal area where strict adherence to the letter of the law overrides distributive justice and rules out free judicial creation. Kraus took issue with those jurists who justified the practice of filling gaps in the criminal code. Rather, an unlawful omission of an act (recklessness, negligence) cannot be punished unless the statute declares it to be punishable: "The judge is prohibited in plain words from punishing violations which are not threatened with punishment ... if the law does not state culpability explicitly and unequivocally, culpability is ruled out explicitly and unequivocally." *The Trial* never defines the nature of Josef K.'s guilt and crime, nor, thus, a possible defense for him, but it makes some conflicting suggestions in this regard. On one occasion K. plans to anchor his projected defense in an ethical norm, that is, to justify or condemn his past actions morally, and offer excuses: "In this defense he would give a short account of his life, and when he came to an event of any importance explain for what reasons he had acted as he did, intimate whether he approved or condemned his way of action in retrospect, and adduce grounds for the condemnation or approval." On another occasion he wants to banish the idea of ethical as well as criminal guilt from his mind altogether and pursue, as if in a business deal, any possible advantage in relation to the court. Both the ethical and the self-interested viewpoints ignore the fact that one's defense in a criminal case cannot be based on an ethical judgment or business savvy but on determining one's criminal culpability, that is, whether one's actions come under a section

The principle usually referred to was "nullum crimen, nulla poena sine lege." For Kraus, however, the criminal statute as a whole must accord with an ethical norm ("Strafe und Schuld," *Zeitschrift für Schweizer Strafrecht* 10 [1897]: 291).

[40]TR 234; P 197. Lohsing, *Strafprozeßrecht* 536.

of the criminal statute. The determination of exactly this question is impossible since the statute is secret. One of the warders correctly refers to the impossible dilemma K.'s defense is facing: "he admits that he doesn't know the Law and yet he claims he's innocent."[41]

Since K. has not been charged formally but only implicitly or obliquely and thus may be merely suspected of a wrongdoing, it is plausible initially that he assume his innocence: "There was no such guilt." At other times he entertains the possibility that there exist charges against him (whatever they may be) and that he might be guilty. This reflection would explain his playing with the idea that the court's hall of investigation itself might draw and guide him to it, since the court is said to be drawn to the guilty. In addition, declaring his innocence gives him pleasure because it happens before a private person (the painter) without fear of consequences, that is, without (presumably) the danger of perjuring himself. Besides guilt and innocence, K. contemplates a third status regarding culpability: "the Court of Inquiry might have discovered, [that I was innocent or at least] not so guilty as they had assumed." This possibility could easily be seen in connection with something else he mentions, the concept of causing someone harm or discomfort without willfulness ("it was done by strange people against my will, and yet ... the fault was mine") or without guilt ("on my account but not by any fault of mine"). Thus Josef K.'s phrase "not so guilty as they had assumed" could be seen in analogy to the lesser degrees of criminal culpability (such as recklessness or negligence[42]) that most criminal laws accept as "defeating" criminal intent, foreknowledge and malice. K.'s belated "Where there arguments in his favor that had been overlooked? Of course there must be" suggests some mitigation that could have changed the outcome.[43]

---

[41]Kraus, "Rechtsphilosophie und Jurisprudenz" 789–91. TR 113; P 98. P 109; TR 127. P 82 ("Strafprozeß"); TR 94. TR 6; P 11. In a broader sense than the merely criminal the law's secrecy is addressed in "The Problem of Our Laws": "it is an extremely painful thing to be ruled by laws that one does not know" (CS 437; E 314).

[42]TR 127; P 109. P 35; TR 35. P 128; TR 149. TR 25; P 27. TR 24; P 26. TR 43; P 41. In the proposed revision of the Austrian criminal code statutory negligence can consist in a lack of attentiveness: "Someone acts with negligence if he could have anticipated the endangering ... with the attentiveness his duty required of him" (Alexander Löffler, "Die Abgrenzung von Vorsatz und Fahrlässigkeit," Österreichische Zeitschrift für Strafrecht 2 [1911]: 159). Kraus traced inattentiveness as an ethical deficiency to Aristotle (Kraus, Die Lehre von Lob, Lohn, Tadel und Strafe bei Aristoteles [Halle: Niemeyer, 1905] 58–68).

[43]TR 228; P 194. Kafka considered adding to "In the Penal Colony": "Had something been forgotten? A decisive word? A [hold]? A charity? Who can penetrate this entanglement?]" (D 2: 178–79); "War etwas vergessen? Ein entscheidendes Wort? Ein Griff? Eine Handreichung? Wer kann in das Wirrsal eindringen?" (T 327).

The phrase *not so guilty*, however, may also refer to the neo-Aristotelian, partially utilitarian theorem of degrees of guilt that Oskar Kraus developed and discussed over a period of fifteen years. Measured on a scale of intrinsic values from the highest practical good to the greatest evil, the degree of a person's moral as well as criminal guilt (wrongful willing) is proportionate to the social evil that would be effected by the respective wrongful action: "The subjective culpability increases in proportion to the anticipated evil."[44] Moreover, as for Aristotle, a person's guilt is greater or smaller in reverse proportion to the number of others disposed to the same degree of wrongful willing in similar circumstances: "*Guilty* are only those ... who in regard to certain of their volitional dispositions appear less ethically strong than others .... A person should be called *guilty* only if he merits no excuses, that is, if the case is not such that if everybody, or nearly everybody else, were they in his mental circumstances, would be determined to a consciously immoral decision." In short, the degree of a person's guilt depends on both how the willed outcome measures on the scale of intrinsic values and to what degree other people's dispositions for wrongful willing match his or her own. Both measurements are inversely related to each other since "the greater is the prospective evil the smaller is the percentage of people who make the immoral decision."[45] For Kraus, the degree of a person's criminal guilt is always proportional to the degree of his or her implied moral guilt (blameworthiness). The former is distinguished from the latter by being realized, through commission or omission of an action, in the external world. When Josef K. sees himself as less guilty than assumed, he conceivably could be contemplating a diminution of his guilt by comparing himself with others. When he argues that no person can be called guilty and, consequently, he is innocent because he is just one of them, he excuses himself from all degrees of guilt. According to the tradesman Block, however, the court insists that each crime is unique and incomparable, that guilt, therefore, cannot have degrees based on comparison with other people's conduct: "Each case is judged on its own merits ... [there is no commonality]." The novel never explains or proves K.'s actual criminal guilt, although the priest clearly states that the court considers K. guilty at least for now. If at first the priest appears to agree with K.'s claim that no one

[44]Intrinsic value refers to Aristotle (Kraus, "Die aristotelische Werttheorie in ihren Beziehungen zu den Lehren der modernen Psychologenschule," *Zeitschrift für die gesamte Staatswissenschaft* 61 [1905]: 573–92), Bentham (Kraus, *Zur Theorie des Wertes* 35) and Brentano (Kraus, "Rechtsphilosophie und Jurisprudenz" 769–88). Kraus, "Das Motiv," *Zeitschrift für die gesamte Strafrechtswissenschaft* 17 (1897): 481. Almost identically: Kraus, "Über den Begriff der Schuld und den Unterschied von Vorsatz und Fahrlässigkeit," *Monatsschrift für Kriminalpsychologie und Strafrechtsreform* 9 (1913): 324.

[45]Kraus, "Über den Begriff der Schuld" 324–26. Kafka's "not so guilty" (TR 25; P 27) vaguely resembles Kraus's concept of a "less guilty violator" (340).

should be found guilty since people are merely people, he quickly adds that K. argues the way all guilty people do. In his diary the author himself once pronounced Josef K. guilty, leaving it open whether *guilty* has an existential, ethical, or criminal meaning. All these attributions of guilt are in flat contradiction to the fact that the trial's specific procedures are unjust and legally perverse, the court system a constitutional outlaw, and K. not only innocent (not charged with a crime) but convicted and executed no matter what.[46]

---

[46]P 180; TR 210. TR 175; P 150. P 180; TR 210. T 299; D 2: 132. Cf. "K. is not punished for anything he does, whether blameworthy or not. He has *done* nothing. That is the joke on him" (Richard A. Posner, *Law and Literature: A Misunderstood Relation* [Harvard UP, 1988] 124).

7: From Guilt to Individualism

MOST CRITICS AGREE THAT Kafka's strongly felt guilt toward his father, and especially toward Felice Bauer, led to his writing *The Trial*. The greater part of this chapter tries to shed some light on how the writing, and aftermath, of this novel modified Kafka's feelings of guilt as well as his ethical views. In the famous letter to his father he directly connects his guilt toward him with the last line of *The Trial:* "I developed a boundless sense of guilt. (In recollection of this boundlessness I once wrote of someone, accurately: 'He is afraid the shame will outlive him, even.'" Until late in his life the symbolic figure of the father represents an inescapable law ("the father-juryman who filled all the doors") that blocks the doors, the escape routes. Kafka's feelings of personal inadequacy and self-condemning guilt with respect to his father not only help to shape "The Judgment," "The Metamorphosis," and this novel but also produce his extreme ethical individualism: the rejection of notions (such as Oskar Kraus's) of blameworthiness based on comparisons with the ethical dispositions of others. Kafka started the novel in August 1914, one month after his formal breakup with Felice, which he experienced as a court proceeding against himself.[1] Almost from the start of his relationship with her, he had let on that he could not help but "poison" and deceive her, because he neither wanted to keep her nor lose her.[2] He saw his guilt toward her as primarily existential and ethical ("[before] the Judges on High") but predicted that it would increase until it became guilt before a court of law ("human judges"). He admitted to himself that at no point was he ever willing to marry her because her sheer presence threatened his ability to write. He told her as

---

[1]DF 170; H 143. Similarly: B 195; L 166; cf. H 159 ("mein Schuldbewußtsein stammt ja eigentlich von Dir"); DF 191. L 273; B 317. T 254–56; D 2: 65. As regards Felice's central role for *The Trial*, see, e.g., John Winkelman, "Felice Bauer and *The Trial*," *The Kafka Debate*, ed. Flores, 311–34.

[2]FE 170; F 269. F 78; FE 30. "Ich kann nicht mit ihr leben und ich kann nicht ohne sie leben" (B 122; L 102). In a selection from Kierkegaard's diaries Kafka had read (T 199; D 1: 298) a similar line: "[Es wäre] mir unmöglich gewesen ohne sie zu leben" (Sören Kierkegaard, *Buch des Richters: Seine Tagebücher 1833–1855 im Auszug*, transl. Hermann Gottsched [Jena and Leipzig: Diederichs, 1905] 23).

much: that his courting and proposing to her was a criminal or villainous fraud.[3] Felice just had the misfortune of being the greatest enemy of his life's only authentic concern — his writing. Thus, he caused her, although innocent, to suffer more than if she had been guilty: "As I see it, she is suffering the utmost misery and the guilt is essentially mine ... she is an innocent person condemned to extreme torture; I am guilty of the wrong for which she is being tortured, and am in addition the torturer."[4]

Grete Bloch's letter of mid-October 1914 to Kafka — the first communication from Felice's circle since the breakup — again centered his attention on Felice. In a letter to Felice he strongly implied that he was without blame because, after all, he had never deceived her: there had been nothing unexpressed with regard to his insistence on the priority of his writing over their marriage. On the contrary, the real problem was that she never believed him. In addition, she had expressed — long before their last hostile encounter in his Berlin hotel room — fear of and aversion to his making their relationship secondary to his writing. Perhaps her fear was as justifiable as his own, concerning her threat to his writing, but certainly not more so. Kafka's emphasis on the fear they had of each other is an indication that their renewed contact alleviated his feeling of guilt somewhat.[5] His communication with her contributed to the writing in December 1914 of the famous parable "Before the Law," which presents a less self-condemning, less perverted view of law and justice than Joseph K.'s story.[6] The parable is part of the introduction to the (written) law that governs the court and, consequently, of the criminal law itself. Within the parable, however, the man from the country who comes to the door of the law to ask for admittance describes it as accessible and desirable to everybody: "Everyone strives to attain the Law" recalls the first

[3]FE 56; F 114. T 228; D 2: 24–25. F 400, 468; FE 270, 322. His guilt was sharpened by his belief that marriage in itself was ethically and socially desirable: "Woman, or more precisely put, perhaps, marriage, is the representative of life with which you are meant to come to terms" (BN 50; H 87).

[4]F 617; FE 437. D 2: 185; T 331. See also "Ich bin schuld an allem" (F 425; FE 288), "ganz unanzweifelbar schuld" (M 30; MI 22). Kafka felt that he had contributed to her father's death (T 277; D 2: 100).

[5]F 614–15; FE 436. T 273–74; D 2: 93–94. F 615–21; FE 436–41. In 1922, when his relationship with Milena — which, above all, was plagued by fear (M 202, 296; MI 150, 219) — was thrown into a crisis, he linked the fear he experienced in love to his fear of the burning bush (God, the law), relating fear to guilt (B 297, L 256).

[6]T 279; D 2: 101. P 182–83; TR 213–15. Kafka read it to Felice in January 1915 ("auch sie erfaßte sie richtig" - T 287; D 2: 112) and a year later sent her a published version by registered mail (F 650; FE 463, note 1).

sentence of Aristotle's *Metaphysics*.[7] The doorkeeper[8] in front of the law
tells the man that he is not permitted to enter the law now but that it is possible that he may be permitted to do so later. He gives the man a stool and lets
him sit down. The man waits for this permission in front of the law for the
remainder of his life. Gradually his realistic perspective on the world turns
pathologically narrow, seizes on the immediate obstacle, this particular doorkeeper, and eventually on the fleas in the doorkeeper's collar.[9] Finally, with
failing eyesight, he does not know whether it is becoming darker or whether
his eyes are "deceiving" him. Moments before his death the doorkeeper tells
him "No one but you could gain admittance through this door, since this door
was intended for you." While the statement's first part merely answers the
man's belated question why no one else has requested admittance here, its
second part creates a vast interpretive problem.

In his discussion of the parable the priest strives for "respect for the
written word," but he also offers interpretations that have become part of an
established exegetical tradition.[10] He denies that the doorkeeper's first announcement — prohibiting the man's admittance while indicating its possibility
for the future — and his later one that the door was meant only for him
amount to a contradiction. He calls the doorkeeper's comprehension of this

[7]In Brentano's translation: "Alle Menschen begehren von Natur nach dem Wissen"
(Brentano, *Vom Ursprung sittlicher Erkenntnis*, ed. Oskar Kraus, 4th ed. [Hamburg:
Meiner, 1955] 22). Kafka's phrasing is: "Alle streben doch nach dem Gesetz" (P
183; TR 214). Brentano uses the quote to illustrate men's universal desire for the
practical good.

[8]The doorkeeper allegory has been connected with the Jewish-mystical tradition
(Heinz Politzer, *Franz Kafka: Der Künstler* [Frankfurt: Fischer, 1965] 270); a
Midrash legend (Ulf Abraham, *Der verhörte Held: Verhöre, Urteile, und die Rede
von Recht und Schuld im Werk Franz Kafkas* [Munich: Fink, 1985] 116); the secretaries of Hasidic rabbis (Ritchie Robertson, *Kafka: Judaism, Politics, and Literature*
[Oxford: Clarendon, 1985] 127); the Kabbalistic linkage between God's hierarchical
permanent court and a spatially progressing study of the Torah (Karl E. Grözinger,
Kafka und die Kabbala: Das Jüdische in Werk und Denken von Franz Kafka [Frank-
furt: Eichborn, 1992]; Grözinger, "Himmlische Gerichte in der ostjüdischen Erzählung," *Franz Kafka und das Judentum* 93–112). A probable allusion is to the fact
that during biblical times court sessions were held at the city gates (Amos 5:10; Isa.
29:21).

[9]Jürgen Born, "Kafka's Parable *Before the Law*: Reflections Towards a Positive
Interpretation," *Mosaic* 3 (1970): 155. The stool is an echo of the Austrian criminal
procedure referred to earlier that requires the investigating judge to offer the defendant or witness a chair during the hearing.

[10]"The laws are very ancient; their interpretation has been the work of many centuries, and has itself doubtless acquired the status of law" ("The Problem of Our
Laws" - CS 437; E 314) expresses the spirit of theological (Talmudic, Christian) and
juridical hermeneutics that the priest alludes to.

and other matters merely clouded: the "right perception of any matter and any misunderstanding of the same matter do not wholly exclude each other."[11] K. concludes that the announcements contradict each other in two respects. The "prohibition" to enter is negated by the revelation that the door was intended for the man, that the long-sought-for permission had been granted all along. The statement of possible future admittance appears contradicted by the fact that the apparent permission is revealed seconds before the man's death, thus rendering it ineffective and meaningless. In K.'s view, the man's belief that the possible permission would be given in time for him to take advantage of it deceives him into waiting. One school of interpreters appears to take a middle position between K.'s and the priest's assessments. They construe the doorkeeper's first announcement as an ambiguous judicial decision. The door-keeper's duty, of course, is to take his instructions literally and prohibit the man from entering, but instead he indulges in a bit of free judicial creation: "In suggesting to the man the possibility of future admittance the doorkeeper is exceeding his duty. At that time his apparent duty is only to refuse admittance and indeed many commentators are surprised that the suggestion should be made at all, since the doorkeeper appears to be a precisian with a stern regard for duty." In other words, by stating that it possibly can be reversed in the future, the doorkeeper gives the prohibition a misleading implication.[12] It apparently allows his last statement — which merely confirms that the man had been waiting in front of the right door — to mean that all along the man has had the permission to enter. The priest is intrigued with this jurisprudential criticism; he discusses several motivations for the doorkeeper to embellish a presumably straightforward instruction to prohibit the entry. One is his friendly disposition, something the priest earlier had admitted about himself: "I am too easily influenced and tend to forget my duty." Another is his naiveté and conceit regarding his place within the structure of the law. The priest calls these motivations "[gaps] in the character of the doorkeeper." K. concludes that the doorkeeper should have been dismissed from his job for incompetence. The priest objects, revealing his dogmatic allegiance to institu-

---

[11]TR 216; P 185. Critics often use this dictum to show that the author himself accepted the nondecidability of textual meanings (see Theo Elm, *"Der Prozeß,"* *Kafka-Handbuch* 2: 429), but it merely characterizes this doorkeeper's judicial-hermeneutic ignorance. The priest does assume, however, that the doorkeeper holds other beliefs that exclude each other: the door to the law is always open, yet he thinks he will be able to close it after the man's death (P 182–83; TR 213, 215).

[12]TR 215; P 184. Similarly, Jacques Derrida claims that the man was not prohibited from entering, that "permission had never been denied him: it had merely been delayed, adjourned, deferred." "The discourse of the law does not say *no* but *not yet*, indefinitely" (J. Derrida, "Devant La Loi," *Kafka and the Contemporary Critical Performance*, ed. Udoff, 140–1). Both the parable's literal and legal meanings show that this is not so.

tional legal positivism. The fact that the doorkeeper initially goes beyond his specific instructions and is ill-informed about the law in general is offset by his being in the law's service and his otherwise stern regard for duty: "It is the Law that has placed him at his post; to doubt his dignity is to doubt the Law itself." K. answers that the doorkeeper's inconsistent statements and rulings are "impossible" to accept. The priest, however, who earlier admitted that interpretation of the law is mere opinion as compared to the unalterable text of the law itself, declares them to be "necessary," that is, binding.[13] He would agree with the positivists' demand that a judge's decision be unambiguous and conclusive regardless of its legal rationale: "[It is the reason for the] distinction between the juridical and philological interpretation that the legislator's intent (which the philological interpretation emphasizes) is possibly unclear and full of gaps and contradictions but that the juridical interpreter cannot be satisfied with such a result. As judge he cannot let the parties go home with a *non liquet*, he always must come up with a clear, complete and consistent decision."[14]

The man before the law does not overtly seek a verdict; instead of guilt he feels fear and increasing despair due to the delays in gaining admittance. Yet in other respects his wish to enter is analogous to K.'s wish to be acquitted. K.'s comment that the doorkeeper's belated announcement is "redeeming" — even if too late to benefit the man — presumes that admittance means some kind of deliverance through or from the law, one's acquittal. The statement "since this door was intended for you" — or, in the priest's words, that each individual before the law is provided with his or her own entrance and doorkeeper — expresses a basic truth about all laws. Law is universal, applies to everybody in a like manner. Yet each case is different, and the law is applied by an individual judge. Each application results in a specific verdict, an individualized "admittance." The court confirms *or* denies what the individual plaintiff claims as his or her right (in civil cases), what the defendant has

---

[13]TR 212; P 181. TR 216; P 185. TR 220; P 188. Not only the law but also its application (the verdict) is "beyond human judgment" (TR 220; P 188). The story "The Refusal" suggests that at the moment of pronouncing a verdict a judge is perceived as being above the human: "the colonel, who, as it were, had turned once more into a human being like the rest of us" (CS 267; E 313). *The Castle* suggests that any verdict is arbitrary: "When an affair has been weighed for a very long time ... the decision comes in some unforeseen place ... a decision that settles the matter, if in most cases justly, yet all the same arbitrarily" (C 88; S 68).

[14]The well-known legal theoretician Gustav Radbruch in his review of "Die leitenden Grundsätze der Gesetzesinterpretation," by Oskar Kraus (*Zeitschrift für die gesamte Staatsrechtswissenschaft* 26 [1906]: 259) [*non liquet* means *undecidable*]. By contrast, Derrida (note 12) does not acknowledge this difference between philological-metaphorical and jurisprudential signification — nor that between moral (universalist-Kantian) and positive-legal reasoning.

committed or omitted (in criminal cases). In short, admittance in the parable could be analogous to an acquittal in a trial, and denial of admittance analogous to a conviction. If so, the doorkeeper's prohibition could also mean that the man has been found guilty for now, and the seeming indication of possible future admittance would then mean that the man might yet be proven innocent. By being informed seconds before his death that he has been waiting in front of the right door, he also learns that he has not been so proven during his lifetime.

The law in the parable is less forbidding (everybody strives toward it) and less vindictive than the perverted criminal law that presumes Josef K.'s guilt, condemns him without charge or public trial, and kills him like a dog. In one of his last thoughts before his execution, K. asks himself whether at this stage the logic underlying these proceedings could be questioned: "Logic is doubtless unshakable, but it cannot withstand a man who wants to go on living." This statement expresses — more clearly than the priest's insistence that the doorkeeper's statements and decisions are "necessary" — the opposition between the verdict's rigid finality and an individual's desire to find mitigating circumstances in her or his favor. It recalls von Jhering's well-known polemic against the conceptualism of late-nineteenth-century civil law: "Life is not there for the concepts, the concepts are there for life. Not what logic but what life postulates must be done whether it be logically deducible or impossible." Oskar Kraus, quoting a comment about the role of logic in law ("Nowhere does logic become so practical, so sensitive as in law"), wrote: "The sharpness of reasoning must not lag behind the sharpness of the sword which the conclusion puts into motion."[15] Notwithstanding K.'s belated protest, his question upon meeting his executioners, "So you are meant for me?" — an allusion to the doorkeeper's "this door was meant for you" — had already signaled his resigned acceptance of his verdict as binding. Since the novel places a contradictory structural emphasis on both K.'s responsibility for a disastrously ineffective defense and his foregone, unappealable criminal conviction, it casts the conflict between individual conduct and institutionalized law as the existential paradox that K., and perhaps the man from the country too, somehow "chooses the self he is."[16] As the next section will show, *The Trial* as a whole has given Kafka insight into, and emotional dis-

---

[15]Von Jhering, *Der Geist des römischen Rechts* 3: 321; his critique prefigured, but stopped well short of, the Free Law theorem. Kraus, *Das Recht zu strafen* (Stuttgart: Enke, 1911) 54 [supplementary issue of *Der Gerichtssaal* 79 (1911)].

[16]Walter Sokel, "The Programme of K.'s Court," *On Kafka,* ed. Kuna, 9; K.'s existential guilt, however, does not necessarily entail Oedipal guilt. Brod reports that when Kafka read the first chapter to his friends, he laughed himself into a frenzy (*Über Franz Kafka* 156).

tance from, his self-inflicted and ethically questionable guilt in the act of fictionalizing it.

Self-condemning Guilt Defeated: "The Penal Colony"

Within a few days of Grete Bloch's October 1914 letter to him Kafka wrote "In the Penal Colony," which marks a shift away from how he had conceived guilt in his earlier work, including *The Trial*. Through the writing of this story he discovered the contradiction of deriving an entire penal system from self-condemnation. Acting as legislator, the penal colony's former commandant had decreed that someone who is accused of even a minor violation must be sentenced to sadistic torture and death and must be enlightened about his guilt by having the law he is alleged to have violated written on his body. The officer now running the penal system has embraced these legal maxims. In addition to being the colony's executioner, he serves as its judge. In the latter role his maxim is to convict the accused automatically, without giving him the right to defend himself, and to offer no reasons for this conviction to anybody: "My guiding principle is this: Guilt is never to be doubted." In other words, the officer is a fanatic who believes that every accused is guilty and that the guilty can achieve enlightened redemption through execution. He considers this procedure the "most humane and most in consonance with human dignity," designed to show justice "being done." If we can believe his account of past executions, there were many others in the colony who approved of this penal system.[17] The explorer's role, to observe rather than to reform foreign justice systems, could be a late echo of Lederer's report about his trip to study the U.S. criminal justice system.[18] Lederer was in agreement with Oskar Kraus that punishment should not be retributive but primarily utilitarian, to prevent crime through deterring and reforming the criminal: "The *probation* consists mainly in this that the court abandons the punishment of those convicted in cases where the carrying out of the punishment would be a greater evil than the state is permitted to inflict in the public interest .... We often experience how painful for judges and the public the rigidity of a law is which inexorably demands punishment as atonement for

[17]CS 145; E 104. The officer's maxim reflects Titorelli's assertion that "once [the Court] has brought a charge against someone, [it] is firmly convinced of the guilt of the accused and can ... never be dislodged from that conviction" (TR 149; P 128–9). CS 156; E 113. CS 154; E 111.

[18]See chapter 6, note 36. The story also reflects a German traveler's account of penal colonies. See Walter Müller-Seidel, *Die Deportation des Menschen: Kafka's Erzählung "In der Strafkolonie" im europäischen Kontext* (Stuttgart: Metzler, 1986).

every offense."[19] The explorer has initial doubts about whether he ought to intervene against this system of injustice and cruel capital punishment. The officer hopes that the explorer will not "challenge" his criminal procedure because, he claims, it is part of the national culture supporting the colony. The visitor has "seen and learned to appreciate the peculiarities of many peoples" and, thus, might accept this procedure as just. Kraus condemned ethical and legal relativism, which held, based on ethnographic research, that "there is not a single ethical prescription or a single legal maxim which would have to be considered valid for all places, times or peoples." The explorer has, however, already — perhaps right from the beginning — decided in his mind that this penal procedure is unjust and inhumane. He has done so not because of any emotive or empirical consideration such as a fellow-feeling for the prisoner but on universalist (post-Kantian) moral grounds.[20]

The fanatical (though sincere) officer believes that both his judicial maxim (never to doubt guilt) and his procedure are universally justifiable, are in accordance with human dignity. Yet he is able to understand that the explorer's opposition to the procedure amounts to a powerful twofold condemnation. First, the officer's legal maxim "Be just!" expresses a perverted notion of justness. Second, since the officer universally rules that guilt must never be doubted, any condemnation of his procedure automatically convicts him. To make good on both his maxims, to be just (as he understands it) and never to doubt guilt — in short, to refute the procedure's alleged injustice and to abide by it — the officer must convict himself and have the violated maxim ("Be just!") written on his body.[21] The twists and turns of the plot engender a poignant insight for Kafka. The officer's maxim never to doubt guilt requires that it be applied universally, regardless of someone's guilt. Logically the maxim is contradictory: convictions based on it never prove guilt, and, therefore, quite contrary to the maxim's meaning, guilt must always be doubted.

---

[19]Lederer, "Das *probation system*" 89. See also Kraus, *Das Recht zu strafen*, passim. In reference to Kraus, Utitz commented to Brentano (5 May 1906) about the utilitarian purpose of punishment (prevention, education), indicating that the club's nonlawyers were interested in this issue. Punishment as retribution was still widely accepted in 1914. The released prisoner considers the punishment retribution (E 119; CS 163). Cf. also "The ancient history of our people records terrible forms of punishment. This does not, however, imply anything in defense of the present penal code" (DF 291; H 235).

[20]CS 155; E 113. Kraus, "Rechtsphilosophie und Jurisprudenz" 764–65. E 116; CS 159. E 110; CS 152.

[21]The officer resembles Hare's "idealistically" racist Nazi, who, upon discovering he is a Jew, will have himself killed, "for he thinks that even if the other interests of people (including his own) are sacrificed, the ideal state of society ought to be pursued by producing ideal men and eliminating those that fall short of the ideal (R.M. Hare, *Freedom and Reason* [Oxford: Clarendon, 1963] 161).

The officer's self-conviction and self-execution contain another contradiction. He charges himself with no longer being able to administer justice under his system, but through his self-conviction he renders himself innocent of this charge. This double contradiction is Kafka's metaphorical expression of his discovery that undiscriminating (universal) self-condemnation levels the difference between guilt and innocence and, thus, produces an ethical paradox. Expressing this authorial insight, the killing apparatus rules against writing the maxim "Be just!" on the officer — as it must, if it is to appropriate the maxim as an unperverted moral imperative. Instead, it kills the officer quickly, without producing his enlightenment. This "smooth, [machine-like] refutation" of the officer's unjust notion of criminal guilt fictionalizes the author's self-acquittal from the oppressive guilt he felt toward his father and Felice.[22]

Ethical Individualism

The maxim "guilt is never to be doubted" metaphorically expressed the author's guilt regarding his fathers' perceived condemnation of him as well as his failed obligations toward Felice due to their breakup. The fear that he would never meet society's demand for marriage compounded this guilt. His gradual reconciliation with Felice in 1916 culminated in their summer vacation, which taught him to see his undiminished ambivalence and trauma concerning her not as "summoned up, but rather imposed." For the first time he experienced trust, closeness, and sexual intimacy with her.[23] His self-reproaches yielded to a feeling of blamelessness and existential resignation. A long diary-like entry from the same summer was a remarkable attempt to unmask the parents' and society's alleged universal authority and demands as unjust, opposed to each child's uniqueness and, thus, inevitably breeding resentment against them. In late 1917 and early 1918 in Zürau in northern Bohemia, after the discovery of his tuberculosis and during his final breakup with Felice, Kafka accepts both his failure in achieving a fulfilled social life and his increasing loneliness as a means of concentrating on and clearly recognizing what is essential for his survival as a writer: "As a result I would assume a coherence, not dissipate myself in meaninglessness, and keep a

---

[22]The alleged *enlightenment* could not have been about a violated law written on one's body because all those executed were believed to experience it, including the innocent ones. D 2: 180; T 328.

[23]L 117–18; B 139 (see TKA 1: 795 for the restored entry; cf. T 315; D 2: 159). They agreed to get married right after the war (B 140; L 118). For Kafka the trauma concerning this relationship (see the next chapter) continued to grow until after their second breakup at the end of 1917.

clear-eyed view." In the aphorisms and letters written during this period he becomes aware, in consultation with Søren Kierkegaard's writings, of the thoroughly individualistic, even subjectivist bent of his own ethical beliefs.[24] Through a series of sophisticated reflections he concludes that Christian and philosophical (Hegelian, Aristotelian-utilitarian) explanations of ethics are insufficient in this regard.

He contemplates the Hebrew myth of humanity's Fall and, with Kierkegaard's help, comes to embrace its existential-ethical meaning. The Fall (original sin or guilt) is both the evil itself and the condition of our knowledge of it. Consequently, and paradoxically, a good conscience is evil simply because knowing oneself to be good is based on knowing the difference between good and evil — and that knowledge springs from original guilt: "In Paradise, as always: that which causes the sin and that which recognizes it for what it is are one. The clear conscience is Evil." Therefore, knowledge, especially self-knowledge, cannot be but evil in this sense ("Knowledge of oneself is something only Evil has"). Original sin constitutes both ethical knowledge and mortality and is therefore independent of any secondary ethical or juridical guilt ("The state in which we are is sinful, irrespective of guilt"). The Fall was necessary to our individual development and being in the world. We were driven from paradise not because of guilt, but lest we eat from the tree of life.[25] Kafka's melancholy joke that Adam's first domestic animal after the expulsion was the snake grounds the etiological myth about man's Fall in the repetitiveness of daily life.[26] The ethical paradox that knowledge of one's guilt constitutes that very guilt — in other words, that only ignorance is innocent — is complemented by the apparent logical paradox "Truth is indivisible, hence it cannot recognize itself; anyone who wants to recognize it has to be a lie." One of this aphorism's many possible translations is that truth, as the value of true propositions or sentences, cannot be known but through propositions or sentences about them. Both paradoxes are echoed in the judicial aphorism "Only he who is a party can really judge, but as a party he cannot judge. Hence it follows that there is no possibility of judgment in

---

[24]H 165–69; DF 201–6. The insistence on the child's moral uniqueness can be seen as an educational analogy to the Free Law critique of positive law. L 166; B 196. B 234–40; L 199–203.

[25]BN 33; H 71. BN 24; H 62. BN 37; H 74. H 68; BN 29. H 73; BN 36. See also Sabina Kienlechner, *Negativität der Erkenntnis im Werk Franz Kafkas: Eine Untersuchung zu seinem Denken anhand einiger später Texte* (Tübingen: Niemeyer, 1981) 19–48.

[26]H 71; BN 33. Hans Helmut Hiebel suggests that Kafka views historical repetition as an "atemporal matrix" of culture (*Die Zeichen des Gesetzes: Recht und Macht bei Franz Kafka* [Munich: Fink, 1983] 101).

the world."[27] Only the accused and the accuser — in Kafka's own case conceivably the same person, but in either case the only parties sufficiently informed about the exact circumstances of the alleged violation — can render a truthful assessment. However, a party — someone knowing the specifics — cannot also be the judge, cannot impartially apply the law and thereby give a just judgment. Therefore, so the aphorism implies, all judgments, whether by an informed party or an impartial but uninformed judge, are by nature unjust, go against the accused. The aphorism's oppositional construction of individual and general truth, individual and general justice is more subversive of institutionalized law than the Free Law program.

Kafka felt that Kierkegaard's writings deepened his own understanding of ethical individualism, but only up to a point. *Fear and Trembling* is aimed against the Hegelian theory that the general will (the ethical, communal law) must annul and supersede the singular will (self-interest, conscience): by holding out in his or her subjectivity, the individual will violates the general will, becomes immoral, guilty. Thus, Agamemnon has the ethical (though tragic) duty to sacrifice his daughter; his love for her must yield to the interest of the state (the general will). Kierkegaard argues that Abraham's unquestioning obedience to God's absolute command suspends Hegel's all-encompassing (or any other social) ethics. In other words, the willingness to sacrifice Isaac expresses a "private" (Christian, though absurd) faith because the sacrifice is not demanded by the interest of a state; in fact, it would be murder under almost any law. Despite his toying with an "individualism of faith" — the "imitatio Christi" as a completely individualistic act — Kafka is suspicious of Kierkegaard's emphasis on conscience or faith as blind obedience. Ethics must prove itself in ordinary life; its real problem (even in Agamemnon's case) lies in its "equivocation." The ambiguity of ethical demands forces the individual constantly to "go back and forth between the singular and the general."[28] In his own case, reconciliation with his father and marriage are demands of the general will that he has tried to fulfill time and again ("back and forth") but that have clashed with the needs of his own existence.[29]

[27]BN 35; H 73. BN 25; H 64. The aphorism's first sentence sounds like a version of Jhering's "Partei sein und unparteisch sein, ist nicht miteinander zu vereinigen" ["to be a party and to be impartial cannot be brought together"] (*Der Zweck im Recht* 1: 308).

[28]B 235–39; L 199–203. Søren Kierkegaard, *Fear and Trembling. Repetition*, ed. and transl. Howard Hong and Edna Hong (Princeton UP, 1983) 54–67 ("Problema I"). BN 27; H 65–66. BN 54–55; H 91–92.

[29]T 333 ("Rückkehr zum Vater"); D 2: 187. H 87 (marriage as "Repräsentant des Lebens"); BN 50. See also Claude David, "Die Geschichte Abrahams: Zu Kafkas Auseinandersetzung mit Kierkegaard," *Bild und Gedanke. Festschrift für Gerhart Baumann*, ed. Günter Schnitzler et al. (Munich: Fink, 1980) 83.

Kafka both distinguishes himself from and identifies with Kierkegaard's Abraham; by criticizing his flight from ethical obligations he implies a self-criticism. Abraham has everything socially desirable (house, wife, son), even tries to take his belongings ("moving van") into the hereafter, and, therefore, could hardly be an example for Kafka. In other respects Kafka's situation resembles Abraham's. Through his obedience Abraham effectively negates the "diversity of the world" and its laws and concentrates on his special relationship with God. Because he cannot escape the world, get the moving van through the exit door, he should look for a "springboard into the world": "Abraham is laboring under the following delusion: he cannot endure the monotony of this world. Now the fact is that this world is notoriously and uncommonly manifold, which can be put to the test at any moment if one just takes up a handful of World and looks at it more closely." Kafka sees a narrowing and exclusion of the world happening in his own life and writing: "Stillness keeps impoverishing my world. I ... literally do not have the lung power to breathe into the world the richness and variety that it obviously has, as our eyes teach us."[30] Staying his individual course as a writer by ignoring the world and the people around him, Kafka admits, carries the risk of wrongdoing and delusion.

In response to Kafka's letters from Zürau, Brod claimed that Kierkegaard's playing off of faith against ethics and sexual desire results in self-torture. Opposing this alleged self-denial and devaluation of sexuality, Brod embraced the view (which he thought was based in Jewish mysticism) that God, even if not on the side of ethical duty, does stand on the side of sexuality and life. Kafka felt that he ought to defend Kierkegaard's view of faith against Brod's facile distinction: instead of being antiethical (and, thus, also against desire), faith is ethically inscrutable: "The relationship to the divine is primarily not subject to any outside judgment; perhaps this is so much so that Jesus himself would not be permitted to judge how far a follower of his has come." Kafka quotes to Brod a passage from Kierkegaard's diaries: "As soon as a man comes along ... who says: However the world is, I shall stay with my original nature which I am not about to change to suit what the world regards as good ... dark, uncanny demons, who have long sat idle, gnawing their fingers, leap up and stretch their limbs; for, so they say, here is something for us, for which we have long waited."[31] So Kierkegaard affirms that faith can express an individualistic ethics that disregards the way of the world ("however the world is") and all of society's ethical judgments ("what the world

[30]B 333; L 285. H 92; BN 55. BN 55; H 92. L 199; B 235.

[31]Brod's letter of 19 March 1918 (EF 2: 244–45). L 202–3; B 239. Kierkegaard had added here "denn die Exemplarmenschen geben ihnen nichts zu tun"; "because the exemplary people provide no work for them [the demons]" (Kierkegaard, *Buch des Richters* 160). Kafka first encountered this text in 1913 (T 199; D 1: 298).

regards as good"). Kafka understands that Kierkegaard's construction of the ethical is based on, and directed against, Hegel, yet his own qualifications of this construction effectively criticize Hegel as well. Kierkegaard wrote that Agamemnon, through his daughter's sacrifice, found "rest in the universal." Kafka's phrase "the general interpreted as being at rest" appears to be a reference to this quote; his question "rest in the general?" asks whether the individual's ethics can ever be reconciled to the general will. Two months earlier he had quoted Brod's use of the word *rest* back to him, disputing Brod's claim that a sexual relationship can result in a peaceful rest — a reconciliation with one's partner and (by extension) one's ethics: "The vision you have ... '[rest], complete peace in *eros*' — is something so tremendous that you can't really swallow it; which fact should prove how untenable it is."[32] In the same month he wrote with regard to the Fall that man wants to "reverse" the Fall, "falsify" his knowledge of good and evil, because he wants to return to paradise, experience rest even if only for a moment. Two other aphorisms also deal centrally with the term *rest*. In the first it stands for immortality both in paradise and in the hereafter, where, presumably, the back-and-forth between the singular and the general is not necessary or even possible: "For us there exist two kinds of truth, as they are represented by the Tree of Knowledge and the Tree of Life. The truth of the active [person] and the truth of the [person at rest]. In the first, Good separates itself off from Evil; the second is nothing but Good itself, knowing neither of Good nor of Evil." In the second aphorism *rest* refers to the denial of the world, to pretending that one's movement is really at rest: "In a certain sense you deny the existence of the world. You explain life as a state of rest, a state of rest in motion." In 1922 Kafka wrote that he wanted to "[destroy the 'rest'], to upset the balance." In other words, rest cannot be obtained in life, disturbance and constant movement are our lot. He admired the (Greek) concept of movement, which Kierkegaard explored in *Fear and Trembling* and *Repetition*. Movement — like the notions of transition and repetition — contains both the old and the new. All three concepts are superior to Hegel's dialectical mediation and sublation because they permit the survival of the individual. Kierkegaard's example of the individual's struggle to survive against the general (the dialectic) is the figure of Job: "Job is, so to speak, the whole weighty defense plea on man's behalf in the great case between God and man, the lengthy and appalling trial." Kafka uses similar words to describe his and his sister Ottla's struggle against their father: "We sit together ... [to discuss] this terrible trial that is pending between us and you ... a trial in which you keep on claiming to be the judge, whereas, at least in the main ... you are a party too, just as weak and deluded as we are." The father, and by analogy even God, is not the

---

[32]Kierkegaard, *Fear and Trembling* 79 ("Problema II"). BN 54; H 92. L 191; B 226. The internal quote is from Brod's letter of 16 Jan. 1918 (EF 2: 223).

representative of the general, is not the impartial judge he proclaims himself to be.[33]

Kafka's thoughts on ethics did not culminate in these post-Kierkegaardian reflections. His relentless ethical self-scrutiny was also directed against, among other things, Oskar Kraus's psychology and ethics: "Never again psychology! Two tasks at the beginning of your life: to narrow your orbit more and more, and ever and again to check whether you are not in hiding somewhere outside your orbit." The statement rejects the Aristotelian notion that other people's moral dispositions should have something to do with evaluating one's own conduct. A parable appearing among the aphorisms illustrates this point vividly:

There was once a community of scoundrels, that is to say, they were not scoundrels, but ordinary people. They always stood by each other. If, for instance, one of them had made a stranger, someone outside their community, unhappy in some rather scoundrelly way — that is to say, again, nothing scoundrelly, but just what is usual, just the normal sort of thing — and he confessed to the whole community, they investigated the case, judged it, imposed penances, pardoned, and the like. It was not badly meant, the interests of the individual members and of the community as a whole were strictly safeguarded, and he who confessed was supplied with the complementary color to the color he had shown: "What? You mean you are upset about *that*? But what you did was a matter of course, you acted as you were bound to. Anything else would be incomprehensible. You are in a nervous condition, that's all. Pull yourself together and be sensible." So they always stood by each other, and even after death they did not desert the community, but rose to heaven dancing in a ring. All in all it was a vision of the purest childlike innocence to see them fly. But since everything, when confronted with heaven, is broken up into its elements, they crashed, true slabs of rock.

Some people have banded together to put each other's moral dispositions and wrongdoing in a favorable light, to paint them as ordinary, unremarkable, and forgivable. After their deaths — constituting an inescapable moment of quasi-

[33]H 76; BN 38. BN 43; H 80. BN 47; H 84. D 2: 213; T 353. B 238; L 202. Kierkegaard, *Repetition (Fear and Trembling. Repetition,* ed. H. and E. Hong) 131–87, 210; "It can be very becoming and true ... if a person believes that misfortune has struck him because of his sins, but this belief may also be the case because he vaguely conceives of God as a tyrant" (207). Kafka remarks that the eternal repetition of our expulsion from Paradise means that, knowingly or not, we have remained in Paradise (H 69; BN 31). DF 167–68; H 141. This comment recalls the aphorism, quoted earlier, that a judge, any positive law, is either ignorant or partial.

religious, ethical-individualist truth — their self-serving community breaks apart, their attitudes and actions become incomparable, stand revealed as inexcusable and damnable. In his ethical treatise Brentano had argued against the relativism and positivism of contemporary moral and legal theory, which merely validated what society happened to find acceptable. He wanted to hold ethical, societal, and legal norms to a single intrinsic standard: the love, for its own sake, of the greatest amount of practical good. He agreed with Aristotle that the highest ethical good can only be achieved within society, and that duties and virtues (such as selflessness, charity, or self-sacrifice) can only be exercised by people living in society.[34] In a Kantian (or even Nietzschean) argument directed against the Aristotelian-utilitarian view, however, he discovered that apparent virtues are often not motivated by love for the highest practical good but are self-serving — for instance, that they derive from a prudential belief that to help others will ultimately serve one's own best interest. In other words, purely self-regarding motives at some point became divorced from their original intent and took on the guise of habitual virtues, due to the narrowness of consciousness: "This is caused above all by our narrow-mindedness, the so-called narrowness of consciousness, which prevents us ... from always keeping our eyes on the more distant and ultimate ends. In this way some people may be led by a blind, habitual impulse to love others with a certain unselfishness." In a late aphorism Kafka adopts Brentano's unmasking of virtues but goes him — and, implicitly, Kant's or Nietzsche's dissection of interested motives — one step better by arguing that true virtue can never be realized in society: "[The narrowness of consciousness] is a social imposition. All virtues are individual, all vices social. The things that pass as social virtues, love, for example, disinterestedness, justice, self-sacrifice, are only 'astonishingly' enfeebled social vices." All these virtues are social virtues and, thus, nothing but attenuated social vices. We do not act out the underlying undiminished vices due to the narrowness (the partial unconsciousness) of our consciousness — which thus becomes socially desirable in itself. The aphorism expresses Kafka's radical individualistic ethics: virtue does not really apply to our life among others, it expresses a thoroughly subjective value. This paradoxical stance was burned into him by the early experience that moral authority existed merely to convict him: "I lived under laws that had been invented only for me and which I could, I did not know why, never completely comply with." What is morally wrong is determined by thoroughly subjective reasoning: "When as a child I had done something very bad, although nothing bad or nothing all that bad in the public sense of

[34]BN 42; H 79. BN 21; H 59. Brentano, *Vom Ursprung sittlicher Erkenntnis* 30–34 ("So ist denn der Mensch ethisch bestimmt zum Leben in der Gesellschaft" - 31). The book (1889) provided the philosophical yardstick for most of Kraus's legal theorems.

the word, but something very bad in my private sense ... I was amazed that everything continued along its course unchanged." Knowledge of good and evil is a continuing, throrougly individualistic, self-critical project; it can be viewed "as a foretaste to that torment of hell which consists in having to review one's entire life with the knowledge that comes of hindsight, where the worst thing is not the confrontation with obvious misdeeds but with deeds one once considered worthy." In 1922 Kafka reiterates that any social virtue, even the most pronounced altruism such as "martyrdom, sacrifice of oneself for the sake of another" is outside the individual's truth.[35]

In a 1921 diary entry Kafka reflects on Franz Werfel's *Bocksgesang* which he read from October 30 into early November when it was serialized in the *Prager Presse*. In this play a feudal estate-owner hides his misshapen monster-like son in an outhouse and eventually decides to kill him. The creature escapes and triggers a peasant revolt that causes his (normal) brother's and his own deaths as well as his family's material ruin: "Free command of the world at the expense of its laws. Imposition of the law. The happiness in obeying the law. But the law cannot merely be imposed upon the world, and everything left to go on as before except that the new lawgiver be free to do as he pleases. Such would be not law, but arbitrariness, revolt against law, self-defeat."[36] The play illustrates that if someone violates his community's laws by trying to do away with an undesirable offspring, he will suffer the loss of all his progeny.[37] Kafka's reflection on this dramatized paradox runs as follows: someone powerful enough to be above the law creates a law for his own purpose, or imposes some such law. He experiences happiness but is then bound to obey this law. If he fails in this obedience, he must convict himself for his moral and legal transgression. Kafka applies the paradox to himself: he may seek to modify his self-assigned guilt, and his resulting conviction at the hands of others, through adopting a subjective ethics based on his particular needs. Even an existentially driven, thoroughly individualistic value system, however, generates binding laws of its own.

[35]Brentano, *Vom Ursprung sittlicher Erkenntnis* 39. Kraus calls this virtuous guise mimicry *(Das Recht zu strafen* 153). GW 273; BK 220. DF 148; H 127. MI 202; M 273. MI 12; M 15. D 2: 217; T 355.

[36]D 2: 199; T 342. The restored entry (TKA 1: 873) relates his remarks to Werfel's *Bocksgesang* (Munich: Wolff, 1921). Cf. B 363; L 311.

[37]Producing an offspring for Kafka is closely linked to producing a definitive literary work (T 348; D 2: 206. B 431; L 232). He sees Werfel increasingly bogged down by artistic contradictions, relates Werfel's "Magische Trilogie" *Spiegelmensch* (cf. M 283; MI 209) to his own playful conjecture of a seemingly obedient but prevaricating Abraham who does not even have a son to sacrifice (B 333; L 285). The central metaphor of *Bocksgesang*, the breaking of a self-imposed law, applies to artistic integrity as well.

8: Temporal Experience, Metaphor, Sexuality

KAFKA'S STYLE FROM 1917 on has been described as abstract or parabolic, privileging a distanced, objective narratorial stance. These descriptions ignore the distribution of structural features, such as abstractness or distance, over the earlier and later works and the changes that these features undergo. An objective narrator at a well-calibrated distance to his tale can indeed be found in some of the parables, yet the majority of the later stories as well as *The Castle* still provide the familiar self-narrating, subjective perspective. Furthermore, if any of the works were to be called abstract, it might as well be "The Metamorphosis" and *The Trial*, which blend autobiographical allusion and a generalized sense of guilt with dogged observation *cum* description and conceptually grounded plotting and causalities.[1] Works such as these pay modernism's debt to realism and naturalism by taking representational mimesis to near-parodic heights.[2] By contrast, the fiction from 1917 on blends autobiography, description, and metaphorical structuring into ever more open-ended symbolic meanings.[3] It addresses issues such as temporal existence, historical

---

[1]For descriptions of the late style see Ingeborg Henel, "Periodisierung und Entwicklung," *Kafka-Handbuch* 2: 234. Orson Welles's film *The Trial* conveys the idea of abstractness well: "Mrs. Grubach: ... with your arrest, I get the feeling of something abstract, if you know what I mean. K *looking up at* Mrs. Grubach: I'd say it's so abstract I can't even consider that it applies to me" (*The Trial: A Film by Orson Welles*, ed. Nicholas Fry [London: Lorrimer, 1970] 27). The author alludes to his personal life throughout his work (Malcolm Pasley, "Semi-Private Games," *The Kafka Debate*, ed. Flores, 188–205).

[2]Stephen Dowden argues such a point (*Sympathy for the Abyss* 103). It is not clear, however, whether the truthful depiction of one's inner experience should also fall under realist mimesis, be seen as an "isomorphic doubling of the world into words."

[3]Stanley Corngold argues that Kafka's writerly stance turns away from sensory observation and description to rhetorical, allegorical, semantically undecidable metaphoricity (*Franz Kafka: The Necessity of Form* [Ithaca: Cornell UP, 1988] 105, 149). He overlooks that Kafka's metaphorical and symbolic force always relies on linguistic expressions of perception, cognition, reference, belief, and valuation.

transience, confounding sexual experience, obsessional desire, the seeming explanatory force of myths, and the hope for release through writing.

After his 1916 vacation with Felice in Marienbad, Kafka stayed on alone for ten more days and accompanied the visiting Rabbi of Belz on several sightseeing excursions through this spa. A remark introducing the epistolary report of these events to Brod encapsulates an emphasis on precise description so characteristic of the early mature stories: "I shall only describe [the whole thing], since I cannot speak of more than I [can] see. But all one actually sees is the most minute details." The rabbi shows a voracious attention to even "quite forlorn details" during his daily outings. Yet his relationship to those around him does not bespeak the same perceptual curiosity. No one in his entourage is allowed to stand in front of him, and since he often turns sideways, everyone must move quickly out of his way. Three months later Kafka twists this description around to express his need for self-centeredness in living and writing: "I have an infinite yearning for independence and freedom in all things. Rather put on blinkers and go my way to the limit than have the pack [of my family revolve] around me and distract my gaze." If a family (and, implicitly, a wife) followed his every turn, they would scatter his creative focus. He, therefore, must stick to his own path even if it means disregarding all others, wearing blinders. Right after the vacation with Felice he gives a final summation of all the accumulated reasons why the proposed marriage upon which they had again agreed would have a distracting and destructive effect on his writing. Marriage will scatter his mind ("[you] fly to all quarters of the sky"); only bachelorhood will ensure his physical and mental concentration. This self-acceptance spawns his increasing concern with temporal experience and his growing reservations about theories: "From outside one will always triumphantly impress theories upon the world and then fall straight into the ditch one has dug, but only from inside will one keep oneself and the world quiet and still."[4]

Recent philosophical attempts to clarify the conceptual and linguistic nature of metaphor are helpful in exploring this aspect of Kafka's style. Metaphors can be general propositions, applying a sortally inappropriate predicate to a class of objects: for instance, "Man is a wolf." The predicate *being a wolf* is literally false of all the objects in question (men) but, in spite of this falsity, suggests other predicates (*fierce*) that are true of them. Metaphors can also be singular propositions, applying a sortally incorrect concept to a specific person ("Jim is a wolf") or thing ("The church is a wolf"). As Donald Davidson observes, metaphor is one of the "devices that serve to alert us to aspects of the world by inviting us to make comparisons." Like compari-

---

[4]L 119; B 141. B 145 ("ganz verlorene Kleinigkeiten"); L 122. D 2: 167; T 320 (also F 729; FE 524–5). DF 211; H 173. BN 16; H 55 (the statement, written in late 1917 just before the aphorisms, implies an earlier fascination with theories).

sons and similes, metaphorical statements are open-ended in that they do not specify which of the properties expressed by the concept can be attributed to the object in question. As Davidson further states, "There is no limit to what a metaphor calls to our attention ... we can't provide an exhaustive catalogue of what has been attended to." Metaphorical statements can direct our attention to quite divergent concepts or properties.[5] To narrow down the list of properties that the author (the metaphor's creator) may have meant to attribute, however, "it is necessary to search the text and context for the author's grounds ... that will constrain the basis of the comparison to a plausible set of alternatives."[6] Kafka's semantically deliberative style is better captured by a conceptual construction that situates metaphorical meanings within a logical space than by the post-Nietzschean notion of metaphor's infinitely deferable, undecidable meaning.

In "A Country Doctor" the doctor discovers on a boy a mysterious, metaphorically potent wound, which, it turns out, alludes to several of the author's obsessions. For instance, when, half a year after writing this story, Kafka discovered his tuberculosis, he used the fictional boy's "blood wound" to refer to his own "wound of the lungs." The author then makes his illness a metaphor or symbolic expression of his past trauma regarding Felice, which he describes as a tangle of guilt, insatiable need for justification, sexual desire, misery, abstemiousness, and wretchedness. His semiprivate metaphor conceptually yokes together the fictional wound with both his own physical illness and his emotional trauma. Then, in a further move, he molds this metaphorical relation into a psychophysical one: he sees his tuberculosis as caused by the mental trauma. The gigantic traumatic "mass" never ceases to grow; it can no longer be contained by his "head" or mind and thus creates the physical wound. The trauma is an "overflowing of its banks" into his body. Seeing his tuberculosis as a psychosomatic outgrowth of his emotional wound perhaps derives from first experiencing the physical illness as a "bubbling-up in the throat" of blood, a flowing out of his inner being: "How was I going to plug

[5]Donald Davidson, "What Metaphors Mean," *On Metaphor*, ed. Sheldon Sacks (U of Chicago P, 1978) 38, 44–45; also in: *Philosophical Perspectives on Metaphor*, ed. Mark Johnson (Minneapolis: U of Minnesota P, 1981) 211, 218. This well-argued theory of metaphor has generated a broad array of commentary and debate. See, e.g., David Cooper, *Metaphor* (Oxford: Blackwell, 1986); Eva F. Kittay, *Metaphor* (Oxford: Clarendon, 1987).

[6]George A. Miller, "Images and Models, Similes and Metaphors," *Metaphor and Thought*, ed. Andrew Ortony (Cambridge UP, 1979) 241. For an earlier statement about metaphor's role of making us notice conceptual aspects see Martin Warner, "Black's Metaphors," *British Journal of Aesthetics* 13 (1973): 367–72.

it since I had not opened it?"[7] The image of being wounded, mentally and physically opened up, is connected not only to trauma and illness but also to the experience of literary creation and overwhelming intimacy. After finishing "The Judgment," he called the writing of it a "complete opening out of the body and the soul." From then on writing became for him a pouring of himself out into, an opening up of himself to the work. During his vacation with Felice he experienced emotional closeness as an opening up of himself to her but also as being wounded, torn open, gaping, disgorging something he wants to protect forever. Fifteen months before his death he sees the pouring-himself-out as a metaphor for his life yet also fears that he would "[close off] the opening through which one flows forth into the world. I am not far from it at times. A river flowing upstream."[8]

The central metaphorical proposition of "A Country Doctor" relates directly to Kafka's wounds. The story is written from the first-person perspective; it consists of short paratactic sentences, often divided by semicolons. It opens a vast physical and psychological space, sending a country doctor through a blizzard to a patient and on beyond, without the possibility of return. At the outset he has no horse and, almost unable to move in the snow, stands waiting for something to take him across the vast space. He strides through the courtyard and kicks open the door to the abandoned pigsty. An unknown man (a groom) crawls out on all fours; two horses emerge from the pigsty as if being born or egested: "Two horses, enormous creatures with powerful flanks, one after the other, their legs tucked close to their bodies, each well-shaped head lowered like a camel's, by sheer strength of buttocking squeezed out through the door hole which they filled entirely."[9] The groom,

---

[7]T 329; D 2: 182. B 160–1; L 137–38. B 242; L 239. Kafka, *Briefe an Ottla und die Familie*, ed. Hartmut Binder and Klaus Wagenbach (Frankfurt: Fischer, 1981) 39 (cf. the "Quellen in der Kehle" of this letter with "Quellen aus der Kehle" - F 753; FE 543). Years later he recalls that when he was writing "The Judgment" — he had just met Felice — his emotional wound burst open for the first time (M 235; MI 173–74).

[8]D 2: 276; T 184. Cf. FE 49 (my desire to "pour myself into" my story); F 105. Also: FE 137 (my head "was completely closed" to my novel); F 224 (opening up a mental space occurs within the fiction as well: Bendemann's and Samsa's, Roßmann's and Josef K.'s self-enclosed minds expand). T 315 (the restored passage reads "Also öffne Dich Thor Mensch komme hervor" - TKA 1: 795); D 2: 159. B 139; L 117–18. D 2: 223; T 359.

[9]CS 220; E 124 (*ausmessen* [to measure out] for *striding through* suggests confinement). *Sty* and *man* are potent metaphors of "repressed sexual energies" (Edward Timms, "Kafka's Expanded Metaphors: A Freudian Approach to *Ein Landarzt*," *Paths and Labyrinths*, ed. J. P. Stern and J. J. White [London: U of London, 1985] 72).

about to yoke the horses to the gig, catches hold[10] of the doctor's maid Rosa
and leaves red marks on her cheek with his teeth. Rosa makes frenzied attempts to hide from the man in the depth of the house, but he sends the gig
with the doctor on its way, "whirled off like a [twig] in the freshet," pursues
her, and apparently rapes her. Blinded and deafened for an instant, the doctor
arrives at the patient's farmyard momentarily, as if it opened out just outside
his own gate. The doctor blames the patient's family for instigating his excru-
ciating, seemingly useless summons in the middle of the night.[11] After repeated examinations, however, he discovers the boy's mortal wound. The
attention paid him by his two whinnying horses suggests to him that his examination is "ordained" by some higher authority, though not the Christian one;
the villagers, having lost faith in the parson, expect everything from the doctor
instead.

The story is justly famous for its compact symbolism. The central metaphorical proposition is created not at one stroke but gradually through narrative progression. The word *Rose* occurs in the story's two major segments,
first naming the doctor's maid, who is victimized by the groom, and later the
pink color of his patient's wound. Its singular reference (the maid) and its
conceptual meaning (pinkness) together establish the metaphorical proposition
"The maid is pink" (has a wound's pink color), which translates metonymically into "The maid is the wound." The maid's function in the doctor's
environment is analogous to aspects of Felice's role in Kafka's life, both
women wounding but also being wounded by a male. While Kafka models the
figure of the country doctor largely on himself, he also sees himself as similar
to the boy, possessing the wound of tuberculosis.[12] During his Marienbad
vacation with Felice, he fictionalized the doctor-patient relationship as a form
of self-observation ("the doctor ... observed the sick man who looked at him
in return"). In other words, the doctor discovers his own mortality in the

---

[10]The narrative here switches from past to present tense, emphasizing the narrator's
emotional involvement (Gerhard Kurz, *Traum-Schrecken: Kafkas literarische Existenzanalyse* [Stuttgart: Metzler, 1980] 122). The intermingling of past- and present-
tense passages shows that "all events are translated into the interior language of a
perceiving consciousness" (Cohn, *Transparent Minds* 203), that is, into self-narration.

[11]The tiny house in which Kafka wrote this story thrilled him because he stepped
from the living room directly into the snow-covered alley (F 751; FE 542). In the
story, however, some real time must have elapsed, since the snowing has stopped.
The doctor's being sickened by the father's intellectual narrowness (E 126; CS 222)
echoes Kafka's feelings about his own father (cf. T 331–32; D 2: 185–86).

[12]B 160; L 137. The country doctor also echoes the scientific observer-role of the
ubiquitous doctor in Zola, Fontane, Ibsen, Hauptmann and Chekhov. See Maurice
Larkin, *Man and Society in Nineteenth-Century Realism: Determinism and Literature*
(Totowa, N. J., Rowman & Littlefield, 1977) 134–38.

boy's illness and death wish. His diagnostic experience tells him that the unusual-looking wound is not a natural "endowment" but violently inflicted, resembling a castration injury. The village people undress the doctor and lie him down next to the wound and threaten to kill him if he does not cure the boy ("If he doesn't, kill him dead!"). This scene fictionalizes shamanic practices about which Kafka apparently had read. The doctor's flight from the dying patient's bedside ("But now it was time for me to think of escaping") appears to echo yet another custom among primitive practitioners, but also to refer to a well-known satirical depiction of the allegedly impotent academic medicine that Kafka scorned.[13] Reflecting the author's renewed ambivalence toward Felice, the doctor wants to provide for — that is, sexually renounce — the "beautiful" maid Rosa. He now is ready to attend to and accept his irrevocable old age, incurable wound, and approaching death. Finally forlorn, wandering through the frigid emptiness of this "unhappy age," he laments that he was duped by a "false ring" on his night bell. There is an indication that this lament should not be taken quite as seriously as it sounds. In a diary entry of 1922 Kafka does not see the doctor's nightly summons as a mishap but instead equates it (in view of the miraculously emerged horses) with a disconsolate person's acquiring unexpected "new strength." "A Country Doctor" structurally ties together thematic and narrative modes of attentiveness:[14] the doctor's scientifically informed habits of observation, his gradual insight into the existential significance of the surreal events and the wound, and his unblinking, unflinching, even ironic self-narration.

The doctor's lament is linked to Kafka's obsessively restated belief that his life once took a wrong turn, and subsequently many other wrong turns, and that he, Kafka, was doomed "by the skin of his teeth." This both minuscule and decisive misfortune makes its appearance in many guises — as a fatal distraction, a clumsiness that lets everything in his life fail, the wrong turn of the rudder that spoiled his relation to his father, a seemingly insignificant sexual irritation: "What have you done with your gift of sex? It was a failure, in the end that is all that they will say. But it might easily have succeeded. A mere trifle, indeed so small as not to be perceived, decided between its failure and

---

[13]D 2: 158; T 314. CS 225; E 128. The wound is a symbolic castration, connected to both the doctor's and Kafka's emotional trauma (Hans Helmut Hiebel, *Franz Kafka: "Ein Landarzt"* [Munich: Fink, 1984] 83–93). On Kafka's knowledge of shamanism, the doctor's flight before the patient dies, and other elements of the story's primitive and modern medical background see Paul Heller, *Franz Kafka: Wissenschaft und Wissenschaftskritik* (Tübingen: Stauffenburg, 1989) 86–102.

[14]T 351–52; D 2: 212. In any case, the doctor's emotional self-discovery and resignation due to horses appearing "out of nothing" (T 352) is uplifting compared to the vermin's "birth out of nothing" (H 89; BN 51). Numerous conceptual and structural analogies connect the story's first and second halves (Lawrence O. Frye, "Reconstructions: Kafka's *Ein Landarzt*," *Colloquia Germanica* 16 (1983): 321–36).

success."[15] This sexual failure, somewhat misrepresented here as incidental, really amounts to a deep-seated frustration in Kafka's life, which will be explored below. The experience of one single deciding misfortune is fictionalized hauntingly in the story about the dead hunter Gracchus, written around the same time as "A Country Doctor." The fact that the hunter's life is sealed by bad luck — he dies from a misstep he takes in pursuing a chamois — extends to his afterlife.[16] He willingly slips into his winding sheet like a girl into her wedding dress, but his death ship suffers an irreparable misdirection. The wish to help him is, therefore, futile: "The thought of helping me is an illness that has to be cured by taking to one's bed." The hunter feels that he will never come to his final rest because of this "fundamental error of [his] onetime death": "My death ship lost its way; a wrong turn of the wheel, a moment's absence of mind on the pilot's part, [a] distraction." Making a fatal mistake, navigating the wrong way is linked here to a cognitive mistake, the diversion of one's attention: "Life is a constant distraction that does not even allow for reflection as to what it distracts from."[17]

Another story written that spring, "The Great Wall of China," makes historical inquiry dependent on two more basic requirements, perceptual acquaintance and referential grasp. The narrator questions whether the immense Great Wall has been completed as alleged, since tales persist of remaining gaps. No one can answer this question conclusively since, due to the wall's immeasurable expanse, no one can see the whole of it with his or her own eyes. The wall was built in discontinuous small segments lest the workers, facing a seemingly endless task, be discouraged from the start. Even so, many people became confused during the period of construction (for instance, by the speculative project of a new Tower of Babel) exactly because they sought to concentrate exclusively on one task. In retrospect the narrator seeks explanations for the system of piecemeal construction beyond the reasons initially provided by the government. Yet he admits that, due to his limited mental capacity and the vastness of the questions to be studied, he will never

---

[15]T 17; D 1: 27. H 89; BN 51–52. H 120 ("als hätte ich etwa mit einer Steuerdrehung das Ganze anders einrichten können"); DF 139. D 2: 203; T 346.

[16]E 287; BK 251. *Gemse* (chamois) was a common name for prostitutes in Vienna and Prague; the hunter is modeled on Theodoric of Ravenna, whose sexual lust (attributed by legend) can be associated with the Fall (Frank Möbus, "Theoderich, Julia und die Jakobsleiter: Franz Kafkas Erzählfragment zum *Jäger Gracchus*," *Zeitschrift für deutsche Philologie* 109 [1990]: 259–62). The story, thus, also expresses Kafka's discomfort over his brothel visits (see next section). *Gracchus* is authorial self-reference, since both *kavka* and *gracchio* mean *jackdaw* (Binder, *Schaffensprozeß* 232).

[17]CS 230; E 288. CS 228; E 287; navigating (*lenken*) is linked etymologically to diversion or distraction (*ablenken*). DF 299; H 242.

find the true answer: "The limits that my capacity for thought imposes upon me are narrow enough, but the [field] to be traversed here is infinite." The capacity for knowledge is conceived again in spatial terms (narrowness), the object of knowledge, curiously, through a temporal concept. In a wider sense the known object is China itself. The country is so vast, however, that the heavens can scarcely span it; the narrator's home is so far from Peking that when the news from there reaches his remote region it is necessarily always outdated, to the point of bearing no connection to the current moment. For instance, the news of the wall's construction arrives thirty years after it was first announced. A legend dealing with this space-time lapse has it that the dying emperor sends a message to someone in a remote corner of the empire, but it can never reach its addressee. First, the ring of palaces and courtyards, as well as the capital itself, are so vast (though also called a mere *dot*) that no messenger could ever get through, even if he tried for thousands of years. The narrator surmises that if the messenger could reach the open fields, he would fly and "soon" deliver his message, but even the possibility of the message's arriving soon is merely a seeming one. The country as a whole is so large that any arriving news always has to be out of date. The knowing subject is always dwarfed by the vastness of what can be known.[18]

"A Report to an Academy," written a few weeks later, likewise dwells on the individual's capacity for knowledge. This story is a first-person account by an ape of his five-year-long transformation into a reasoning and narrating human. In line with Kafka's earlier theoretical interests, the expansion of the ape's mind turns the Darwinian concept of gradual, temporal evolution into a spatially conceived series of cognitive events.[19] The story was written half a year before those aphorisms that see humanity's expulsion from paradise as a reiterative, continuing event. The story's printed version removes from the following text the second sentence — an allusion to the gate of paradise, the biblical rationale for ethical knowledge: "It is intended to show the direction by which a former ape has infiltrated the human world and gained a footing in it. The result is that all have taken the same route from the gate of Paradise on, one sooner, another later, all the better, all the worse, and we all lie in

---

[18]The narrator, elusive and ironic, vacillates between factual description and myth-making rhetoric (J. M. Rignall, "History and Consciousness in *Beim Bau der chinesischen Mauer*," *Paths and Labyrinths*, ed. Stern and White, 111–26). What is central, however, is not the elusiveness of history but that of reference. E 289; CS 235. E 292; CS 239. CS 241; E 293. E 295; CS 243. BK 243; CS 248. E 295; CS 243. E 296; CS 244.

[19]By contrast, Clayton Koelb emphasizes the story's temporal aspects, its metaphor-generating uses of Darwinian evolutionary theory (*Kafka's Rhetoric: The Passion of Reading* [Ithaca: Cornell University Press, 1989] 153–59).

each other's arms."[20] The ape's accelerating cognitive acculturation and emerging consciousness are described primarily in terms of spatial (the brain's) dimensions. He "gallops through" the five years that separate him from his life as an ape; he enters the enclosed human world through a gate. This gate alludes to the expulsion from paradise but more plainly conceptualizes the distance the ape has covered: when he looks back at it, the gate appears smaller and smaller. It will ultimately be as minute as the chink at the heel of Achilles' otherwise invulnerable armor.[21] Put differently, the most important requirement for the ape now is to stop clinging to the memories of his origin, to allow his past to "close up against him" more and more. Because of the narrowness of consciousness his new knowledge must drive out his previous apelike thoughts. In effect, his earliest memories now reach back only to the time after his capture, when he woke up in a cage.

The expedition team's report that he was the only one captured from a pack of apes recalls Kafka's disparaging remark about the people around him as the family pack. It suggests that the ape and Kafka have something in common, that they both work hard at finding a way out from a crisis. The recurring term *way out* helps to explain the ape's thought processes, which result in his decision to become human. Because even many of the memories he retained until after his capture have been replaced, the reconstruction of his old thinking process — spatially conceived as a "fine clear train of thought ... constructed somehow with my belly" — can only be an approximation. When he found himself confined in that narrow cage, with a tiny gap that hardly let him perceive the outside world, it dawned on him that for the first time in his life he was "stuck" and that to become unstuck he had to cease being an ape. His cumulative observations of the crew on the freighter taking the expedition team home to Hamburg impel him in the direction of this decision. One of the sailors makes special efforts to teach him human habits such as pipe smoking and drinking alcohol from a bottle. The ape's most eager attention is seen in spatial terms; his eyes follow the drinking lesson right into the man's throat, and he is overjoyed with his gradual understanding of the matter. When for the first time he uncorks and empties a bottle on his own, the sailors follow him with increasing attentiveness and reward his first human sound with speech he can understand ("Listen, he's talking"). The ape soon takes in so much learning that his old nature "speeds away" from him and the rays of knowledge break into his "awakening brain" from all directions. He pursues this development until he is able to ascribe to himself the "average education

---

[20]Wolf Kittler and Gerhard Neumann, "Kafkas *Drucke zu Lebzeiten*: Editorische Technik und hermeneutische Entscheidung," *Franz Kafka: Schriftverkehr*, ed. W. Kittler and G. Neumann (Freiburg: Rombach, 1990) 43–44.

[21]E 147; CS 250. Of course, the heel is also a spot of vulnerability in the biblical account of the Fall, God's curse of enmity between man and snake (Gen. 3:15).

of a European."[22] At the end he wants to spread abroad his exemplary insights into how one acquires knowledge. The network of allusions to man's Fall and the ape's increasing distance from it also suggest that Kafka fictionalizes here his own turning away from the guilt that upbringing and interpersonal experience had imposed upon him.

Gender Relations and Sexuality in The Trial and The Castle

For Kafka the terms *cleanliness* and *dirtiness* (or *purity* and *impurity*) represent ethical values such as sincerity (honesty) and insincerity (lying). For instance, to make literature serve a political aim is untruthful and unclean. Because love relationships are fraught with deception, they also can be impure: "In me, by myself, without human relationship, there are no visible lies. The limited circle is pure." As he later puts it, relationships create unclean misunderstandings and never-ending guilt. One of the most painful divisions in his life is that between unobtainable marriage as the highest moral value[23] and his confounding, somewhat contemptible experience of sexuality. He is aroused by the lure of, and occasionally obtains, casual sexual intercourse but associates it with dirt and uncleanliness.[24] He experiences either nonsexual reciprocal love or, on rare occasions and with reluctance, sexually intimate love. He acknowledges that he did not receive the gift of sexuality as an intimate part of a love relationship and even sometimes qualifies sex as

[22]T 320; D 2: 167. B 195; L 166. CS 253; E 150 (the ape's belly is an allusion to the Fall, the snake being condemned to "measure out the length of the road on his belly" - BN 38; H 75). E 153–54; CS 257–58.

[23]B 210–11; L 179 (cf. B 197; L 168). D 1: 300; T 201. M 136, M 243–44; MI 102, 180. In a letter to Käthe Wohryzek Kafka calls marriage "das höchste Erstrebenswerte auf Erden" (Klaus Wagenbach, "Julie Wohryzek, die zweite Verlobte Kafkas," *Kafka-Symposium*, ed. Jürgen Born, Ludwig Dietz, Malcolm Pasley, Paul Raabe, and Klaus Wagenbach [Berlin: Wagenbach, 1965] 46). An even higher value is marriage with children (52; H 153; DF 183). For the entire traumatic context *marriage* see H 152–58; DF 183–90.

[24]Sex with a prostitute (H 154–55; DF 185–86) or casual sex without love (M 197–99; MI 147–48) are unclean, yet they are also innocent (T 206; D 1: 309), "nothing evil," a "different world" (T 347; D 2: 205). Cf. also Kafka's accounts of sought-after sexual arousal (B 33; L 21. TKA 1: 13. T 202; D 1: 303. T 206; D 1: 309. B 317; L 273. TKA 1: 908) and encounters with prostitutes (B 59; L 45. T 385; D 2: 258–59. T 400–401; D 2: 278–79. TKA 3: 208).

punishment, evil, or shameless.[25] He ponders the paradox that he can love only women who are morally and intellectually superior to him and who, therefore, could arouse no sexual interest in him. Love relationships are impossible due to the seriousness they require, his striving for perfection, his physical and intellectual weakness, and his growing isolation. Yet despite the increasing renunciation of marriage and sexual intimacy in love, up to his last years he is tortured by sex as an inescapable physiological need.[26]

Kafka's relationship with Felice bears directly on understanding one of the women characters in *The Trial*. Fräulein Bürstner, K.'s fellow lodger, not only shares the initials with Felice Bauer but various personal characteristics as well. K.'s warning, subsequently disavowed, to his landlady that Fräulein Bürstner often comes home late,[27] as well as Mrs. Grubach's witnessing the Fräulein's dating of different gentlemen make it plausible that Kafka is here using motifs from an essay by Karl Kraus.[28] In his journalistic forays Kraus made it his chief aim to expose satirically the contradictions between people's diverse sexual conduct, on the one hand, and the hypocrisy of the Viennese public and the Austrian criminal law regarding prostitution and so-called sexual deviancy, on the other. Decriminalizing prostitution became a major focus of his polemics.[29] The essay referred to deals with a trial of a young

[25]T 201–4; D 1: 301–5. T 286; D 2: 111–12. T 315 [TKA 1: 795]; D 2: 159 (his 1916 vacation with Felice). T 346; D 2: 203 ("What have you done with your gift of sex?"). T 198; D 1: 296 ("Coitus as punishment for the happiness of being together"). H 87; BN 50 (sex as evil). According to Milena, Kafka experienced shame in all sexuality (M 370; MI 248).

[26]B 317; L 273. B 289; L 250. B 295; L 254. B 297; L 256. T 353; D 2: 215. See Brod's remark about Kafka's brothel visit in 1922 (TKA 3: 208). Two 1922 diary entries, among many others, address the physiological need for sexual intercourse: T 346; D 2: 203–4. T 361 ("Notdurft"); D 2: 227 ("needs"). TKA 1: 916. Sexual abstinence by the adult male was thought to cause headaches and nervousness (Christian von Ehrenfels, *Sozialethik* [Wiesbaden: Bergmann, 1907] 2). This book was known to the members of the club (Bergmann referred to it forty years later ["Briefe Franz Brentanos an Hugo Bergmann" 107]).

[27]See Binder, *Kafka Kommentar zu den Romanen* 205–8. Kafka learned from Felice that she sometimes returned home late (F 53; FE 12).

[28]P 24, 69; TR 21, 76. For Kafka's interest in the writings of Kraus see Kurt Krolop, "Prager Autoren im Lichte der *Fackel*," *Schriftenreihe der Franz-Kafka-Gesellschaft* 3 (1989): 92–117.

[29]He saw his articles against the criminalization of *Gelegenheitsmacherei* or pandering (collected in his *Sittlichkeit und Kriminalität* [1908]) as contributions to the debate on penal reform (*Die Fackel* 290 [1909]: 13). Kraus showed hypocrisy at work in all areas of public life. See e.g. his publishing of a letter by Ernst Lohsing, author on criminal procedure, about plagiarism in the establishment press (*Die Fackel* 186 [1905]: 23).

woman who was wrongfully charged with prostitution because, among other things, she often came home late. It also berates the courts for expecting landlords and caretakers to give testimony about their tenants' private conduct and denounces the criminal justice system's immorality, its hypocritical condemnation and prosecution of prostitutes:

> There is not a week that passes without judicial infamy. Blinded by political megalomania and moralistic persecution mania the judicial system measures out to men and women the same amount of torture and injustice .... God created the caretaker so that he could evict Adam and Eve from Paradise .... In its zeal to discover the most secret things justice tears off her blindfold so that she can cover her private parts.[30]

His seeing parallels between the judiciary and prostitution — "The justice system is a whore who will not let herself be snubbed, who collects her shameful fee even from the poor"[31] — probably helps to account for one of the most enigmatic features of Kafka's novel. Lewd, promiscuous women are connected with and seem to exert an influence on the court system. Kafka (like Karl Kraus himself) felt a strong affinity to, and thus appears to have based many of his female characters on, Otto Weininger's influential, outrageously antifeminist 1903 treatise on gender differences. For Weininger the basic male characteristics are memory, attentiveness, apperception, logic, knowledge of law, ethical will, and individuality. Women show, in varying degrees, only traces of these qualities; they cannot overcome their basic narrowness of consciousness and are, therefore, amoral and completely sex-driven.[32] The court usher's wife is sexually drawn to the officials as well as to Josef K., and he fleetingly senses that she is trying to "entrap" him on the court's behalf. Leni, the defense attorney's helper, finds all accused men indiscriminately irresistible. On the way to his execution K. catches sight of someone he

[30]Karl Kraus, "Aus dem dunkelsten Österreich," *Die Fackel* 214–15 (1906): 1–6; 2. The word *Scham* means shame, infamy as well as private parts. Fräulein Bürstner's lifestyle (her seeming availability) make Josef K. believe that he can seduce her (P 29–31; TR 28–29).

[31]"Denn die Justiz ist eine Hure, die sich nicht blitzen läßt und selbst von der Armut den Schandlohn einhebt" (Kraus, "Das Ehrenkreuz," *Die Fackel* 272–73 [1909]: 2–5; 5). The essay was part of a public reading by Kraus in Prague in December 1910 (*Die Fackel* 313–14 [1910]: 59).

[32]See Nike Wagner, *Geist und Geschlecht: Karl Kraus und die Erotik der Wiener Moderne* (Frankfurt: Suhrkamp, 1982). Politzer, *Franz Kafka* 289. Otto Weininger, *Geschlecht und Charakter: Eine prinzipielle Untersuchung* (Vienna and Leipzig: Braunmüller, 1903) 269, 290, 306, 378. The book became known not only for its infamous definitions of gender but also for declaring the bisexual nature of each woman and man.

believes to be Fräulein Bürstner. The admonition her late appearance represents for him suggests an awareness that his attraction to the women connected
with the court, their possible attempts to entrap him, and his inattentiveness
to the affairs of his trial are all unhappily intertwined. The fact that the court
officials control and use these women underscores — more even than their
ability to humiliate the defendants — judicial arbitrariness and unpredictabili-
ty.[33]

Kafka's love relationship in 1920 with Milena Jesenská, her reservations
about him, and his attempts and hopes to make the relationship more lasting
— he considered her his intellectual peer — trigger feelings of wretchedness,
impurity, and despondency over his health. This prolonged crisis (until 1922)
was aggravated by a circumstance not addressed by previous biographies. Kafka told Milena that he considered her marriage to Ernst Polak inescapable,
sacramentally insoluble. Max Brod viewed his own extramarital affairs as
near-religious experiences and celebrated them as "intermittently divine," as
grace and miracle. He did not understand his friend's fear of a sexual relationship with Milena, who, after all, was a married woman. Brod told him,
naively, that his misgivings about an involvement with her were groundless
since initially (presumably, because she was married) it would be without
obligations or consequences. What he could not fathom was that Kafka considered a relationship with a married woman forbidden because of the Torah's
prohibition of adultery.[34] As late as 1922 Kafka was buoyed by the hope for
an "honest" relationship with Milena because her marriage to Polak was
finally coming to an end.[35] In a long diary entry Kafka agrees with Milena's
assessment that the cause of his unhappiness is his fear of sexual intimacy. Yet
the only antidote, fearlessness, cannot be obtained simply by forcing oneself
to overcome one's fear. He admits both that his sexual need tortures him and
that he is able to overcome or ignore his fear and shame when the opportunity

---

[33]P 52, 191; TR 56, 225. Reiner Stach (*Kafkas erotischer Mythos: Eine ästhetische
Konstruktion des Weiblichen* [Frankfurt: Fischer, 1987]) discusses the women's
diversionary tactics which prove so destructive to Josef K. (41, 60, 74–75) but
overstates their alleged utopian, saving role as mediators between K. and court, or
K. and castle (141–42, 174–75).

[34]M 134, 214, 216; MI 101, 159–60. EF 2: 244, 301–3 (cf. B 229; L 194); Brod
justifies this celebration in light of the Jewish mystical tradition while feeling a bit
uneasy about his free-floating sexual "addiction." Kafka objects to his friend's (EF
2: 302) characterization of sex as intermittently divine and counters, at least as his
own relation to Milena is concerned, with a reference to the "burning bush" (B 297;
L 256). Yet he admires Brod's extramarital affair (B 313; L 270).

[35]"Ehrenhaftigkeit" (T 359; D 2: 223). See Hannelore Rodlauer, "Kafka und Wien:
Ein Briefkommentar" 203. Ernst Pawel has written an insightful account of their
relationship (*The Nightmare of Reason: A Life of Franz Kafka* (New York: Farrar,
Straus, Giroux, 1984) 389–411.

for casual sex offers itself. Since this ability is born of physiological necessity, it does not represent genuine fearlessness and, thus, is abominable. Kafka concludes that the physiological and ethical contradictions of his sexual disposition cannot be resolved. He sees himself sacrificed to the Torah, his blood seeping away between the temple stones.[36]

The Castle, Kafka's most extensive fictional view of the social world, portrays female sexuality and gender characteristics in a less biased, more sympathetic way than does *The Trial* (and, previously, *Amerika*). One of the most offensive aspects of castle power is the officials' ability to lord it over the village women. Most women are eager to submit, and they remain loyal to the officials even decades after an affair has come to an end. Klamm, the highest one to appear, remains important to Frieda long after she has become engaged to K., raising the justifiable fear in K. that Klamm's influence reaches into his, K.'s, own bedroom.[37] The officials' sexual presumptions and conduct violate both traditional decorum and the desirable mutual respect between men and women. Yet Olga, K.'s most important native informer, and the villagers in general do not subscribe to K.'s condemnation of this type of behavior. In fact, Olga explains that the officials' coarseness is really their intense and proper attention to official matters, and a corresponding lack of it to their sexual affairs. This motif, a variation on the fashionable preoccupation with apperceptive cognition — and its specific significance in Weininger's theory of maleness as the union of memory, attentiveness, apperception, and will — is pervasive to the point of satirical exaggeration. The officials must display "vigilance, energy and alertness." Gardena believes that Klamm's sexual affairs are not private at all but part of his official role and that he completely forgets a woman once he is through with her. Secretary Erlanger insists to K. that, because of the incomparable importance of his work, Klamm has to be protected from even the smallest distraction such as the loss of a particular sexual interest — Frieda, in this instance.[38]

[36]T 346–47; D 2: 203–4: "Herbeilocken der Gelegenheit" here means both solicitation of prostitutes and of casual sex (cf. the expressions *Gelegenheit machen* and *Gelegenheit schaffen* for procuring and solicitation). Kafka associates *stones* with the temple - H 94; BN 57). Cf. also notes 25–27.

[37]S 188; C 256 ("women can't help loving the officials"). S 79; C 104. S 59; C 75–76. K.'s relation to Klamm is partly modeled on how Kafka perceived his relation to Milena's husband (M 37, 61, 75, 99, 122–23, 129, 154, 195; MI 28, 46, 56, 74–75, 92–93, 96–97, 115, 145) and his guilt or fear concerning his involvement with her. See also Binder, *Kafka in neuer Sicht* 314–18.

[38]S 187; C 254. C 85; S 66. S 317; C 437. S 82; C 108. S 257; C 353–54. In a deleted passage Momus indicates that apperception is constantly required of the officials: "If one has the strength to look at things unceasingly, so to speak without blinking, one sees a great deal; but if one falters only once and shuts one's eyes, everything instantly slips away into darkness" (C 447; S 323).

Frieda is occasionally helpless and tearful and always domestic and solicitous toward K., her fiancée. She also hints at a deadening possessiveness: "I
dream of a grave, deep and narrow, where we could clasp each other in our
arms as with clamps." One part of her represents a domesticated version of
the sexual solicitation by the women of *The Trial*.[39] The sisters Olga and
Amalie are the opposites of these women. Amalie challenges the castle's male
power structure; she decides to preserve her complete independence at the risk
of becoming a pariah. She keeps silent about her action and displays moral
superiority (to the point of arrogance), a disdain for other people's opinions
about her, and the ability to face the truth concerning herself.[40] Olga is the
more realistically drawn character, courageous, intelligent, independent, and
able to see through some of the castle's machinations. Her admission that
women never had the ability to think things through and her prostitution to the
castle's servants may be faint echoes of Weininger's demeaning views of
female intelligence and sexuality. Her sexually unattractive appearance and
her utterly utilitarian prostitution, however, can be seen as Kafka's attempt to
counteract the traditionally biased view of inferior female intelligence. He
probably was aware of Freud's claim, critical of a Weininger-type gender
theory, that women's alleged intellectual inferiority was merely the inhibition
of their natural intelligence as part and parcel of the socially imposed repres-
sion of their sexuality.[41]

Olga's attempt to ingratiate her family with the castle by sleeping with the
castle's menservants does not duplicate the subservient role women have in
The Trial. Further illuminating the rakishness of all male officials in these two
novels, the menservants are driven by insatiable lust rather than laws. Their

---

[39]S 155; C 211. S 48; C 61. C 182; S 134. Frieda later displays similar attitudes
towards Jeremiah, her second fiancée (S 240; C 328–29). Elizabeth Boa observes
that Frieda's behavioral contradictions are mostly due to the ideological (male)
perspective of K., who sees her "now as a prize wrested from the Other Man, now
a slut who runs off with the Other Man; now as the highest aim in life, now as a
drag on his higher aims" ("Feminist Approaches to Kafka's *The Castle*," *New Ways
in Germanistik*, ed. Richard Sheppard [New York: Berg, 1990] 117).

[40]S 161; C 219. S 190; C 259. S 196; C 267. S 339; C 472. S 162 ("Nachbeten der
allgemeinen Meinung"); C 221. S 200; C 272. Amalia perhaps can be seen as
monstrously egocentric — a quality that Kafka criticized in Abraham (B 236; L
200); she also can be seen as the female "slave who said no ... who speaks the
truth" (Evelyn Torton Beck, "Kafka's Traffic in Women: Gender, Power, and
Sexuality," *Literary Review* 26 [1983]: 570–72.

[41]S 220; C 300. S 334; C 464. S 174; C 237 ("it's amazing how well you grasp it
all" - C 237). S 165; C 225. S 338; C 470. Sigmund Freud, *Die kulturelle Sexual-
moral und die moderne Nervosität* [1908], *Gesammelte Werke: Chronologisch
geordnet*, 18 vols. (London: Imago, 1940–52) 7: 162. Freud here addresses questions raised by Christian von Ehrenfels's *Sexualethik* [1907] (see note 26).

shamelessness is boundless, and they are not permitted to leave the officials' inn except by express order. Later Pepi claims that they are dirty and make their masters' rooms so dirty that not even the Flood could clean them.[42] The portrayal of these men — who are affiliated with the officials, the keepers of the law — as excessively lawless, lascivious, and unclean not only undercuts men's self-indulgent claim of ethical and jurisprudential superiority over women but also mocks the very idea of a law to be obeyed and venerated. On another level *The Castle* expresses the author's despair and remnants of guilt over his ill-fated sexuality as well as his resigned acceptance of the failure to make his intensely desired relationship with Milena work. He rationalizes both his despair and his resignation through portraying love and sexual relation-ships as marred by selfishness, deceit, gross dependencies, and unequal power relations between men and women. As the last chapter will show, *The Castle* is also his attempt to counteract this existential resignation through sweeping theological and political analyses.

[42]S 210 ("statt von den Gesetzen von ihren unersättlichen Trieben beherrscht"); C 285 ("ruled by their insatiable impulses instead of by [the laws]"). The servants cannot leave the Herrenhof without permission (S 210; C 2840); Kafka knew from reports in Kraus's *Die Fackel* that Vienna's officially registered prostitutes were confined to their brothels. S 275; C 380. K. attributes lewdness and dirtiness to his two assistants as well (S 239; C 328).

9: Religion, Delusion, and Prejudice

THE RURAL CUSTOMS, THE monoethnic communal cohesiveness, and the feudal-administrative paternalism portrayed in *The Castle* could very well represent a remote Central or Eastern European backwoods region before the turn of the century. Most characters display unenlightened beliefs, ignorance of legal basics, passive, even submissive civic attitudes — all remnants of a feudal-authoritarian tradition. Other features, however, — a sent-for foreign professional, widespread ideological (postreligious) prejudice, a well-organized civil service, airtight administrative procedures — suggest that this community could be connected to an ethnically diverse, centrally governed early modern state such as Austria-Hungary at the turn of the century. The novel also employs an array of religious, ethnic, and legal motifs — the ancient strife between Judaism and nascent Christianity, the competing cultural anthropological assumptions underlying Jewish assimilation and Zionism, and the Jews' threatened legal equality within the German-speaking, increasingly anti-Semitic environment. These motifs capture the individual anxieties and the collective paranoia of a community threatened by the social and political transition to modernity.

Compared to Karl Roßmann and even to Josef K., K. in *The Castle* deals with less tractable problems and faces more baffling explanations. On the night of his arrival in the village the castle administration appoints him land surveyor. It apparently believes that K. is the person who, as he himself claims, previously had been offered the job and whose arrival it has been expecting. The mayor maintains that K. had been made the offer due to a partly erroneous, partly well-considered administrative decision but also that it can no longer be ascertained whether the letter of appointment had been sent or not. It turns out later that K. was well informed about the castle before his arrival.[1] Two divergent — religious and sociohistorical — allusions illuminate Kafka's reasons for making K. a land surveyor. The first is the more important, as it brings out a hidden ethnic-ideological dynamics in the village. In

---

[1] S 10; C 7. S 60; C 78. S 62; C 80. S 69; C 89. S 73; C 95. S 177; C 241. Contrary to this textual evidence Beda Allemann argues that K. could not have been hired before his actual arrival ("Scheinbare Leere: Zur thematischen Struktur von Kafkas *Schloß*-Roman," *Mélanges offerts à Claude David,* ed. Jean-Louis Bandet [Bern: Lang, 1986] 17, 28).

Hebrew the word for surveyor closely resembles *Messiah*, and, thus, the figure of K. may be seen to reflect Jewish Messianism — an oppressed minority's periodically recurring hope for divine political intervention. Many of the village inhabitants appear to expect great things from K.s arrival, but his persistent outsider status and occasional fumbling make it clear that their hopes are misplaced. Second, Kafka had read about corrupt land surveyors in nineteenth-century Russia whose surveying activities struck the fear in many peasants that they would be cheated out of their lands.[2] In that vein, and perhaps also due to their antimodern beliefs, the tanner Lasemann and the mayor look at K.s surveyor role with suspicion; they see no need for him in this village.

Upon learning of his appointment as surveyor, K., in a rush of thoughts, concludes that the castle is well informed about him and perceives him as an aggressor and that, due to the official appointment, he has greater freedom to maneuver than he could have hoped for. He intends to fight and considers the mere pursuit of his self-interest as an attack on the castle. His assessment may be based on the assumption that a newcomer to this tightly knit community will necessarily fare badly. K. wants to get ahead socially — or at least desires a home, a position, a wife, and membership in the community — but, paradoxically, also believes that he has come here not to lead an honored and trouble-free life. As he becomes more frustrated, he decides to win by any means possible, including lies and cunning. Whatever his quest, he comes to identify its success with meeting Klamm, the highest castle official, face to face, either to talk to him about Frieda, to talk to him as a private person, to let him know his, K.'s, wishes, to explain the actual work he is doing for the village, to seek reconciliation with him, or to justify to him his actions up till now. At one point K. defiantly waits for Klamm in the official inn's courtyard, which is supposed to be off limits to him. Though he knows that his wait will be in vain, his defiance gives him a gratuitous sense of freedom and invulnerability.[3]

---

[2]W. G. Sebald, "The Law of Ignominy: Authority, Messianism and Exile in *The Castle*," *On Kafka*, ed. Kuna, 42–58. S 29; C 34. S 145; C 197. S 216–17; C 294–95. S 273; C 377. Robertson stresses the novel's allusions to the historical critique of Messianism and unmasking of Messianic pretenders within Judaism (*Kafka* 228–35). S 17; C 17–18. S 60–72; C 77–94. See Axel Dornemann, *Im Labyrinth der Bürokratie: Tolstois "Auferstehung" und Kafkas "Das Schloß"* (Heidelberg: Winter, 1984) 102.

[3]S 10; C 7–8. S 58–59; C 74–75. S 40–41; C 50. S 154; C 210. S 190; C 258. S 147; C 200. S 159; C 217 ("all the guile of which he was capable"). K.'s aims: S 49; C 62. S 154; C 209. S 51; C 65. S 84; C 112. S 107 ("mit seinen ... Wünschen an Klamm herankam"); C 145. S 115–16; C 155–56. S 151; C S 163; S 103. The inconsistency of some of these aims is discussed by Richard Sheppard (*On Kafka's "The Castle": A Study* [London: Croom Helm, 1973] 140–47).

After this incident both Gardena, the landlady of the Bridge Inn, and Klamm's village secretary, Momus, tell him that a meeting with Klamm is completely unattainable, that his pursuit is futile, his hope empty. This news can only fortify K.'s sense of an epistemic, and possibly ontological, gap separating him from the castle. For instance, the mayor had claimed that, despite the appointment letter from Klamm and K.'s telephone call to the castle, K. has not come into contact with any real authorities. K. is also told that Klamm never speaks to anybody in the village and nobody in the village can ever speak to Klamm. Even worse, it is said that Klamm never reads the reports his secretaries file about the village, and K. has it firsthand that Klamm is completely misinformed about K.'s current employment. To K., Klamm appears like an eagle who draws his incomprehensible circles high above, although presumably he observes the world below with a downward-pressing, penetrating gaze. K., on the other hand, is compared to a blind-worm who does not understand what is going on. Olga claims that the villagers never understand fully the smallest matters concerning themselves in relation to the castle, and never would, even if they took a lifetime trying to do so.[4]

After K.'s failed attempt to meet and communicate with Klamm in the courtyard, his further attempts become somewhat delusional. He believes that the village officials are interfering with his access to the castle. His talk with the boy Hans Brunswick raises hopes in him that he can no longer forget but that are, admittedly, completely groundless. He absurdly believes that a surreptitious meeting with the boy's mother could open a way to Klamm. He recalls a recent message to Klamm "word for word, not however as he had given it to Barnabas, but as he thought it would sound before Klamm." K.'s attitudes and actions toward villagers and officials range from interest in economic security and membership in the community to arrogance, legally improper behavior, lying, and gross opportunism. For instance, he trespasses by climbing into Klamm's sleigh and seeks admittance to the Brunswick household under false pretenses. He lies to gain Hans's trust and pretends to share Frieda's antipathy toward the Barnabas family. Above all, it appears that he gets involved with Frieda largely because of her intimate relation with Klamm.[5] Yet despite these questionable character traits K. achieves, for the reader, independent moral authority by analyzing the castle's illegal conduct and insisting on individual rights denied him and others by the village and

[4]S 109–11; C 148–51. S 72; C 93. S 50; C 64. S 49; C 62. S 111; C 151. S 114–15; C 154. S 112; C 151. S 56; C 72. S 205; C 279. Henry Sussman sees an ontological difference of realms: K.'s presence "is literally the condition for Klamm's absence and vice versa"; "Klamm cannot be met because he embodies the condition of absence itself" (*Franz Kafka: Geometrician of Metaphor* [Madison: Coda, 1979] 118, 131).

[5]S 144; C 195. S 146; C 199. S 154; C 210. C 162; S 121. S 100; C 133–34. S 151; C 206. S 141–42; C 191. S 235; C 321. S 132; C 179. S 151–52; C 206.

castle administrations. Initially, K. believes that the castle is lenient with him, letting him slip through at his own discretion, and he even suggests at one point that this bureaucracy might be legally and morally acceptable. But Olga's tales point him to the castle's arbitrary and immoral power. With the villagers' consent, she and her whole family are being punished for Amalie's refusal to respond to an official's obscenely worded request to share his bed as well as for her alleged insult to his messenger. K. describes this summons to Amalie as an abuse of power, a crime, a crying injustice.[6]

In many ways the castle functions like a secret court system: the officials decide and carry out policies that are conceived as stipulations of law; they lean on their law books, try to serve the law, and know the clandestine ways of law. Many decisions are arrived at arbitrarily and remain secret; even legal actions such as an official indictment can be kept hidden for some time. Amalie's father has been unable to prove that the family has been indicted or is being blackballed by the castle for his daughter's noncompliance: "Before he could be forgiven he had to prove his guilt, and that was denied in all the departments." The sanctions against them are as elusive and reiterative as the admissions procedure to the castle service is for someone who has fallen out of official favor: "for years he waits in fear and trembling for the result ... then after years and years, perhaps as an old man, he learns that he has been rejected, learns that everything is lost and that all his life has been in vain." Whereas in *The Trial* it was never resolved whether Josef K.'s past or present behavior was on trial, here, evidently, K.'s current rather than past conduct matters to the officials. The landlady, Gardena, tells K. that she went to see Klamm's secretary, Momus: "I have come here to Herr Momus ... to give the office an adequate idea of your behavior and your intentions."[7] Echoing legal positivism, Secretary Bürgel construes the bureaucrats' ruthlessness in dealing with the villagers as a kind of rigid impartiality, as consideration in the petitioner's favor. Actually, official goodwill is a mere facade, since the aim always is to disadvantage the petitioners, to render their demands futile. When Frieda, having left K., returns to her former job as a bartender and, concur-

---

[6]S 74; C 96 (I want "my rights"); K.'s insistence on such rights is argued by Richard J. Arneson ("Power and Authority in *The Castle*," *Mosaic* 12 [1979]: 99–113). S 58; C 74–75. S 175–76; C 239 ("fear of the authorities is born in you here"). S 184; C 251 ("abuse of power"). S 186; C 253 ("Sortini's criminal actions"). S 189; C 257 ("crying injustice").

[7]S 212 ("sie müssen sich sehr fest an die Gesetzbücher halten"); C 288. S 248; C 340. S 251; C 345. S 68; C 88. S 166; C 226–27. C 275–77 ("Since he had failed in proving his guilt"); S 203–4. C 287–88; S 211–12; other entry procedures are postponed indefinitely and broken off at the applicant's death; the Austrian code stipulated that a criminal trial cannot be continued or appealed after the defendant's death: "The ability to be party to a trial expires with the defendant's death .... Against a dead person you cannot start a criminal trial nor continue it on the initial or appeals level" (Lohsing, *Strafprozeß* 197). C 146; S 108.

rently, the castle orders K. to return Frieda to this job, the coincidence of
these causally unrelated events drives home to him that orders from the castle,
no matter whether favorable or unfavorable, are issued without any regard for
the individual concerned. This bureaucracy never acknowledges any errors
and, ultimately, shows no gaps in its total system.[8]

Many episodes in the novel are linked metaphorically to important events
in the Hebrew Bible and especially to the New Testament. K.'s first lovemaking with Frieda is described in ways similar to the biblical account of the Fall.
Although K. experiences it as the breathing of air so unfamiliar that it becomes suffocating, he soon shares Frieda's view of their sexual union as
providential. K.'s arrival in the village alludes beyond the mere Messianic to
the birth of the Messiah-Christ: K. was "at the very first hour of his arrival
… quite helpless on his sack of straw … at the mercy of any official action."
During his visits at the castle offices Barnabas has doubts, similar to the
Apostle Thomas's doubts about the Resurrection, about the true identity of the
official who is designated as Klamm: "it's a matter of life and death for
Barnabas whether it's really Klamm he speaks to or not".[9]

The allusions to Christ hint at a more extensive network of New Testament
references: issues and attitudes addressed by the Apostle Paul in his Epistle to
the Galatians. They are connected to those of the novel's events and concepts
that define criteria for social inclusion and exclusion, accepted and unaccept-
able behavior, the notions of cleanliness and dirtiness. More specifically, they
refer to disputes between Jews and the earliest Christians over the meaning of
the Messiah and definitions of religious group membership, communal rules,
and ritual law — and then show modern anti-Semitism's expropriation of these
definitions. A castle official who occasionally acts as Klamm's deputy is called
Galater (the German word for *Galatians*). The messenger who carries letters
and oral messages between K. and the castle is named after the Apostle Barnabas, who, together with Paul, founded the Christian congregations in Galatia. The Hebrew name Barnabas means son of consolation; Klamm's second
letter promises K. consolation. K., however, rejects this letter because it
reveals Klamm's ignorance about K.'s situation. Paul's epistle urges the

---

[8]S 247; C 338. S 248; C 340. S 253; C 348 ("futile demands"). S 258; C 355. S
65; S 250; C 343 ("the foolproofness of the official organization"); S 253; C 347
("the incomparable sieve"). Kafka himself is aware of bureaucracy's absurd unre-
sponsiveness to human needs (B 377; L 327). He also echoes contemporary critical
analyses of bureaucratic power (see Dornemann, *Im Labyrinth der Bürokratie*
106–57).

[9]S 43–44; C 54 (see also Hulda Göhler, *Franz Kafka: "Das Schloß." "Ansturm
gegen die Grenze": Entwurf einer Deutung* [Bonn: Bouvier & Grundmann, 1982]
90–91). K. fears suffocation: breathable air is one of Kafka's metaphors for desire
beyond sexuality: T 348, 353, 357; D 2: 206, 215, 220). S 52 ("gesegnet, nicht
verflucht sei die Stunde"); C 67. C 216; S 158. S 168; C 229. Cf. John 20:25–29.
C 231; S 170.

replacement of the Torah with the faith in Christ; it lashes out against Jewish-Christian missionaries in Galatia who insist that gentiles must adopt circumcision and obedience to the Jewish law as preconditions for their Christian faith.[10] He points out that the Apostle Peter acted with duplicity when he shared meals with his gentile-Christian brothers but broke off table fellowship with them when members of the Jerusalem congregation were present. Paul accuses Barnabas, a born Jew, of the same hypocrisy. His point is that many Christian Jews do not yet fully accept his belief that faith in the redeeming significance of Christ's death invalidates all of the Torah.[11] After the turn of the century, in the wake of pioneering philological and archaeological research into the origins of the New Testament writings, Jewish and Christian theologians engaged in debates over the continued role of Jewish law and faith for Christianity. For the Christian side, as seen by a present-day scholar, Paul's break with Judaism was "his argument that the covenant *skips* from Abraham to Christ, and now includes those in Christ, but not Jews by descent." "What is wrong with the law, and thus with Judaism, is that it does not provide for God's ultimate purpose, that of saving the entire world through faith in Christ."[12] On the Jewish side, the orthodox-nationalist and liberal-assimilationist theologians perceived the ancient strife between the Jews, the Jewish Christians, and Paul differently. The former tried to show that everything Jesus and the earliest Christians taught can be traced to the Hebrew Bible and

[10]Acts 4:36. S 115–16 ("seien Sie getrost"); C 154. Consolation alludes to both the Jews' Messianic hope and the Christian gospel. When Klamm calls out for Frieda (he sounds like God calling Adam after the Fall), K. experiences the interruption of his lovemaking (the Fall) as a "tröstliches Aufdämmern," a glimmer of consolation (S 44, C 54). Paul thinks that the Jewish-Christian preachers have bewitched the Galatians (Gal. 3:1). Analogously, K. notices that he is being bewitched by Barnabas (S 34; C 40), that Frieda is bewitched by the assistants (S 239; C 328).

[11]Gal. 2:12–13; 2:16. See the conceptual similarity of Kafka's wish at a sanitarium, ostensibly because of his vegetarian food, to be served separately: "I asked to be served at a separate little table in the common dining room" (L 233; B 270). Kafka apparently knew the anti-Jewish *Letter of Barnabas* (included in an early version of the New Testament canon), which admonishes Christians to read the Jewish dietary laws spiritually and allegorically (Barnabas 10:1–10; cf. John 6:26–27). Two of the novel's passages satirize the desire to mistake linguistic meanings for foodstuffs: "He licked his lips as if news were [a nourishment]" (C 33; S 29). "Wenn Sie nur nicht immer ... wie ein Kind alles gleich in eßbarer Form dargeboten haben wollten!" (S 111; C 150).

[12]E. P. Sanders, *Paul, the Law, and the Jewish People* (London: SCM Press, 1985) 207, 47. For the then available knowledge of Paul's life and his writing of the epistles see Theodor Zahn, *Einleitung in das Neue Testament* (Leipzig: Deichert, 1900).

its rabbinical interpretations.[13] The latter diminished the differences between the particularist, nationalist Jewish law and the universalist Christian gospel (or its alleged philosophical successors). For instance, Ignaz Ziegler reinterprets the Talmud in the tradition of German Idealist philosophy, seeing it as an ethical guide for any individual to raise himself or herself up to God. This position was a departure from his orthodox insistence, only five years earlier, on the irreducible significance of Jewish law, arguing that if the Jews had gone along with Paul and abandoned circumcision and the dietary laws Christian monotheism would have succumbed to Christian paganism. Even so, instead of making the Jewish faith universal (Christian), Paul made it merely Greco-Roman, replacing monotheism with the Trinity.[14] For Moriz Friedländer, Judaism does not have to fall back on the continuing importance of the Jewish law, let alone Idealist-universalist ethics. He radically historicizes the Christian critique of Talmudic Judaism: Paul's opposition to the law merely continues the non-Talmudic moral, spiritual, and universalist reading of the Torah favored by Jews of the Greek-speaking diaspora before and during the life of Jesus. Paul's mission to convert gentiles to Christianity grows out of the Hellenistic Judaic faith that dismissed the ritual meaning of the Torah and gave religious equality to all converted gentiles. Jesus himself taught a Hellenistic (antipharisaic) spiritual law, addressing it not to a nation but each individual.[15]

Kafka's religious views at first are close to such Judaic-universalist reinterpretations of the Torah. In 1916, pointing to upbringing, inclination, and environment, he professes his indifference to the Talmudic faith and ritual

[13]Joseph Eschelbacher, for instance, argues that no Hellenistic Jew would have dismissed the Torah. Thus, the Apostle Paul's so-called epistles are falsely attributed to him; they issue from a much later (second-century) pagan Christianity. See Eschelbacher, *Das Judentum und das Wesen des Christentums: Vergleichende Studien* (Berlin: Poppelauer, 1908) 143–46.

[14]Ignaz Ziegler, *Die Geistesreligion und das jüdische Religionsgesetz: Ein Beitrag zur Erneuerung des Judentums* (Berlin: Reimer, 1912) 82, 99. Kafka owned this book. Ziegler, *Der Kampf zwischen Judentum und Christentum in den ersten drei christlichen Jahrhunderten* (Berlin: Poppelauer, 1907) 73–75, 53, 78; this historical assessment is similar to the Zionist insistence on the Jews' separate cultural and religious identity, such as Jakob Klatzkin's (see notes 22, 24, 28).

[15]Moriz Friedländer, *Die religiösen Bewegungen innerhalb des Judentums im Zeitalter Jesu* (Berlin: Reimer, 1905) viii–xiii, 4–21. Kafka owned this book also. Friedländer has been called an "irreconcilable adversary of pharisaic Judaism" and "antirabbinical" (Gösta Lindeskog, *Die Jesusfrage im neuzeitlichen Judentum: Ein Beitrag zur Geschichte der Leben-Jesu-Forschung* [Uppsala: Lundequistska, 1938] 149, 156).

observance.[16] He begins to acknowledge, however, that within a Christian (often anti-Semitic) environment Jews advert to religious and even ritual differences as a means of maintaining their identity. His 1917 story "Jackals and Arabs" portrays the irreconcilable hatred between jackals (Jews) and Arabs (non-Jews) in terms of their oppositional use or expropriation of a core element of Judaism, the Talmudic dietary and purity laws. The jackals consider themselves clean while labeling the Arabs unclean. They feed on the carcasses of camels under the pretense that they have to rid the world of them.[17] In turn, the Arabs barely tolerate the jackals as useful but unclean (carcass-eating) parasites. The story furthermore alludes to Jewish Messianism and the anti-Semitic propaganda about Jewish ritual murders of gentiles: for ages the jackals have been waiting for someone to help them cut the Arabs' throats and take their blood.[18]

As suggested earlier, Kafka employs cleanliness and dirtiness as value concepts with regard to literary and sexual matters. In his letters to Milena from 1920 he attributes impurity to himself as a westernized Jew, largely based on his existential self-doubt and feeling of sexual insufficiency. Less personally motivated, however, he derives this self-ascribed quality from both the Zionist critique of the assimilated western Jew and the Austrian cultural anti-Semitism. According to these two structurally similar views, assimilation and urbanization have estranged the Jews from their historical and national roots and made them culturally degenerate.[19] Kafka's self-criticism as a Jew

---

[16]See F 700; FE 502–3. On the other hand, Kafka would not subscribe to Paul's substitution of the Torah with Abraham's "Christian" faith (Gal. 3:16). Abraham cannot have faith since he has no way of knowing that it is he who is called upon ("[kann nicht glauben,] daß er gemeint ist" - B 333; L 285).

[17]E 132–35; CS 407–11. Jens Tismar shows that many German writers portrayed (originating with Jer. 9:10) the Jews as jackals ("Kafkas *Schakale und Araber* im zionistischen Kontext betrachtet," *Jahrbuch der deutschen Schillergesellschaft* 19 [1975]: 306–23). He and Robertson (*Kafka* 164) see the jackals as referring to the westernized Jews whom the Zionists painted as parasitical. They can also be seen, however, as orthodox eastern Jews who cannot, due to their exile, keep all ritual laws and who thus see themselves as unclean (see Helen Milful, "*Weder Katze noch Lamm?* Franz Kafkas Kritik des *Westjüdischen*," *Im Zeichen Hiobs: Jüdische Schriftsteller und deutsche Literatur im 20. Jahrhundert*, ed. Gunter Grimm and Hans-Peter Bayerdörfer [Königstein: Athenäum, 1985] 184–86). About the Arabs representing all non-Jews cf. Gen. 16:10; about the uncleanliness of camels cf. Lev. 11:4; 17:10.

[18]Kafka knew about the charges of ritual murder against the Jews (M 68; MI 51). In his diary of a trip to Egypt, Flaubert describes Arabs around a campfire in the presence of jackals (Gustave Flaubert, "Tagebuch des jungen Flaubert," *Pan* 1 [1910–11] 187). Flaubert appears to have served as a model for Kafka's emotionally removed European narrator.

[19]For the Zionists' (e.g. Martin Buber's) critique of the westernized Jew see Robertson, *Kafka* 146, 161–65. *Cultural* anti-Semitism refers here to the culturally (not

and experience of anti-Semitism gradually suggest to him what will become an important subplot of *The Castle*: concepts of ethnic difference such as impurity can be used as instruments of social exclusion.[20] At the same time, despite his increasing national self-assertion as a Jew[21] and doubts about Jewish-German assimilation he retains a strong sense of belonging within the Western cultural and ethical tradition. For instance, he is unconvinced by Max Brod's oppositional construction of Judaism and Christianity and his religious critique of non-Jewish German culture in his *Paganism, Christianity, Judaism*. Brod boldly declares that Christian theologians merely allege the superiority of Christianity over Judaism, that it is conceptually inferior to Judaism. Somehow at odds with the Jewish-nationalist stance against diluting Judaism down to a universal ethical idea or spiritual identity,[22] Brod claims that Judaism is the more universalist, Christianity the more particularist religion. The former gives open individual access to God, the latter allows one way only, mediation through Christ, excluding all non-Christians. In contrast to the alleged Christian universalism, Jewish universalism preserves and tolerates national distinctions. Brod uses Kafka's parable "Before the Law" — about the door to the law that, against all appearances, is meant for one person only — to illustrate that God reveals his grace to the chosen individual uncondition-

politically) motivated polemics against Jews by conservative (antiliberal, antimodernist) journals such as *Der Brenner* (see Sigurd P. Scheichl, "Aspekte des Judentums im *Brenner* [1910–1937]," *Untersuchungen zum "Brenner,"* Festschrift für Ignaz Zangerle, ed. Walter Methlagl et al. [Salzburg: Müller, 1981] 70–121. Kafka was a reader of this journal and owned several issues.

[20]M 294; MI 217–18 ("I'm the most Western-Jewish of them all ... everything must be earned, not only the present and the future, but the past as well. If the Earth turns to the right ... then I would have to turn to the left to make up for the past"). M 25 (the western Jew as problematic marital partner for a "clean" Christian woman); MI 19. Kafka does not attribute impurity to all assimilated Jews. For example, the courage, independence, and truthfulness of his sister Ottla or Ernst Polak merit the description *clean* (F 730; FE 525. M 47; MI 36). He was alarmed and warned by personal encounters with anti-Semites (M 26, 288; MI 20, 213. B 275, 298; L 237, 256) and (see below) the increasing groundswell of anti-Semitism in the Austrian press (B 273; L 235–36).

[21]Starting with his interest in the Yiddish theater in 1911 and then especially since 1915 (Binder, in *Kafka-Handbuch* 1: 390–95, 468–72, 499–510. Robertson, *Kafka* 12–37, 141–84).

[22]See Jakob Klatzkin, "Grundlagen des Nationaljudentums. Erstes Kapitel: Irrwege des nationalen Instinkts," *Der Jude* 1 (1916–17): 534–36. Max Brod, *Heidentum, Christentum, Judentum: Ein Bekenntnisbuch*, 2 vols. (Munich: Wolff, 1921) 2: 66–159 ("Die falsche Grundkonstruktion des Christentums"), 2: 160–232.

ally, without mediation.[23] To assert a modern Jewish identity completely divorced from Christianity, Brod argues that in antiquity a mutual exclusion of Judaism and Hellenic paganism existed that has continued into the present. Greek religion and culture, concerned exclusively with the visible world, eschewed anything that might transcend it. During the war Brod taught ancient literature to Jewish teenagers, refugees from Galicia, and found them unable to take the Homeric gods seriously in the slightest.[24] Kafka finds his friend's appraisal of the Hellenic tradition inconsistent. In light of Brod's repeated celebrations of existential and sexual joy in his letters and in this book, Kafka even suggests that next to Judaism Brod's spiritual home is paganism. He himself strongly sympathizes with the Hellenic religion since it concedes to the individual the possibility of happiness in the everyday world without his needing to strive for the divine. Above all else, Kafka remains unconvinced of Brod's plea for cultural segregation of Jews from Germans based on the differences between the Judaic and the Christian faiths.[25]

Several months into the writing of *The Castle*, Kafka took a serious interest in Hans Blüher's just-published *Secessio Judaica*. It claims that both Zionism and German anti-Semitism are comparable expressions of the Jews' eventual and unavoidable racial segregation from the German people. No one can be both German and Jewish; the two races are opposed to each other. Through Darwinian adaptation and mimicry the Jews vainly try to blend in with their German hosts. Intermarriage is against the Germanic blood law; Jewish blood, sexual attitudes, and economic outlook are unclean. The complete secession of the Jews from the Germans, the unmasking of their mimic-

[23]Brod, *Heidentum, Christentum, Judentum* 1: 242–4; to fight off Paul's gospel and to preserve their national identity, however, the Jews initially had to exercise a narrow ritual observance (2: 132, 204). 2: 71–72; Brod ignores the parable's paradoxical appearance of promise, and ultimate denial, of legal absolution.

[24]Brod, *Heidentum, Christentum, Judentum* 2: 258–73 ("Vom Heidentum einst und immer"). Brod's claim of "Unvermischbarkeit" [the inability to mix (2: 263)] echoes Jakob Klatzkin's critique ("Deutschtum und Judentum," *Der Jude* 2 (1917–18): 246–50) of Hermann Cohen's booklet *Deutschtum und Judentum* (Gießen: Töpelmann, 1915) which insisted on important links between Judaism and Hellenism (5–11). Brod, *Heidentum, Christentum, Judentum* 2: 263. Kafka refers to this passage when he playfully identifies himself (B 279; L 242) with such youngsters Brod taught.

[25]B 279; L 242 (7 Aug. 1920). Cf. Brod's "Von allen Boten Gottes spricht Eros am eindringlichsten. Er reißt den Menschen am schnellsten vor das Angesicht der Herrlichkeit Gottes" ["Of all of God's messengers eros speaks most forcibly. It snatches man most quickly before the face of God's glory"] (Brod, *Heidentum, Christentum, Judentum* 1: 34).

ry, has begun and is irreversible.[26] Beneath the book's seeming objectivity
Kafka suspects in Blüher an "enemy of the Jews."[27] And yet, somewhat
taken in by the philosophically dressed racist speculations, Kafka does not
think him a traditional anti-Semite but someone who points up insurmountable
ethnic differences. To him Blüher's employment of segregationist vocabulary
approximates certain aspects of Jewish religious and national thought. His
suggestion that a critique of Blüher should be undertaken by a Talmudist and
"after the fashion of the Jews" illustrates, like "Jackals and Arabs" and *The
Castle*, his understanding of how firmly ethnic and cultural value differences
and exclusions are based on religious concepts.[28] He eventually recognizes
a certain facile prejudice in Blüher's thesis when he recalls it upon browsing
in a chauvinist German literary history by Friedrich von der Leyen. This work

[26]Hans Blüher, *Secessio Judaica: Philosophische Grundlegung der historischen
Situation des Judentums und der antisemitischen Bewegung* (Berlin: Der Weiße
Ritter, 1922) 15–16, 37–38, 42–43, 63–64. The book exploits Hegelianism ("law
of pure history"; the *idea* of a people), claims that the Jews have lost their "historical substance" (are sick as a people and as individuals) from early on because they
were fated to produce Christ from their midst, kill and reject him (19–20); cf. also
Blüher, *Die Aristie des Jesus von Nazareth: Philosophische Grundlegung der Lehre
und Erscheinung Christi* (Prien: Kampmann, 1921) 304–6. *Secessio Judaica* has
been placed squarely within the increasing anti-Semitism in the political parties on
the far right as well as the professional and trade associations in Germany during
and after the First World War (Werner Jochmann, *Gesellschaftskrise und Judenfeindschaft in Deutschland 1870–1945* [Hamburg: Christians, 1988] 149, 152, 168).

[27]"Judenfeind" (T 363–64; D 2: 231). Blüher insisted that his anti-Semitism was
objective, without ill will against individual Jews. As late as 1933 the Jewish assimilationist critic — and, with Brod, editor of the first edition of unpublished Kafka
stories *Beim Bau der chinesischen Mauer* (1931) — Hans-Joachim Schoeps labeled
the book *judengegnerisch* (antagonistic towards the Jews) as distinct from anti-
Semitic (Hans Blüher and H. J. Schoeps, *Streit um Israel: Ein jüdisch-christliches
Gespräch* [Hamburg: Hanseatische Verlagsanstalt, 1933] 7).

[28]B 380; L 330 (30 June 1922); the Zionists stressed cultural and religious segregation: cf. Richard Lichtheim, *Das Programm des Zionismus* (Berlin: Zionistische
Vereinigung für Deutschland, 1913) 14–16, 33 [Kafka owned this book]; Jakob
Klatzkin, "Grundlagen des Nationaljudentums," 610, 613; Felix Weltsch, *Nationa-
lismus und Judentum* (Berlin: Welt-Verlag, 1920). For Arnold Zweig all modern
nations engage in mutual rejection ("Abstoßung"); Zionism merely reciprocates and
duplicates the anti-Semitic rejection of all (even assimilated) Jews by their host
nations ("Der heutige deutsche Antisemitismus," *Der Jude* 5 [1920–21]: 373, 629);
he did not construe Blüher's rejection of Jews as anti-Semitic (6 [1921–22]: 142).
The fact that Kafka refers to Brod's *Heidentum, Christentum, Judentum* when
speaking of the fateful assassination of the German foreign secretary Walther Rathenau by anti-Semites (B 378; L 328) suggests that he has become more aware of
how the perception of religious differences between Germans and Jews can be
perverted into racial exclusion and rejection.

claims that even mediocre German (non-Jewish) writers are distinguished by their being rooted in their respective Germanic tribal traditions and regions, a distinction Jewish authors (such as Jakob Wassermann) can only strive for in vain. "And even if Wassermann should rise at four in the morning day after day and his whole life long plow up the Nuremberg region from end to end, the land would still not respond to him and he would have to take pretty whisperings in the air for its response." Despite the scorn Kafka pours over this blood and soil presumption, he himself previously had adopted a self-critically segregationist stance with regard to the most important aspect of his life — literature. He suggested that Jewish-German writers such as himself appropriate somebody else's possessions, perform a mimicry of German language and literature.[29] Blüher's call for radical segregation appears to confirm Kafka's feeling that Jewish assimilation to German culture is doomed, hopelessly nonreciprocal.[30]

Kafka incorporates motifs from the Epistle to the Galatians into *The Castle* almost from the beginning. As the new critical edition shows, the author introduces the castle messenger by titling the second chapter "Barnabas." Through the figure of Barnabas the missionary role of the historical Barnabas, his wavering between adherence to the Judaic law and faith in Christ, becomes a symbol for K.'s crossing of quasi-ethnic borders and for the Barnabas family's outsider status within their own society. The foreigner K. suspects that the family must have committed some sin to be so despised by Gardena, the proprietress of the Bridge Inn.[31] At this point her reservations about the family look like an exclusion on moral or religious grounds — like an orthodox sanction against mixing with gentiles, a Christian ban on dealing with

[29]L 346–47 (von der Leyen's book as an "accompanying music to the *Secessio Judaica*"); B 400. B 336–68; L 287–89 (the German spoken by many Jews is an "appropriation of someone else's property ... it remains someone else's property, even though there is no evidence of a single solecism").

[30]B 479; L 410 (Jewishness within German culture as an "incurable" affliction). Two years earlier he felt that through their accelerating modernist influence on traditional German culture the Jews had helped to create anti-Semitism (B 274; L 236). In direct response to *Secessio Judaica* Felix Weltsch argued, in a letter to Hugo Bergmann, that anti-Semitism is caused by the Jews' disproportionate influence on German society, and, thus (from his Zionist perspective), rejection by the Germans is understandable, segregation desirable (*Max Brod: Ein Gedenkbuch 1884–1968*, ed. Hugo Gold [Tel-Aviv: Olamenu, 1969] 102). In an obituary for Walther Rathenau in *Selbstwehr* Weltsch wrote that the assimilationist Jews never received reciprocating love ("Gegenliebe") from the Germans (quoted by Hartmut Binder, "Franz Kafka und die Wochenschrift *Selbstwehr*," *Deutsche Vierteljahrsschrift für Literatur- und Geistesgeschichte* 41 [1967]: 294).

[31]According to Malcolm Pasley (SKA 2: 81, 88), the title "Barnabas" appears to have been conceived together with the first chapter's title "Ankunft" ("Arrival" [a Messianic notion]). S 55; C 70–71.

infidels. Chapter 15 suggests[32] that Olga views her brother's castle service in the light of the Messianic hope that underlies both Judaism and the gospel. She sees Barnabas "entrusted with relatively important letters, even with orally delivered messages." She cautions K., however, not to take the Messianic meaning of her brother's service too literally, so as not to "pin too many hopes on him and suffer disappointment"; it may yet turn out to be a "completely vain hope." K.'s request that Barnabas deliver his messages without delays conflicts with the castle's views of what his service requires. According to Olga, despite his doubts Barnabas must pretend to K. that his messenger role is officially approved. If he were to express doubts about its legitimacy, it would mean "to undermine his very existence and to violate grossly laws that he believes himself still bound by." Furthermore, Barnabas dares not ask the officials at the castle what goes on there "for fear of offending in ignorance against some unknown rule."[33] Especially the first of the two remarks echoes the Christian Jews' attempts to reverse Paul's dismissal of the Jewish law, as well as his scorn for his fellow apostles' (Peter's, Barnabas's) backsliding.

At this point in the text Kafka composed (and immediately deleted) a long speech by Olga that reveals the delusional and prejudicial — in fact, anti-Semitic — nature of the villagers' reservations about her family. He appears to have written it under the direct impact of *Secessio Judaica*.[34] Frieda considers it intolerably shameful that K. returns from his visits to the family with their domestic odor in his garments. In other words, the Barnabas family suffers the kind of prejudice a Jewish family might experience within a turn-of-the-century Christian environment.[35] K. asks Olga why the villagers have

---

[32]The critical edition's new chapter 15 (the first part of the old chapter 15) runs SKA 1: 270–94 (S 165–79; C 224–43). It was written before Kafka's departure for Planá on June 23, 1922 (see Pasley, SKA 2: 68).

[33]C 226; S 166. C 229; S 168. C 234; S 172. The fact that Barnabas is not permitted to pass certain barriers in the castle offices (S 168; C 228–29) echoes the parable "Before the Law." It turns out later (S 222; C 302) that it was Galater who assigned the two assistants to K. to dissuade him from thinking that having settled in the village was a big deal. C 230; S 169 ("Gesetze ... unter denen er ja noch zu stehen glaubt"). C 238; S 175 ("Verletzung unbekannter Vorschriften").

[34]S 332–37 (initially composed for and stricken from S 175); SKA 2: 352–67; C 438–69. The passage was deleted immediately: prior to it Olga speaks of Barnabas's fear, right after it K. criticizes this fear (S 175). See Pasley about Kafka's habit of making immediate deletions and corrections (SKA 2: 73–77). Kafka recorded his first comment on Blüher's book on 16 June (T 363; D 2: 231), his second on 30 June (B 380; L 330). Chapter 15 was written prior to 23 June (SKA 2: 68). Rathenau was assassinated on 24 June.

[35]S 234 ("den Geruch ihrer Stube in den Kleidern"); C 320. This anti-Semitic reproach was well-known. Arthur Schopenhauer, e.g., characterized the Jews and Jewish tradition with the term *foetus Judaicus* (Jewish odor). See his *Parerga und*

so much contempt for them. He recalls his own initial antipathy toward them, which was not based on any particular thing one could explain. "How revolting all that had been, and all the more revolting because this impression could not be explained by details, for though one listed the details in order to have something to hold on to, they [the Barnabas family] were not bad, it was something else about it all that one could not put a name to."[36] Only after the whole family had, for him, broken up into individual persons, some of whom he could understand and feel friendly toward, did his revulsion subside. K. recognizes that the antipathy against the Barnabas family, a contempt mixed with fear, grips all the villagers, and that they have no rationale or explanation for it, either:

> I am now convinced that you are all being done an injustice. But though I don't know the reason, it must be difficult not to do you an injustice. One must be a stranger in my special situation in order to remain free of this prejudice. And I myself was for a long time influenced by it, so much influenced by it that the mood prevailing where you are concerned — it is not only contempt, there is fear mixed with it too — seemed a matter of course to me, I did not think about it, I did not inquire into the causes, I did not in the least try to defend you all ... one has to get to know you all, particularly you, Olga, in order to free oneself from the prevailing delusion.

Only a foreigner such as K. can see beyond the prejudice, can get to know the individual family members well enough not to succumb to this delusion. The deleted passage also reflects on the Messianic hope. Barnabas's phrase, "A Land-surveyor has arrived, he seems to have come for our sake," sounds both the Messianic motif of rescue from one's enemies and the Christian one of God's becoming man to atone for mankind's sins. The prevailing prejudice makes it plain, however, that such hopes are futile. The old letters Barnabas carries to K. are "no good to anyone and only [cause] confusion in the

Paralipomena, vol. 2, sections 177, 184 [Kafka owned a copy of this work]. See also the corresponding term *anrüchig* (for *disreputable*), in this context (S 211–12) applied to people out of official favor. Cf. also "Jackals and Arabs": "ein bitterer ... Geruch entströmte den offenen Mäulern" (E 133; CS 408). Brod passingly suggested that the Barnabas family's ostracism represents anti-Semitism (*Der Prager Kreis* 108); similarly Gerald Stieg, "Wer ist Kafkas Bote Barnabas?," *Austriaca* 17 (1983): 153.

[36]C 463; S 333. This refers to Blüher, who argued that the Germans had to make a universal break from the Jews because the old anti-Semitism's reliance on specific reproaches against Jews could always be refuted by specific counterexamples: "to each particular charge the anti-Semites make, the Jew will be able to give a particular answer in justification. Blüher makes a very superficial survey ... of the particular charges" (D 2: 231; T 364).

world." In the text that follows (or rather, replaces) the deleted passage Kafka steers away from an overt portrayal of anti-Semitism. K. cautions Olga not expect too much from Barnabas's messages, not to scrutinize "each single word of his as if it were a [word of] revelation, and base one's own life's happiness on the interpretation." Barnabas may not be able to recognize Klamm, and the letters he carries are discarded old ones, yet there is something of value offered to him at the offices.[37]

Olga's second deleted speech explains that the villagers' prejudice is so strong that if they did not despise her family, they would despise themselves. K. assures her that he will try to treat her and her family exactly the way he himself wants to be treated by others.[38] The best way to understand K.'s role is to see him as an assimilated Jew. He is well aware of the significance of his marrying Frieda, a "local woman," as a means of overcoming his outsider status and becoming an accepted member of the community. His remarks that as long as he is not married to Frieda and settled down in the village he is still free to choose his own company, and that he might consider a more intimate connection with Olga's family, show that he feels more at home with them than he does with the villagers. And yet he respects the force of the villagers' prejudice (almost that of an inviolable law) enough to consider avoiding any unnecessary contact with the family.[39] Whereas the deleted passages try to explain the social sanctions against the Barnabas family through racial prejudice, the chapter following them (called "Amalia's Secret") reinterprets the casting out of Amalia's family as a social exclusion or, rather, obscures it by making it a consequence of her disobedience to Sortini's illicit request. Frieda is the first of the villagers to spread the news about the incident involving Amalia and, along with Gardena, repeatedly justifies the ostracism. The villagers dread Amalie's refusal of the official's sexual request as if the refusal equaled some moral uncleanliness; they do not want to be "touched" by it,

---

[37]C 463–64; S 333–34. C 467; S 336 ("für uns gekommen"). C 462; S 332. C 239; S 176. S 176–77; C 240–41.

[38]S 338–42 [deleted from S 178]; SKA 2: 369–77; C 470–76. This deletion also happened instantly because prior to it K. reproaches Olga, and right after it Olga responds to the reproach (S 178; C 242); Olga's deleted phrase "Du verstehst unsere Not noch nicht" (S 336; C 467) is almost verbatim repeated in the passage that follows the deleted text ("Du kennst nicht unsere Not" - S 178; C 242). K.'s behavioral precept echoes Rabbi Hillel's summation of the Judaic faith and law: "What is hateful to you, do not do to your neighbor" (referred to by Eschelbacher, *Das Judentum und das Wesen des Christentums* 31, 74).

[39]S 74 ("eine Hiesige"); C 96. Cf. S 323 ("Gemeindemitglied — Rechte und Pflichten — kein Fremder"); C 447. According to Frieda, as a foreigner K. is treated here with severity and "injustice," he needs permission from the authorities to get married (S 329–30; C 457–58); in Austria before 1849, only the oldest son of a Jewish family could get a license to marry. Kafka's grandfather had been subject to this law (Wagenbach, *Franz Kafka* 16). S 340–41; C 474.

want to keep clear of it, want to preserve the purity of their institutions by excluding her family. Frieda calls Amalie the "most shameless of them all," unsuitable for marrying anyone in the village.[40] Kafka's initial portrayal of anti-Semitism reflects his own experience in Austria, intensified by Blüher's polemic, its immediate erasure his strong reserve toward lament over ethnic discrimination.[41] Pride in one's Jewish identity distinguishes his generation from "an older generation which mistook differentiating for exclusion."[42] Olga feels that it is necessary to speak of her family's misery but also realizes that their lament over being discriminated against feeds on itself. As has been pointed out already, the community's bias against the family is abetted by the elusive castle. The administrative (and, implicitly, constitutional) protection of their rights is undermined by an unspoken officious bias that Olga's father is unable to prove: "Could he perhaps refer to some official decree that had been issued against him? Father couldn't do that. [Or did an official agency commit an infringement? Father knew of none.] Well then, if he knew of nothing and nothing had happened, what did he want?" The father's hope of proving his innocence is as delusional as K.'s desire to penetrate the castle. During the distribution of files to the officials residing at the inn, one of the officials "did not want consolation, he wanted files." The bureaucracy is governed by its own self-preserving rationality; it rules out consolation, a term for Messianic hope.[43]

Calling the quasi-social racial prejudice a prevailing delusion, K. insists on distinguishing between false belief or deception — which the author put

[40]Olga says: "Three years ago we were [middle class] girls and Frieda an [orphan], a servant" (C 259; S 191). Olga's description of the menservants' lust ("ruled by their insatiable impulses instead of by [the laws]" - CS 285; S 210) matches Paul's admonition that Christian freedom from the law does not license fornication and lasciviousness (Gal. 5:19); Sortini's request can be seen in this light. S 198-99 ("in keiner Weise von ihr berührt werden"; "auf das sorgfältigste fernzuhalten"); C 268-69. S 194; C 264 ("the spotlessness of its reputation"). C 319; S 233. S 241; C 330.

[41]He is well aware of the lament's familiarity, speaking of the "Klagegeheul" and "Klageton" of the jackals (E 133-34; CS 407, 409) — "they were all lamenting and sobbing" (CS 409; E 134) — but his reaction against it is excessive. He chastises Arthur Holitscher's "Judenklage" (B 479; L 410), which is really minuscule (*Lebensgeschichte eines Rebellen: Meine Erinnerungen* [Berlin: Fischer, 1924] 108).

[42]Gustav Krojanker, preface, *Juden in der deutschen Literatur: Essays über zeitgenössische Schriftsteller*, ed. G. Krojanker (Berlin: Welt, 1922) 7-16; 12 [Kafka owned this book]. The remark was directed at Jakob Wassermann, who had just given a vivid account of the poisonous and pervasive German anti-Semitism in the late nineteenth century (*Mein Weg als Deutscher und Jude* [Frankfurt: Fischer, 1921]) 38-39, 46-47, 117-23).

[43]S 190 ("fangen wir zu klagen an, reißt es uns fort"); C 259. C 275; S 202. C 358; S 260.

forth in the parable about a man expecting to be admitted to the law though he never would — and delusion as a persistent (in *The Castle*, collective) disregard for veridical evidence. In his own encounters with anti-Semitism Kafka considers the question of veridical evidence decisive. Reading in 1920 in a Meran newspaper a lead article about Zionism and the anti-Semitic pamphlet *Protocols of the Learned Elders of Zion*, he notes that the article goes to a suspicious length to insist that the Russian scholar who published the secret protocols "really exists."[44] By the time of writing *The Castle,* he has realized that anti-Semitic hatred is beyond rational comprehension and cure. Contemplating the fateful assassination of Rathenau, he admits that this matter goes far beyond his mental horizon and later indicates that he has given up on the conflict-ridden Jewish-German relationship and on assimilation as "incurable." In *The Castle*, especially in several deleted passages, he brings together the cognitive and juridical themes found in his earlier works with religious-social techniques of inclusion and exclusion. As a puzzling deflection from his life-long struggle to free himself from an all-powerful law perceived as unjust, he realizes that exclusion from the community means to be left out of the law, without all legal protection.[45] The novel portrays a community in which officials and citizens are incapable of veridical cognition and belief, instituting just laws and applying them equally, or accepting a common humanity.

"The Hunger Artist," written shortly before or at the time of the deleted passages discussed above, alludes to the paradisiacal state before the institution of the Torah as well as to the expulsion from paradise.[46] The story con-

---

[44]L 235–36; B 273; the article reviewed a book by Friedrich Wichtl that quoted from the *Protocols* [later discovered to be a forgery]. During the same stay in Meran, confronted with rumors about Jewish soldiers infecting themselves with gonorrhea to avoid serving at the front, Kafka asks Brod whether this could possibly be true (B 275; L 237). A rigged 1916 survey by the Prussian War Ministry alleged that many Jews were shirking their military duty in the war (Jochmann, *Gesellschaftskrise und Judenfeindschaft* 110–11; Helmut Berding, *Moderner Antisemitismus in Deutschland* [Frankfurt: Suhrkamp, 1988] 168–70, 184).

[45]B 378; L 328. L 410; B 479. In 1910 he had seen his outsider role as a bachelor, his nonmembership in the community, as an exclusion from the law: "We are outside the law, no one knows it and yet everyone treats us accordingly" (D 1: 27; T 17).

[46]The story apparently was written on 23 May 1922 (SKA 2: 67). The fasting can be seen as a wish to undo the Fall, the eating of the fruit (Gerhard Neumann, "Hungerkünstler und Menschenfresser: Zum Verhältnis von Kunst und kulturellem Ritual im Werk Franz Kafkas," *Franz Kafka: Schriftverkehr*, ed. Kittler and Neumann, 415). The hunger artist's "stories out of his nomadic life" (CS 269; E 165) allude to the expulsion as well as to the motif of the wandering Jew; they also point to the professional hunger artists from the turn of the century (see Breon Mitchell, "Kafka and the Hunger Artists," *Kafka and the Contemporary Critical Performance* 236–55).

nects these motifs to the events of Christ's life.[47] One metaphorically dense passage suggests a connection between the semantic and the religious issues discussed in the present book: "[the hunger artist's] legs in a spasm of self-preservation clung close to each other at the knees, yet pawed [or scraped on] the ground [in such a way] as if it were not [the real one; the real one] they were only trying to find." The passage entails a double metaphor: it employs a word that expresses both pawing and scraping and plays on the meaning of *real*. The first part of the statement suggests that the hunger artist's legs are hobbled but he is pawing the ground with them as if eager to start running (as a horse might do). The second part suggests that he scrapes on the real ground as if it were not real, to uncover the real ground beneath it. The latter motif has mostly been understood as the hunger artist's search for a spiritual meaning or reality.[48] The connotations of *ground* in Kafka's later work, however, link both motifs — eagerness to start running and reaching out beyond the everyday real — to a communal (Jewish) home or ground.[49] Wanting to get away from a present condition and searching for a real ground, Kafka is saying here, encompasses, beyond the everyday reality we ascertain, something we hope for.

[47]Christ's birth: the hunger artist sat "not even on a seat but down among straw" (CS 268; E 164) [*seat* would have connoted the early stages of a criminal proceedings]. Temptation: the hunger artist fasts for forty days (Matt. 4:2). Crucifixion: the hunger artist takes "a sip ... of water to moisten his lips" (CS 268), "his head lolled on his breast ... his body was hollowed out" (CS 271); "sich die Lippen zu feuchten" (E 164), "der Leib war ausgehöhlt" (E 166).

[48]CS 271; "scharrten aber doch den Boden, so, als sei es nicht der wirkliche, den wirklichen suchten sie erst" (E 167). *Scharren* in German means both scraping and pawing. Kurz sees the scraping as a hermeneutic search for an allegorical meaning of existence (*Traumschrecken* 80). Of course, *ground* also has a literal meaning for Kafka; cf. Gregor's search for solid ground in "The Metamorphosis": "die Beinchen hatten festen Boden unter sich" (E 68; CS 102).

[49]"Most young [Jewish writers] wanted to leave Jewishness behind them ... with their posterior legs they were still glued to their father's Jewishness and with their waving anterior legs they found no new ground" (L 289; B 337); "The absence of any firm Jewish ground under my feet"(L 349; B 404). Robertson shows that Kafka was aware of the Zionists' use of *soil* as a term for tradition, cultural roots, membership in a community, and, ultimately, the soil of Palestine (*Kafka* 146–47, 159–60).

Appendix of German-Language Sources

[In quotes from unpublished sources, punctuation and spelling have been made to conform to standard grammar. Most words abbreviated in the original are here given in full.]

Introduction:

[1] "Aber doch freue ich mich des besonders guten Eindruckes, den beide eifrigen jungen Leute empfangen und der ihnen und Anderen, denen sie ja hier davon erzählen, so lebendig gezeigt hat, was für eine anderer Geist unsere Schule belebt als wie er in den Tempeln der Tagesgötzen zu Leipzig, Wien, München usw. waltet" (Anton Marty to Franz Brentano, 15 Sept. 1905).

[2] "Sie haben richtig vorausgesehen, daß Höfler hier auch eine philosophische Gesellschaft (als Dependance der Wiener) gründen wollte. Aber es ist ihm niemand hingegangen. Dagegen hat sich diesen Winter ein kleiner Verein von Philosophen gebildet, die ganz zu uns halten und von Christl [Christian von Ehrenfels] und Loisl [Alois Höfler] nichts wissen wollen" (Marty to Brentano, 13 Mar. 1905).

[3] "Die philosophischen Abende des Vereins, den unsere kleine Gemeinde hier bildet, scheinen heute sehr animiert und anregend werden zu wollen. Ich habe darauf gedrungen, daß man weniger oft zusammen komme, daß aber dafür die selteneren Abende regelmäßig besucht werden und einen mehr akademischen und weniger familiären Charakter haben. Bisher haben Aufzeichnungen, die sich Bergmann und Utitz bei Ihnen gemacht haben, als Grundlage der Diskussion gedient und sehr anregend und erfrischend gewirkt. Ich habe aber darauf aufmerksam gemacht, daß man vorsichtig sei, nicht auf diesem Wege zu Entlehnungen und Verballhornungen Anlaß zu geben. Da Bergmann sein Freiwilligen-Jahr hier abdient, kann auch er mit an den Versammlungen teilnehmen, und ebenso tuen es in der Regel die drei Dozenten" (Marty to Brentano, 19 Oct. 1906).

[4] "Bergmann ist durch das Seminar (das die beiden Frauen [Berta Fanta and Frieda Freund] besuchten) und den philosophischen Klub, dem sie angehörten

und der öfter in Ihrer Wohnung in Prag oder wohl auch hier in Podbaba sich versammelte, mit der Familie bekannt geworden" (Marty to Brentano, 20 Aug. 1906).

[5] "Hier haben wieder die philosophischen Abende begonnen, deren Thema bisher war, das, was wir bei Ihnen erfahren haben, nun gemeinsam zu besprechen. So führte uns auch der gestrige Abend zu den mannigfachen Fragen, von denen besonders zwei unsere Gemüter stark bewegten. Und da würde unsere Gesellschaft — der in diesem Jahre auch die drei Dozenten als ständige Besucher angehören — sehr gern wissen, wie Herr Professor dazu Stellung nehmen" (Emil Utitz to Brentano, 7 Oct. 1906).
"Unsere philosophische Gesellschaft hat nun wieder ihre Sitzungen im Sommer-Semester aufgenommen; vorige Woche brachte ich ein kritisches Referat über K. Langes 'Illusionstheorie'; diese Woche wird uns Dr. Lederer über seine — in Amerika gepflogenen — Studien an Kindergerichtshöfen berichten, die er auch gern in Österreich einführen möchte" (Utitz to Brentano, 1 May 1907).
"Morgen eröffnen wir die philosophischen Abende mit der Vorlesung meiner Abschrift Ihrer Abhandlung. So wird also ihr Geist über uns schweben" (Utitz to Brentano, 2 Oct. 1907). [According to Marty (Marty to Brentano, 4 Oct. 1907), the treatise referred to is Brentano's "Vom Begriff des Schönen." See Franz Brentano, *Grundzüge der Ästhetik*, ed. F. Mayer-Hillebrand (Bern: Francke, 1959) 123–35.]

[6] "[Ehrenfels hatte] seit langer Zeit weder mit mir, noch mit Eisenmeier und Kraus, irgend einen philosophischen Verkehr. Er nimmt auch nicht an den Abenden des philosophischen Klubs teil. (Freilich wünschen wir alle selbst nicht, daß er es tue.) Dagegen hat er eben am Tage, bevor ich Ihren Brief (der eine Abschrift des seinigen enthielt) erhalten habe, in der Höfler-Gesellschaft einen Vortrag gehalten" (Marty to Brentano, 14 May 1907).

[7] "[Es besteht nicht die mindeste Chance,] daß einer von unseren jungen Leuten, soweit sie Semiten sind, (und leider auch trotz empfangener Taufe nicht) an eine deutsche Universität berufen werde. So muß man in Österreich um so wachsamer sein und keine mögliche Stelle unberücksichtigt lassen, sonst erstickt in Folge an Mangel an genügend freier Luft Ihre ganze Schule" (Brentano to Marty, 17 Nov. 1908).

Chapter 1:

[8] "Das Umgewandeltwerden einer jüngeren (schwächeren) Vorstellung durch eine ältere, ihr an Macht und innerer Ausgeglichenheit überlegene führt den Namen der Apperception, im Gegensatz zur unveränderten Aufnahme

derselben, der Perception .... Die Apperception bringt in unser Seelenleben eine gewisse Stetigkeit und Festigkeit hinein ... [sie] ist die Reaction des Alten gegen das Neue — in ihr offenbart sich das Übergewicht, das die älteren, feststehenden und in sich geschlossenen Vorstellungskreise gegenüber den neu auftretenden Vorstellungen haben. Diese Übermacht kann sich bis zur Verfälschung der äußeren Wahrnehmung versteigen" (Gustav Lindner and Franz Lukas, *Lehrbuch der Psychologie* 93–94).

[9] "Da wir vermöge der Enge des Bewußtseins jeweilig nur eine sehr beschränkte Menge von Vorstellungen zu überschauen vermögen, so ist eine freie Reproduktion des weiten Gebietes der schon einmal bewußt gewesen Vorstellungen nur dadurch möglich, daß sie in wohlgefügte Reihen gebracht werden und wir mittels des Anschlages der Anfangsglieder beliebige und selbst entfernte Punkte der Reihen leicht erreichen können, ohne durch die von allen Seiten sich herandrängenden Vorstellungen behindert zu werden" (Lindner and Lukas, *Lehrbuch der Psychologie* 85–86).

[10] "Durch die Beziehung der Empfindung auf das äußere, durch sie zu unserem Bewußtsein gelangende Object wird die Empfindung zur Wahrnehmung" (Lindner and Lukas, *Lehrbuch der Psychologie* 16).
"Farbe, Klang, Geruch, Geschmack, Härtegrad, Gewicht, Wärme und Kälte sind Eigenthümlichkeiten im Verhalten der Außendinge, die wir mittelst der Empfindungen wahrnehmen und als Eigenschaften auf die Außendinge übertragen" (Lindner and Lukas, *Lehrbuch der Psychologie* 53).
"Projicieren wir nun diese mit dem Bewußtsein von der räumlichen Ausdehnung der berührten Hautstelle verbundene Empfindung auf den äußeren Gegenstand, von dem der Reiz herrührt, so gelangen wir zur Wahrnehmung der räumliche Ausdehnung des Gegenstandes" (Lindner and Lukas, *Lehrbuch der Psychologie* 61).

[11] "Während Gesichtswahrnehmungen nur zu Flächenbildern führen, die nicht selten auf 'optische Täuschungen' hinauslaufen, verschaffen wir uns mittelst der 'Handgreiflichkeit' des Hautsinnes die Überzeugung von der Solidität der Außendinge und von ihrer materiellen Eigenthümlichkeit. Beide Sinne wirken aufs innigste zusammen, so daß der Hautsinn nur ein derberes Schauen auf die unmittelbare Nähe (Tasten des Blinden), der Gesichtssinn nur ein feineres Tasten in die Ferne darstellt .... Die Hand wirkt mit dem Auge auf das innigste zusammen; ohne sie würde das Gebiet optischer Wahrnehmungen nur auf dasjenige beschränkt bleiben, was sich dem Auge von selbst zufällig darbietet, während wir gegenwärtig durch die Geschicklichkeit unserer Handgriffe die Objecte zwingen, ihr innerstes unserem Auge zu erschließen" (Lindner and Lukas, *Lehrbuch der Psychologie* 70–71).

[12] "Der Hallucinant sieht Landschaften, die nicht vorhanden (Visionen), und hört Stimmen von Personen, die nicht anwesend sind (Akoasmen). Dabei sind diese Erscheinungen so deutlich und die Stimmen so laut, daß er sie mit Wahrnehmungen verwechselt …. In den meisten Fällen fehlt nämlich die Grundbedingung für die Entstehung der sinnlichen Lebhaftigkeit, der physische Reiz, auch bei den Hallucinationen nicht ganz. Oft entstehen beim Hallucinanten directe Reizungen der centralen Theile des Nervensystems" (Lindner and Lukas, *Lehrbuch der Psychologie* 76).

[13] "Der Psychologe hat es nur mit diesen 'Sehdingen' zu tun, nicht aber mit dem, was etwa in Wirklichkeit unseren Sinnesqualitäten entspricht. Seine Aufmerksamkeit richtet sich auf das, was wir 'erleben', auf unsere Bewußtseinstatbestände" (Utitz, *Grundzüge der ästhetischen Farbenlehre* 1).

[14] "Zunehmende Dunkelheit legt sich nicht bloß *auf* die Dinge, sondern auch *zwischen* uns und die Dinge, um sie endlich ganz zu verdecken und allein den Raum zu füllen. Blicke ich in einen dunklen Kasten, so sehe ich denselben vom Dunkel *erfüllt*, und dasselbe wird nicht bloss als dunkle Farbe der Wände des Kastens gesehen" (Ewald Hering, "Der Raumsinn und die Bewegungen des Auges," *Handbuch der Physiologie*, ed. L. Hermann, 3.1: 573).

[15] "[a) Es ist] sicher, daß es neue Vorstellungen gibt, welche wir nicht ästhetisch werten. Welchen Teil der neuen Vorstellungen werten wir also ästhetisch? Die Frage bleibt. b) Es wäre notwendig, die 'ästhetische Apperception', einen bisher vielleicht nicht eingeführten Ausdruck, ausführlicher oder eigentlich überhaupt zu erklären. Wie entsteht jenes Lustgefühl und worin besteht seine Eigenart, wodurch unterscheidet es sich von der Freude über eine neue Entdeckung oder über Nachrichten aus einem fremden Land oder Wissensgebiet. c) Der hauptsächliche Beweis für die neue Ansicht ist eine allgemeine physiologische, nicht nur ästhetische Tatsache, und das ist die Ermüdung. Nun ergibt sich einerseits aus deinen vielen Einschränkungen des Begriffes 'neu', daß eigentlich alles neu ist, denn da alle Gegenstände in immer wechselnder Zeit und Beleuchtung stehn und wir Zuschauer nicht anders, so müssen wir ihnen immer an einem anderen Ort begegnen. Andererseits aber ermüden wir nicht nur beim Genießen der Kunst, sondern auch beim Lernen und Bergsteigen und Mittagessen, ohne daß wir sagen dürften, das Kalbfleisch sei keine uns entsprechende Speise mehr, weil wir heute ihrer müde sind. Vor allem aber wäre es unrecht zu sagen, daß es dieses doppelte Verhältnis zur Kunst gebe. Lieber also: der Gegenstand schwebt über der ästhetischen Kante und Müdigkeit (die es eigentlich nur zur Liebhaberei der knapp vorhergehenden Zeit gibt), also: der Gegenstand hat das Gleichgewicht verloren, und zwar im üblen Sinn. Und doch drängt deine

Folgerung zum Arrangieren dieses Gegensatzes, denn Apperception ist kein Zustand, sondern eine Bewegung, also muß sie sich vollenden. Es entsteht ein wenig Lärm, dazwischen dieses bedrängte Lustgefühl, aber bald muß alles in seinen gehöhlten Lagern ruhen. d) [Es] gibt einen Unterschied zwischen ästhetischen und wissenschaftlichen Menschen. e) Das Unsichere bleibt der Begriff 'Apperception'. So wie wir ihn kennen, ist es kein Begriff der Ästhetik" etc. (Franz Kafka, in Max Brod, *Der Prager Kreis* 94–95).

[16] "Die rasche Abnahme der Empfindung bei starker Zunahme des Reizes schützt das empfindende Wesen. Die Tatsache der Schwelle sichert uns erst die Möglichkeit der Ruhe, die wir nicht genießen könnten, wenn jeder Reiz auf uns einstürmen könnte" (Hugo Bergmann, rev. of *Psychophysik: Historisch-kritische Studien über experimentelle Psychologie*, by Constantin Gutberlet, *Philosophische Wochenschrift* 3 (1906): 116).

[17] "[Stumpf] denkt gar nicht daran, daß das Gefühl in Einem Akt untrennbar mit der anschaulichen Vorstellung einer Sinnesqualität zusammengegeben sein und darum an ihrer Intensität und überhaupt an ihrem ganzen Charakter Teil haben kann, ohne eine Eigenschaft eines der Momente des Sinnesinhalts selbst zu sein, indem es vielmehr eine neue (zur Gattung: Liebe und Haß gehörige) Beziehungsweise zu diesem Inhalt ist" (Marty to Brentano, 2 Feb. 1907).

[18] "Allem Gefühl muß doch zumindest eine Vorstellung zugrundeliegen; ich liebe und hasse ja immer etwas. — Nun gibt es Fälle, wo anscheinend diese Vorstellung fehlt! der Schmerz einer entzündeten Stelle; eine Temperaturempfindung, die allmählich beim Stärkerwerden ganz durch die Schmerzempfindung verdrängt wird und in beiden Fällen richtet sich meiner Meinung nach das Gefühl nur auf die Schmerzempfindung; die wird gehaßt. Soll die Schmerzempfindung wieder ein Gefühl sein, müßte sie wieder an eine Vorstellung anknüpfen; die ist aber rein descriptiv gar nicht gegeben; so wie bei einer zu heißen Suppe keine Geschmacks- sondern nur eine Temperaturempfindung gegeben ist, da kann dann auch die Geschmacksempfindung nicht wirken" (Utitz to Brentano, 12 Jan. 1907).

[19] "Es handelt sich um eine Frage, über die wir diese Woche lebhaft disputierten: Werden Interessenphänomene direkt physiologisch verursacht (wie Empfindungen) oder psychologisch durch andere psychische Phaenomene? Oder in manchen Fällen so, in anderen Fällen wieder auf die erste Art? Das letztere (nämlich eine bejahende Antwort auf die zweite Frage) scheint uns das wahrscheinlichste" (Utitz to Brentano, 19 Oct. 1907) [*Interessenphänomen* is the term for the [Brentanoan] intellectual acts of love and hate as the basis for pleasure and pain].

Chapter 2:

[20] "Ein Percipieren ist jedes Sehen. Ich sehe etwas vor mir, könnte aber nicht genau Gestalt, Größe, etc. beschreiben. Das alles appercipiere ich hinterher, vielleicht eines nach dem anderen oder mehreres auf einmal. Ich sehe einen Baum, dann aber appercipiere ich im einzelnen Äste, Blätter und Blüten. Das sind lauter Apperceptionen, welche explicite Gegenstand des Beurteilens wurde (*sic*), während es implicite bereits im Percipieren vorhanden war .... Man geht durch eine Straße, wieviel sieht man da, wie wenig wird bemerkt, d.h. appercipiert" (MA 25-28).

[21] "Wir haben im Zimmer vieles unter Perception gegeben, wenn ich nun einen Gegenstand nenne, so wird er appercipiert. Je genauer die Bezeichnung, desto schärfer wird die Apperception sein. Eigentlich ist ja der Name etwas ganz anderes, ein Laut. Warum appercipiert man nun beim Aussprechen des Lautes eine Farbe beispielsweise? Das ist die Association, wodurch verschiedenes in der Seele verkettet werden kann. Durch die Bennennung von etwas wird die Apperception des Betreffenden begünstigt" (MA 48).

Chapter 3:

[22] "Man spricht wohl auch von der äußeren Wahrnehmung, wie es das Wahrnehmen eines Tones ist, aber das ist nicht ein unmittelbar einsichtiges Erfassen des Objectes, vielmehr bloß ein blindes Anerkennen desselben, was schon daraus hervorgeht, das ja dieses Führwahrhalten des Tones falsch ist. Der Ton existiert nicht in Wirklichkeit, in Wirklichkeit existieren Schwingungen. Man hat das nur Wahrnehmung genannt, weil man fälschlich meinte, man erfasse eine Tatsache mit unmittelbarer Sicherheit. In Wahrheit hat eine nähere Untersuchung gezeigt, daß alles, was wir von der Außenwelt mit Sicherheit wissen nur erschlossen ist. Was wir unmittelbar wahrzunehmen glauben, ist nur eine Erscheinung" (MA 123).

[23] "Warum nehmen wir denn überhaupt eine Außenwelt an, wo sich doch unsere Erfahrung nur aus *unsern* psychischen Zuständen zusammensetzt und wir weder das Dasein von Körpern, noch das von anderen Seelenleben unmittelbar ersehen? Offenbar ist der Glaube an eine Außenwelt nur durch eine Hypothese gestützt .... Meine psychischen Zustände verlaufen so, *als ob* sie durch Körper und andere psychische Wesen mitgewirkt wären. Über dieses 'als ob' kommen wir nicht hinaus. Und wenn wir von einem 'du' und 'er' sprechen, so ist das ein Bild, eine Analogie, nicht mehr" (Bergmann, "Das philosophische Bedürfnis in der modernen Physik," *Philosophische Wochenschrift* 1 (1906): 337).

[24] "In jedem psychischen Akte ist tatsächlich eine Mehrheit von psychischen Beziehungen gegeben, indem jeder psychische Akt nebenher ein Bewußtsein von sich selbst ist .... Wenn ich mir bewußt bin, daß ich jetzt etwas höre, so sind in diesem Akt zwei Beziehungen gegeben[:] das eine ist gerichtet auf den Ton, das andere auf das Bewußtsein des Tones, nämlich das Hören .... Jeder psychische Akt involviert eine doppelte Beziehung, und diese sind zwar unterscheidbar aber nicht tatsächlich trennbar" (MA 106-107).

[25] "Und warum kann diese Selbstgegenwart, wodurch wir uns als sehend, hörend, liebend, hoffend, anerkennend beurteilen, den Charakter eines unmittelbar evidenten Erfassens haben. Weil dieses innere Urteil nicht ein zweiter Akt ist neben dem Sehen und Hören, Fürchten und Hoffen, welche darin wahrgenommen werden, sondern weil es zum Akte gehört, wie das Wahrgenommene selbst ... weil hier das Wahrgenommene und Wahrnehmen, d.h. das anerkennende Urteil, zu derselben Realität gehört, ist es möglich, daß das innere Urteil unmittelbar evident ist" (MA 123-24).

Chapter 4:

[26] "Hier hat [Helmholtz] die für die *zweckmäßige Funktion unserer Sinne* wichtige Tatsache konstatiert, daß wir auf unsere Sinnesempfindungen nur soweit aufmerksam werden, als wir für die Erkenntnis äußerer Objekte verwerten können, daß wir dagegen von allen jenen Bestandteilen des Empfundenen abzusehen gewohnt sind, welche keine Bedeutung für unsere Orientierung in der Außenwelt haben. So werden die subjektiven Gesichtserscheinungen, ebenso die Nach- und Doppelbilder gar nicht bemerkt" (Bergmann, rev. of *Hermann von Helmholtz' psychologische Anschauungen*, by Friedrich Conrat, *Philosophische Wochenschrift* 2 [1906]: 251–52).

Chapter 6:

[27] "Indem der Verwaltungsgerichtshof die angefochtene Entscheidung oder Verfügung lediglich vernichtet, ohne eine andere an ihre Stelle zu setzen, bleibt seine Einwirkung zweifellos auf die Feststellung des durch das administrative Vorgehen tangierten individuellen Rechtskreises beschränkt; die Angelegenheit kehrt in den administrativen Machtkreis zurück und ist im ganzen neuerlich Gegenstand der administrativen Einflußnahme" (Karl Freiherr von Lemayer, "Die Verwaltungsgerichtsbarkeit und der Verwaltungsgerichtshof," Österreichisches Staatswörterbuch, ed. Mischler and Ulbrich [1909] 4: 33).

[28] "Der Richter [empfängt] nicht nur das Gebot der Gesetzestreue, sondern die wichtigsten Vorschriften für sein Verhalten überhaupt nicht von dem positiven Recht, sondern von der Ethik. Ich denke hier nicht nur an jene Fälle, wo das Gesetz selbst den Richter anweist, nach den Grundsätzen der Billigkeit, nach 'billigem Ermessen' vorzugehen; hierher gehören insbesondere auch jene Situationen, in denen es die Pflicht des Richters ist, die Lücken des gesetzten Rechtes auszufüllen ... wo uns das Gesetz im Stich läßt, ist die Entscheidung im Sinne des natürlich Gerechten, d. h. dessen, was in Erwägung aller Umstände recht und billig ist, zu erfüllen" (Oskar Kraus, "Rechtsphilosophie und Jurisprudenz," *Zeitschrift für die gesamte Strafrechtswissenschaft* 23 [1903]: 778–79).

[29] "Es ist nun recht merkwürdig, daß die Gesetze nichts darüber sagen, was denn rechtens sei, wenn der als *criminal* Erklärte die Bewährungsfrist gut besteht; sie erklären lediglich, daß dann die Aufsicht aufgehoben werden solle; nur das Gesetz des Staates Kalifornien hat auf die Wichtigkeit der Regelung dieser Frage Bedacht genommen und bestimmt, daß der unter Aufsicht Gestellte dann freigesprochen werden solle; freilich ist dies inkonsequent: denn er wurde doch vorher schuldig gesprochen! ... drei der vorerwähnten Spezialgesetze [laws of three states] ... bestimmen, daß nach günstigem Ablauf der Bewährungsfrist der Schuldspruch ungiltig wird" (Herbert Lederer, "Das *probation system* in den Vereinigten Staaten von Nordamerika," *Allgemeine österreichische Gerichtszeitung* 59 [1908]: 99).

Works Consulted

Abraham, Ulf. *Der verhörte Held: Verhöre, Urteile, und die Rede von Recht und Schuld im Werk Franz Kafkas*. Munich: Fink, 1985.

——. *Franz Kafka: Die Verwandlung*. Frankfurt: Diesterweg, 1993.

Die Advokatenordnung. Commentary by Hanns Christl. *Österreichische Gesetzkunde: Kommentare zum Gebrauch für Juristen und Nichtjuristen*, edited by Max Leopold Ehrenreich, vol. 3, 785–830. Vienna: Patriotische Volksbuchhandlung, 1912.

Allemann, Beda. "Scheinbare Leere: Zur thematischen Struktur von Kafkas *Schloß-Roman*." In *Mélanges offerts à Claude David*, edited by Jean-Louis Bandet, 1–35. Bern: Lang, 1986.

Anderson, Mark M. *Kafka's Clothes: Ornament and Aestheticism in the Habsburg Fin-de-Siècle*. Oxford: Clarendon, 1992.

Anscombe, G. E. M. *The Collected Philosophical Papers*. 2 vols. Minneapolis: University of Minnesota Press, 1981.

Arneson, Richard J. "Power and Authority in *The Castle*." *Mosaic* 12 (1979): 99–113.

Auerbach, Erich. *Mimesis: The Representation of Reality in Western Literature*. Translated by Willard Trask. Princeton: Princeton University Press, 1953.

Ayer, A. J. *Russell and Moore: The Analytic Heritage*. London: MacMillan, 1971.

Bahr, Hermann. *Die Überwindung des Naturalismus: Zweite Reihe von "Zur Kritik der Moderne."* Dresden: Pierson, 1891.

Beck, Evelyn Torton. *Kafka and the Yiddish Theater*. Madison: University of Wisconsin Press, 1971.

——. "Kafka's Traffic in Women: Gender, Power, and Sexuality." *Literary Review* 26 (1983): 565–76.

Beicker., Peter U. *Franz Kafka: Eine kritische Einführung in die Forschung*. Frankfurt: Athenaion, 1974.

———. "*Berechnung* und *Kunstaufwand* in Kafka's Erzählrhetorik." In *Franz Kafka: Eine Aufsatzsammlung nach einem Symposium in Philadelphia*, edited by Maria Luise Caputo-Mayr, 216–34. Berlin: Agora, 1978.

———. "Erzählweise." In *Kafka-Handbuch*, edited by Hartmut Binder, 2: 36–48.

Bergmann, Hugo. "Das philosophische Bedürfnis in der modernen Physik." *Philosophische Wochenschrift* 1 (Jan.–Mar. 1906): 332–38.

———. Review of *Johannes Müllers philosophische Anschauungen*, by Karl Post. *Philosophische Wochenschrift* 2 (Apr.–June 1906): 186–88.

———. Review of *Hermann von Helmholtz' psychologische Anschauungen*, by Friedrich Conrat. *Philosophische Wochenschrift* 2 (Apr.–June 1906): 251–52.

———. Review of *Psychophysik: Historisch-kritische Studien über experimentelle Psychologie*, by Constantin Gutberlet. *Philosophische Wochenschrift* 3 (July–Sept. 1906): 114–22.

———. *Untersuchungen zum Problem der Evidenz der inneren Wahrnehmung*. Halle: Niemeyer, 1908.

———. "Das philosophische Werk Bernard Bolzanos," *Deutsche Arbeit* 8 (1908–09): 81–89.

———. *Das philosophische Werk Bernard Bolzanos*. Halle: Niemeyer, 1909.

———. "Über den analytischen Charakter des Existenztheorems in der reinen Mathematik." *Annalen der Naturphilosophie* 8 (1909): 495–502.

———. "Über Bücher und über das Lesen." *Herder-Blätter* [Johann Gottfried Herder Vereinigung, Prague] 1.1 (1911–12): 4–8.

———, ed. "Briefe Franz Brentanos an Hugo Bergmann." *Philosophy and Phenomenological Research* 7 (1946–47): 83–158.

Bergman, Shmuel Hugo. "Erinnerungen an Franz Kafka." *Universitas* 27 (1972): 739–50.

Bergman, Schmuel Hugo. *Tagebücher und Briefe*. Edited by Miriam Sambursky. 2 vols. Königstein: Athenäum, 1985.

Berding, Helmut: *Moderner Antisemitismus in Deutschland*. Frankfurt: Suhrkamp, 1988.

Binder, Hartmut. "Kafka und die Wochenzeitschrift *Selbstwehr.*" *Deutsche Viertel-jahrsschrift für Literatur- und Geistesgeschichte* 41 (1967): 283–304.

———. *Kafka Kommentar zu sämtlichen Erzählungen.* Munich: Winkler, 1975.

———. *Kafka in neuer Sicht: Mimik, Gestik und Personengefüge als Darstellungsformen des Autobiographischen.* Stuttgart: Metzler, 1976.

———. "Der Mensch." In *Kafka-Handbuch*, edited by Hartmut Binder, 1: 103–584.

———. *Kafka Kommentar zu den Romanen, Rezensionen, Aphorismen und zum Brief an den Vater.* 2nd ed. Munich: Winkler, 1982.

———. *Kafka: Der Schaffensprozeß.* Frankfurt: Suhrkamp, 1983.

———. *"Vor dem Gesetz": Einführung in Kafkas Welt.* Stuttgart and Weimar: Metzler, 1993.

Blüher, Hans. *Secessio Judaica: Philosophische Grundlegung der historischen Situation des Judentums und der antisemitischen Bewegung.* Berlin: Der Weiße Ritter, 1922.

———. *Die Aristie des Jesus von Nazareth: Philosophische Grundlegung der Lehre und Erscheinung Christi.* Prien: Kampmann, 1921.

———, and Hans-Joachim Schoeps. *Streit um Israel: Ein jüdisch-christliches Gespräch.* Hamburg: Hanseatische Verlagsanstalt, 1933.

Boa, Elizabeth. "Feminist Approaches to Kafka's *The Castle*," In *New Ways in Germanistik*, edited by Richard Sheppard, 112–27. New York, Oxford, and Munich: Berg, 1990.

Born, Jürgen, Ludwig Dietz, Malcolm Pasley, Paul Raabe, and Klaus Wagenbach, eds. *Kafka-Symposium.* Berlin: Wagenbach, 1965.

Born, Jürgen. "Kafka's Parable *Before the Law*: Reflections Towards a Positive Interpretation." *Mosaic* 3 (1970): 153–62.

———, ed. *Franz Kafka: Kritik und Rezeption zu seinen Lebzeiten, 1912–1924.* Frankfurt: Fischer, 1979.

———. *Kafkas Bibliothek: Ein beschreibendes Verzeichnis.* Frankfurt: Fischer, 1990.

Brentano, Franz. *Psychologie vom empirischen Standpunkt.* Vol. 1. Leipzig: Duncker & Humblot, 1874.

———. *Untersuchungen zur Sinnespsychologie.* Leipzig: Duncker & Humblot, 1907.

——. *Psychologie vom empirischen Standpunkt*. Edited by Oskar Kraus. 2 vols. Leipzig: Meiner, 1924–25.

——. *Vom Ursprung sittlicher Erkenntnis*. Edited by Oskar Kraus, 4th ed. Hamburg: Meiner, 1955.

——. *Die Lehre vom richtigen Urteil*. Edited by Franziska Mayer-Hillebrand. Bern: Francke, 1956.

——. *Die Abkehr vom Nichtrealen*. Edited by Franziska Mayer-Hillebrand. Bern: Francke, 1966.

——. *Deskriptive Psychologie*. Edited by Roderick Chisholm and Wilhelm Baumgartner. Hamburg: Meiner, 1982.

Brod, Max. "Zwillingspaar von Seelen: Ein skizzirter Roman." *Die Gegenwart* (7 Oct. 1905): 220–21.

——. "Zur Ästhetik." *Die Gegenwart* (17 Feb. 1906): 102–4; (24 Feb. 1906): 118–19.

——. *Tod den Toten: Novellen des Indifferenten, 1902–1906*. Berlin: Juncker, 1906.

——. *Jüdinnen*. Leipzig: Wolff, 1915.

——. "Die erste Stunde nach dem Tode," *Die weißen Blätter* 3 (1916): 223–56.

——. *Heidentum, Christentum, Judentum: Ein Bekenntnisbuch*. 2 vols. Munich: Wolff, 1921.

——. *Der Prager Kreis*. Stuttgart: Kohlhammer, 1966.

——. *Streitbares Leben, 1884–1968*. Munich, Berlin, and Vienna: Herbig, 1969.

——. *Über Franz Kafka*. Frankfurt: Fischer Taschenbuch, 1974.

——, and Felix Weltsch. *Anschauung und Begriff: Grundzüge eines Systems der Begriffsbildung*. Leipzig: Wolff, 1913.

——, and Hans-Joachim Schoeps. *Im Streit um das Judentums: Briefwechsel*. Eited by Julius H. Schoeps. Königstein: Athenäum, 1985.

——, and Franz Kafka. *Eine Freundschaft*. Vol. 1, *Reiseaufzeichnungen*. Edited by Malcolm Pasley and Hannelore Rodlauer. Frankfurt: Fischer, 1987.

——, and Franz Kafka. *Eine Freundschaft*. Vol. 2, *Ein Briefwechsel*. Edited by Malcolm Pasley. Frankfurt: Fischer, 1989.

Bühler, Karl. "The Psychophysics of Expression of Wilhelm Wundt." In: Wilhelm Wundt, *The Languages of Gestures*, edited by Arthur Blumenthal, 30–54. The Hague: Mouton, 1973.

Busse, Ludwig. *Geist und Körper: Seele und Leib*. Leipzig: Dürr, 1903.

Buxton, Claude E., ed. *Points of View in the Modern History of Psychology*. Orlando: Academic Press, 1985.

Caputo-Mayr, Maria, and Julius Herz. *Franz Kafka: Eine kommentierte Bibliographie der Sekundärliteratur, 1955–1980 (mit einem Nachtrag 1985)*. Bern und Stuttgart: Francke Verlag, 1987.

——, and Julius Herz. "Franz Kafka: Articles in Periodicals and Books. An Update, 1980–1992." *Journal of the Kafka Society of America* 14.1.2 (1990): 4–50.

Chisholm, Roderick. *Brentano and Intrinsic Value*. Cambridge: Cambridge University Press, 1986.

——. "Brentano's Theory of Pleasure and Pain." *Topoi* 6 (1987): 59–64.

Cohen, Hermann. *Deutschtum und Judentum*. Gießen: Töpelmann, 1915.

Cohn, Dorrit. "K. Enters *The Castle*." *Euphorion* 62 (1968): 28–45.

——. *Transparent Minds: Narrative Modes for Presenting Consciousness in Fiction*. Princeton: Princeton University Press, 1978.

——. "The Encirclement of Narrative." *Poetics Today* 2.2 (1981): 157–82.

Cooper, David. *Metaphor*. Oxford: Blackwell, 1986.

Corngold, Stanley. *The Fate of the Self: German Writers and French Theory*. New York: Columbia University Press, 1986.

——. *Franz Kafka: The Necessity of Form*. Ithaca: Cornell University Press, 1988.

Dasenbrock, Reed W., ed. *Literary Theory After Davidson*. Pennsylvania State University Press, 1993.

David, Claude, ed. *Franz Kafka: Themen und Probleme*. Göttingen: Vandenhoeck & Ruprecht, 1980.

——. "Die Geschichte Abrahams: Zu Kafkas Auseinandersetzung mit Kierkegaard." In *Bild und Gedanke*. Festschrift für Gerhart Baumann, edited by Günter Schnitzler, Gerhard Neumann, and Jürgen Schröder, 79–90. Munich: Fink, 1980.

Davidson, Donald. "What Metaphors Mean." In *On Metaphor*, edited by Sheldon Sacks, 29–45. University of Chicago Press, 1978.

———. "What Metaphors Mean." In *Philosophical Perspectives on Metaphor*, edited by Mark Johnson, 200–220. Minneapolis: University of Minnesota Press, 1981.

Delbrück, Bertold. Grundfragen der Sprachforschung. Straßburg: Trübner, 1901.

Deleuze, Gilles, and Félix Guattari. *Kafka: Toward a Minor Literature.* Translated by Dana Polan. Minneapolis: University of Minnesota Press, 1986.

Demetz, Hans. "Meine persönlichen Beziehungen und Erinnerungen an den Prager deutschen Dichterkreis." In *Weltfreunde: Konferenz über die Prager deutsche Literatur*, edited by Eduard Goldstücker, 135–45. Prague: Academia, 1967.

Derrida, Jacques. "Devant La Loi." In *Kafka and the Contemporary Critical Performance*, edited by Alan Udoff, 128–49.

Descartes, René. *The Philosophical Works of Descartes.* Translated by Elizabeth Haldane and G. R. T. Ross. 2 vols. Cambridge: Cambridge University Press, 1970.

Devitt, Michael, and Kim Sterelny. *Language and Reality: An Introduction to the Philosophy of Language.* Oxford: Blackwell, 1987.

Dodd, W. J. *Kafka and Dostoyevsky: The Shaping of Influence.* New York: St. Martin's Press, 1992.

Doležel, Lubomír. "Kafka's Fictional World." *Canadian Review of Comparative Literature* 11 (1984): 61–83.

Dornemann, Axel. *Im Labyrinth der Bürokratie: Tolstois "Auferstehung" und Kafkas "Das Schloß."* Heidelberg: Winter, 1984.

Dowden, Stephen D. *Sympathy for the Abyss: A Study in the Novel of German Modernism: Kafka, Broch, Musil, and Thomas Mann.* Tübingen: Niemeyer, 1986.

Ehrenfels, Christian von. "Über Gestaltqualitäten." *Vierteljahrsschrift für wissenschaftliche Philosophie* 14 (1890): 249–92.

———. *System der Werttheorie.* 2 vols. Leipzig: Reisland, 1897–98.

———. *Sozialethik.* Wiesbaden: Bergmann, 1907.

Ehrenstein, Albert. "Ansichten eines Exterritorialen." *Die Fackel* 323 (1911): 1–8.

Ehrlich, Eugen. "Freie Rechtsfindung und freie Rechtswissenschaft." In Eugen Ehrlich, *Recht und Leben*, edited by Manfred Rehbinder, 170–202. Berlin: Duncker & Humblot, 1967.

Eisenmeier, Josef. *Untersuchungen zur Helligkeitsfrage.* Halle: Niemeyer, 1905.

——. Review of *Physiologische Optik*, by Ewald Hering (*Handbuch der gesamten Augenheilkunde*, edited by A. K. Graefe and Th. Saemisch, vol. 3, pt. 1). *Deutsche Arbeit* 5 (1905–1906): 155–58.

Ellis, John. "The Bizarre Texture of *The Judgment*." In *The Problem of "The Judgment*," edited by Angel Flores, 73–96.

Elm, Theo. *"Der Prozeß."* In *Kafka-Handbuch*, edited by Hartmut Binder, 2: 420–40.

Emrich, Wilhelm, and Bernd Goldmann, eds. *Franz Kafka: Symposium, 1983.* Mainz: v. Hase & Koehler, 1985.

Engländer, Richard. "Die Renaissance des Naturrechts." *Der Kampf* 1 (1907–1908): 547–52.

Eschelbacher, Joseph. *Das Judentum und das Wesen des Christentums: Vergleichende Studien.* Berlin: Poppelauer, 1908.

Fechner, Gustav Th. *Vorschule der Ästhetik.* 2 vols. Leipzig: Breitkopf & Härtel, 1876.

Fingerhut, Karlheinz. "Die Phase des Durchbruchs." In *Kafka-Handbuch*, edited by Hartmut Binder, 2: 262–313.

Fischer, Jens Malte. *Fin de siècle: Kommentar zur einer Epoche.* Munich: Winkler, 1978.

Flaubert, Gustave. "Tagebuch des jungen Flaubert." *Pan* 1 (1910–11): 181–88.

Flores, Angel, ed. *The Problem of "The Judgment": Eleven Approaches to Kafka's Story.* New York: Gordian, 1977.

——, ed. *The Kafka Debate: New Perspectives for Our Time.* New York: Gordian, 1977.

Frege, Gottlob. *Translations from the the Philosophical Writings of Gottlob Frege.* Edited by Peter Geach and Max Black. Totowa, N. J.: Rowman & Littlefield, 1952.

Freud, Sigmund. *Gesammelte Werke: Chronologisch geordnet.* Edited by Anna Freud. 18 vols. London: Imago, 1940–52.

Friedländer, Moriz. *Die religiösen Bewegungen innerhalb des Judentums im Zeitalter Jesu.* Berlin: Reimer, 1905.

Frye, Lawrence O. "Reconstructions: Kafka's *Ein Landarzt*." *Colloquia Germanica* 16 (1983): 321–36.

Fuchs, Ernst. *Schreibjustiz und Richterkönigtum*. Leipzig: Teutonia, 1907.

——. *Gerechtigkeitswissenschaft*. Edited by Albert Foulkes and Arthur Kaufmann. Karlsruhe: Müller, 1965.

Gabriel, Gottfried. "Why a Proper Name has Meaning: Marty and Landgrebe vs. Kripke." In *Mind, Meaning and Metaphysics*, edited by Kevin Mulligan, 67–75.

Geach, Peter. *Mental Acts: Their Content and Their Object*. London: Routledge & Kegan Paul, 1957.

Genette, Gérard. *Narrative Discourse Revisited*. Translated by Jane E. Lewin. Ithaca: Cornell University Press, 1988.

Göhler, Hulda. *Franz Kafka: Das Schloß "Ansturm gegen die Grenze": Entwurf einer Deutung*. Bonn: Bouvier & Grundmann, 1982.

Gold, Hugo, ed. *Max Brod: Ein Gedenkbuch 1884–1968*. Tel-Aviv: Olamenu, 1969.

Gorman, David. "Discovery and Recovery in the Philosophy of Language: Dummett and Frege." *Diacritics* 31 (1983): 43–62.

Gray, Ronald. "Through Dream to Self-Awareness." In *The Problem of "The Judgment,"* edited by Angel Flores, 63–72.

Grimm, Robert H. and Daniel D. Merrill, eds. *Contents of Thought*. Tucson: University of Arizona Press, 1985.

Grözinger, Karl Erich, Stéphane Mosès, and Hans Dieter Zimmermann, eds. *Kafka und das Judentum*. Frankfurt: Athenäum, 1987.

Grözinger, Karl Erich. "Himmlische Gerichte, Wiedergänger und Zwischenweltliche in der ostjüdischen Erzählung." In *Franz Kafka und das Judentum*, edited by Karl Erich Grözinger, Stéphane Mosès, and Hans Dieter Zimmermann, 93–112.

——. *Kafka und die Kabbala: Das Jüdische in Werk und Denken von Franz Kafka*. Frankfurt: Eichborn, 1992.

Groß, Alfred. "Zur psychologischen Tatbestandsdiagnostik." *Monatsschrift für Kriminalpsychologie und Strafrechtsreform* 2 (1905–1906): 182–84.

——. "Zur psychologischen Tatbestandsdiagnostik als kriminalistisches Hilfsmittel." *Allgemeine österreichische Gerichtszeitung* 56 (1905): 133–34.

——. "Die Assoziationsmethode im Strafprozeß." *Zeitschrift für die gesamte Strafrechtswissenschaft* 26 (1906): 19–40; 27 (1907): 175–212.

Groß, Hans. "Zur Frage des Wahrnehmungsproblems." *Allgemeine österreichische Gerichtszeitung* 56 (1905): 51–54; 59–60.

——. "Zur psychologischen Tatbestandsdiagnostik." *Archiv für Kriminalanthropologie und Kriminalistik* 19 (1905): 49–59.

——. "Über Zeugenprüfung." *Monatsschrift für Kriminalpsychologie und Strafrechtsreform* 3 (1906–1907): 577–80.

Grossmann, Reinhardt. *Meinong*. London: Routledge & Kegan Paul, 1974.

Hacking, Ian. *Why Does Language Matter to Philosophy?* Cambridge: Cambridge University Press, 1975.

Haldane, John. "Brentano's Problem." *Grazer philosophische Studien* 35 (1989): 1–33.

Haller, Rudolf, ed. *Jenseits von Sein und Nichtsein: Beiträge zur Meinong-Forschung*. Graz: Akademische Druck- und Verlagsanstalt, 1972.

Hare, R. M. *Freedom and Reason*. Oxford: Clarendon, 1963.

Harris, Roy. *Reading Saussure: A Critical Commentary*. London: Duckworth, 1987.

Hart, H. L. A. "The Ascription of Responsibility and Rights." In *Logic and Language*. First Series. Edited by Anthony Flew, 145–66. Oxford: Blackwell, 1960.

Heanue, James. "Editor's Introduction." In: Alexius Meinong, *On Assumptions*, ix–xlviii.

Hecht, Hugo. "Zwölf Jahre in der Schule mit Franz Kafka." Prager Nachrichten 17.8 (1966): 1–7.

Hegel, Georg Wilhelm Friedrich. *Grundlinien der Philosophie des Rechts*. Edited by Georg Lasson. Leipzig: Meiner, 1911.

Heidsieck, Arnold. "Logic and Ontology in Kafka's Fiction," *Germanic Review* 61 (1986): 11–17.

——. "Logic and Ontology in Kafka's Fiction," In *The Dove and the Mole: Kafka's Journey into Darkness and Creativity*, edited by Moshe Lazar and Ronald Gottesman, 199–212. Malibu: Undena, 1987.

——. "Kafka's Narrative Ontology," *Philosophy and Literature* 11 (1987): 242–57.

——. "Kafka's narrative Ontologie und Erzählhaltung: Ihre Beziehungen zur österreichischen Philosophie der Jahrhundertwende," *Poetica* 21 (1989): 389–402.

——. "Physiological, Phenomenological and Linguistic Psychology in Kafka's Early Works," *German Quarterly* 62 (1989): 489–500.

Heller, Paul. *Franz Kafka: Wissenschaft und Wissenschaftskritik.* Tübingen: Stauffenburg, 1989.

Hemecker, Wilhelm. "Sigmund Freud und die herbartianische Psychologie des 19. Jahrhunderts." *Conceptus* 21.53-54 (1987): 217-31.

Henel, Ingeborg. "Periodisierung und Entwicklung." In *Kafka-Handbuch,* edited by Hartmut Binder, 2: 220-41.

Herbart, Johann Friedrich. *Sämtliche Werke.* Edited by G. Hartenstein. 12 vols. Leipzig: Voss, 1850-52.

Hering, Ewald. "Der Raumsinn und die Bewegungen des Auges." In *Handbuch der Physiologie*, edited by Ludimar Hermann, 3.1: 343-601.

Hermann, Ludimar, ed. *Handbuch der Physiologie.* 6 vols., 12 parts. Leipzig: Vogel, 1879-83.

Hiebel, Hans Helmut. *Die Zeichen des Gesetzes: Recht und Macht bei Franz Kafka.* Munich: Fink, 1983.

——. *Franz Kafka: "Ein Landarzt."* Munich: Fink, 1984.

Hofmannsthal, Hugo von. *Gesammelte Werke,* 15 vols. Frankfurt: Fischer, 1946-59.

Holitscher, Arthur. *Lebensgeschichte eines Rebellen: Meine Erinnerungen.* Berlin: Fischer, 1924.

Husserl, Edmund. *Logische Untersuchungen.* 2 vols. Halle: Niemeyer, 1900-1901.

——. *Logical Investigations.* Translated by J. N. Findlay. 2 vols. New York: Humanities Press, 1970.

——. *Aufsätze und Rezensionen 1890-1910.* Husserliana, vol. 22. Edited by Bernhard Rang. The Hague: Nijhoff, 1979.

——. "Reminiscences of Franz Brentano." In *The Philosophy of Brentano.* Edited by Linda McAlister, 47-55. London: Duckworth, 1976.

Hutchinson, Peter. "Red Herring or Clues?" In *The Kafka Debate,* edited by Angel Flores, 206-15.

Jhering, Rudolph von. *Geist des römischen Rechts auf den verschiedenen Stufen seiner Entwicklung.* 3rd and 4th ed. 3 vols. vol. 2 in 2 pts. Leipzig: Breitkopf & Härtel, 1875-80.

——. *Der Zweck im Recht.* 4th ed. 2 vols. Leipzig: Breitkopf & Härtel, 1904.

Janik, Allan, and Stephen Toulmin. *Wittgenstein's Vienna*. New York: Touchstone, 1973.

Janka, Karl. *Das österreichische Strafrecht*, 3rd ed. Revised by Friedrich Rulf. Prague and Vienna: Tempsky, 1894.

Janz, Rolf-Peter. "Franz Kafka, *Vor dem Gesetz* und Jacques Derrida, *Préjugés*." *Jahrbuch der deutschen Schillergesellschaft* 37 (1993): 328–40.

Jayne, Richard. "Kafka's *In der Strafkolonie* and the Aporias of Textual Interpretation." *Deutsche Vierteljahrsschrift für Literatur- und Geistesgeschichte* 66 (1992): 94–128.

Jochmann, Werner. *Gesellschaftskrise und Judenfeindschaft in Deutschland 1870–1945*. Hamburg: Christians, 1988.

Kafka-Handbuch in zwei Bänden. Edited by Hartmut Binder. Vol. 1, *Der Mensch und seine Zeit*. Vol. 2, *Das Werk und seine Wirkung*. Stuttgart: Kröner, 1979.

Kafka, Franz. *Amerika: Roman* [*Der Verschollene*]. Edited by Max Brod. Frankfurt: Fischer, 1953. Fischer Taschenbuch, 1956.

——. *Amerika*. Translated by Willa Muir and Edwin Muir. New York: Schocken, 1946; 1974. Schocken Kafka Library, 1962.

——. *Amtliche Schriften*. Edited by Klaus Hermsdorf. Berlin: Akademie-Verlag, 1984.

——. *Beschreibung eines Kampfes: Novellen, Skizzen, Aphorismen aus dem Nachlaß*. Edited by Max Brod. Frankfurt: Fischer 1954. Fischer Taschenbuch, 1980.

——. *Beschreibung eines Kampfes: Die zwei Fassungen. Parallelausgabe nach den Handschriften*. Edited by Ludwig Dietz. Frankfurt: Fischer, 1969.

——. *The Blue Octavo Notebooks*. Edited by Max Brod. Translated by Ernst Kaiser and Eithne Wilkins. New York: Schocken, 1954. Cambridge, Mass.: Exact Change, 1991.

——. *Briefe, 1902–1924*. Edited by Max Brod. Frankfurt: Fischer, 1958. Fischer Taschenbuch, 1975.

——. *Briefe an Felice und andere Korrespondenz aus der Verlobungszeit*. Edited by Erich Heller and Jürgen Born. Frankfurt: Fischer, 1967. Fischer Taschenbuch, 1976.

——. *Briefe an Milena*. Edited by Jürgen Born and Michael Müller. Frankfurt: Fischer, 1983. Fischer Taschenbuch, 1986.

——. *Briefe an Ottla und die Familie*. Edited by Hartmut Binder and Klaus Wagenbach. Frankfurt: Fischer, 1974. Fischer Taschenbuch, 1981.

——. *The Castle*. Translated by Willa Muir and Edna Muir. With additional materials translated by Eithne Wilkins and Ernst Kaiser. New York: Schocken, 1954; 1982. Schocken Kafka Library, 1988.

——. *The Complete Stories*. Edited by Nahum Glatzer. New York: Schocken, 1971. Schocken Kafka Library, 1988.

——. *Dearest Father: Stories and Other Writings*. Edited by Max Brod. Translated by Ernst Kaiser and Eithne Wilkins. New York: Schocken, 1954.

——. *The Diaries of Franz Kafka, 1910-1913*. Edited by Max Brod. Translated by Joseph Kresh. New York: Schocken, 1948. Schocken Paperback, 1965.

——. *The Diaries of Franz Kafka, 1914-1923*. Edited by Max Brod. Translated by Martin Greenberg, with the cooperation of Hannah Arendt. New York: Schocken, 1949. Schocken Paperback, 1965.

——. *The Great Wall of China: Stories and Reflections*. Translated by Willa Muir and Edna Muir. New York: Schocken, 1946.

——. *Hochzeitsvorbereitungen auf dem Lande und andere Prosa aus dem Nachlaß*. Edited by Max Brod. Frankfurt: Fischer, 1953. Fischer Taschenbuch [2067], 1980.

——. *Letters to Felice*. Edited by Erich Heller and Jürgen Born. Tanslated by James Stern and Elizabeth Duckworth. New York: Schocken, 1973.

——. *Letters to Friends, Family, and Editors*. Edited by Max Brod. Revised, and with additional letters edited by Beverly Colman, Nahum Glatzer, Christopher Kuppig, and Wolfgang Sauerlander. Translated by Richard Winston and Clara Winston. New York: Schocken, 1977. Schocken Kafka Library, 1977.

——. *Letters to Milena*. Edited by Jürgen Born and Michael Müller. Translated by Philip Boehm. New York: Schocken Kafka Library, 1990.

——. *Nachgelassene Schriften II*. Kritische Ausgabe. Edited by Jost Schillemeit. Frankfurt: Fischer, 1992.

——. *Nachgelassene Schriften II: Apparatband*. Kritische Ausgabe. Edited by Jost Schillemeit. Frankfurt: Fischer, 1992.

——. *Der Prozeß: Roman*. Edited by Max Brod. Fischer: Frankfurt, 1950. Fischer Taschenbuch, 1979.

——. *Der Proceß*. Kritische Ausgabe. Edited by Malcolm Pasley. Frankfurt: Fischer, 1990.

——. *Der Proceß: Apparatband*. Kritische Ausgabe. Edited by Malcolm Pasley. Frankfurt: Fischer, 1990.

——. *Sämtliche Erzählungen*. Edited by Paul Raabe. Frankfurt: Fischer, 1970. Fischer Taschenbuch, 1970.

——. *Das Schloß: Roman*. Edited by Max Brod. Frankfurt: Fischer, 1951. Fischer Taschenbuch, 1968.

——. *Das Schloß*. Kritische Ausgabe. Edited by Malcolm Pasley. Frankfurt: Fischer, 1982.

——. *Das Schloß: Apparatband*. Kritische Ausgabe. Edited by Malcolm Pasley. Frankfurt: Fischer, 1982.

——. Schriften - Tagebücher - Briefe: Kritische Ausgabe. Edited by Jürgen Born, Gerhard Neumann, Malcolm Pasley, and Jost Schillemeit. Frankfurt: Fischer, 1982–.

——. *Tagebücher, 1910–1924*. Edited by Max Brod. Frankfurt: Fischer, 1951. Fischer Taschenbuch, 1973.

——. *Tagebücher*. Kritische Ausgabe. Edited by Hans-Gerd Koch, Michael Müller, and Malcolm Pasley (Frankfurt: Fischer, 1990).

——. *Tagebücher: Apparatband*. Kritische Ausgabe. Edited by Hans-Gerd Koch, Michael Müller, and Malcolm Pasley. Frankfurt: Fischer, 1990.

——. *Tagebücher: Kommentarband*. Kritische Ausgabe. Edited by Hans-Gerd Koch, Michael Müller, and Malcolm Pasley. Frankfurt: Fischer, 1990.

——. *The Trial*. Translated by Willa Muir and Edwin Muir. Revised, and with additional material translated by E. M. Butler. New York: Schocken, 1956; 1984. Schocken Kafka Library, 1988.

——. *Der Verschollene*. Kritische Ausgabe. Edited by Jost Schillemeit. Frankfurt: Fischer, 1983.

——. *Der Verschollene: Apparatband*. Kritische Ausgabe. Edited by Jost Schillemeit. Frankfurt: Fischer, 1983.

Kantorowicz, Hermann [Gnaeus Flavius]. "Der Kampf um die Rechtswissenschaft." In: Hermann Kantorowicz, *Rechtswissenschaft und Soziologie*, edited by Thomas Würtenberger, 13–49. Karlsruhe: Müller, 1962.

Kastil, Alfred. Review of *Psychologische Tatbestandsdiagnostik*, by Max Wertheimer and Julius Klein. *Deutsche Arbeit* 3 (1903–1904): 788–89.

——. *Studien zur neueren Erkenntnistheorie*. Vol. 1, *Descartes*. Halle: Niemeyer, 1909.

——. Review of *Untersuchungen zum Problem der Evidenz der inneren Wahrnehmung*, by Hugo Bergmann. *Zeitschrift für Psychologie* 53 (1909): 390–92.

Kienlechner, Sabina. *Negativität der Erkenntnis im Werk Franz Kafkas: Eine Untersuchung zu seinem Denken anhand einiger später Texte*. Tübingen: Niemeyer, 1981.

Kierkegaard, Sören. *Buch des Richters: Seine Tagebücher 1833–1855 im Auszug*. Translated by Hermann Gottsched. Jena and Leipzig: Diederichs, 1905.

Kierkegaard, Søren. *Fear and Trembling. Repetition*. Edited and translated by Howard Hong and Edna Hong. Princeton University Press, 1983.

Kirchberger, Lida. *Franz Kafka's Use of the Law in Fiction*. New York: Lang, 1986.

Kittay, Eva F. *Metaphor: Its Cognitive Force and Linguistic Structure*. Oxford: Clarendon, 1987.

Kittler, Wolf, and Gerhard Neumann, eds. *Franz Kafka: Schriftverkehr*. Freiburg: Rombach, 1990.

Kittler, Wolf, and Gerhard Neumann. "Kafkas *Drucke zu Lebzeiten*: Editorische Technik und hermeneutische Entscheidung." In *Franz Kafka: Schriftverkehr*, edited by Wolf Kittler and Gerhard Neumann, 30–74.

Klatzkin, Jakob. "Grundlagen des Nationaljudentums." *Der Jude* 1 (1916–17): 534–44; 609–18; 677–84; 825–33.

——. "Deutschtum und Judentum." *Der Jude* 2 (1917–18): 245–52; 358–70.

Klein, Franz. "Freie Rechtsfindung." *Das Recht: Rundschau für den deutschen Juristenstand* 10 (1906): 916–19.

Kobs, Jürgen. *Kafka: Untersuchungen zu Bewußtsein und Sprache seiner Gestalten*. Edited by Ursula Brech. Bad Homburg: Athenäum, 1970.

Kluge, E.-H. *The Metaphysics of Gottlob Frege: An Essay in Ontological Reconstruction*. The Hague, Boston, and London: Nijhoff, 1980.

Knobloch, Clemens. *Geschichte der psychologischen Sprachauffassung in Deutschland von 1850 bis 1920*. Tübingen: Niemeyer, 1988.

Koelb, Clayton. *Kafka's Rhetoric: The Passion of Reading*. Ithaca: Cornell University Press, 1989.

Kraus, Karl. "Aus dem dunkelsten Österreich." *Die Fackel* 214–15 (1906): 1–6.

——. "Das Ehrenkreuz." *Die Fackel* 272–73 (1909): 2–5.

Kraus, Oskar. "Strafe und Schuld." *Zeitschrift für Schweizer Strafrecht* 10 (1897): 290–313.

——. "Das Motiv." *Zeitschrift für die gesamte Strafrechtswissenschaft* 17 (1897): 467–87.

——. "Das Dogma von der Ursächlichkeit der Unterlassung." *Juristische Vierteljahrsschrift* 30 (1898): 1–82.

——. *Zur Theorie des Wertes: Eine Bentham-Studie.* Halle: Niemeyer, 1901.

——. "Rechtsphilosophie und Jurisprudenz." *Zeitschrift für die gesamte Strafrechtswissenschaft* 23 (1903): 763–94.

——. "Die aristotelische Werttheorie in ihren Beziehungen zu den Lehren der modernen Psychologenschule." *Zeitschrift für die gesamte Staatswissenschaft* 61 (1905): 573–92.

——. "Die leitenden Grundsätze der Gesetzesinterpretation." *Zeitschrift für das Privat- und Öffentliche Recht der Gegenwart* 32 (1905): 613–36.

——. *Die Lehre von Lob, Lohn, Tadel und Strafe bei Aristoteles.* Halle: Niemeyer, 1905.

——. "Psychologische Tatbestandsdiagnostik." *Monatsschrift für Kriminalpsychologie und Strafrechtsreform* 2 (1905–1906): 58–61.

——. Review of *Das juristische Denken,* by Karl Georg Wurzel. *Juristische Vierteljahrsschrift* 38 (1906): 73–77.

——. *Das Recht zu strafen.* Der Gerichtssaal, vol 79 [supplementary issue]. Stuttgart: Enke, 1911.

——. "Über den Begriff der Schuld und den Unterschied von Vorsatz und Fahrlässigkeit." *Monatsschrift für Kriminalpsychologie und Strafrechtsreform* 9 (1913): 321–46.

Krojanker, Gustav, ed. *Juden in der deutschen Literatur: Essays über zeitgenössische Schriftsteller.* Berlin: Welt, 1922.

Krolop, Kurt. "Prager Autoren im Lichte der *Fackel.*" In *Prager deutschsprachige Literatur zur Zeit Kafkas. Schriftenreihe der Franz-Kafka-Gesellschaft* 3 (1989): 92–117.

Kudszus, Winfried. "Erzählhaltung und Zeitverschiebung in Kafkas *Prozeß* und *Schloß.*" *Deutsche Vierteljahrsschrift für Literatur- und Geistesgeschichte* 38 (1964): 192–207.

——. "Erzählperspektive und Erzählgeschehen in Kafka's *Prozeß*." *Deutsche Vierteljahrsschrift für Literatur- und Geistesgeschichte* 44 (1970): 306–17.

——. "Changing Perspectives in *The Trial* and *The Castle*," In *The Kafka Debate*, edited by Angel Flores, 385–95.

Künne, Wolfgang. "Edmund Husserl: Intentionalität." In *Philosophie der Neuzeit*, 6 vols. Grundprobleme der großen Philosophen, edited by Josef Speck, 4: 165–215. Göttingen: Vandenhoeck & Ruprecht, 1983–92.

Kuna, Franz, ed. *On Kafka: Semi-Centenary Perspectives*. New York: Barnes & Noble, 1976.

Kurz, Gerhard, ed. *Der junge Kafka*. Frankfurt: Suhrkamp, 1984.

——. *Traum-Schrecken: Kafkas literarische Existenzanalyse*. Stuttgart: Metzler, 1980.

Lambert, Karel. *Meinong and the Principle of Independence*. Cambridge: Cambridge University Press, 1983.

Larkin, Maurice. *Man and Society in Nineteenth-Century Realism: Determinism and Literature*. Totowa, N. J., Rowman & Littlefield, 1977.

Lederer, Max: "Zur Frage der psychologischen Tatbestandsdiagnostik." *Zeitschrift für die gesamte Strafrechtswissenschaft* 26 (1906): 488–506.

——. "Die Verwendung der psychologischen Tatsbestandsdiagnostik in der Strafrechtspraxis." *Monatsschrift für Kriminalpsychologie und Strafrechtsreform* 3 (1906–1907): 163–72.

——. "Das *probation system* in den Vereinigten Staaten von Nordamerika." *Allgemeine österreichische Gerichtszeitung* 59 (1908): 89–91; 97–100.

——. "Das *probation system* in Nord-Amerika," *Zeitschrift für die gesamte Strafrechtswissenschaft* 28 (1908): 391–432.

——. "Amerikanische Kriminalpolitik (unbestimmte Verurteilung, bedingte Entlassung, Behandlung der Gewohnheitsverbrecher)," *Allgemeine österreichische Gerichtszeitung* 60 (1909): 102–103.

Lemayer, Karl Freiherr von. "Die Verwaltungsgerichtsbarkeit und der Verwaltungsgerichtshof." In *Österreichisches Staatswörterbuch*, edited by Ernst Mischler and Josef Ulbrich, 4: 23–46.

LePore, Ernest, ed. *Truth and Interpretation: Perspectives on the Philosophy of Donald Davidson*. Oxford: Basil Blackwell, 1986.

Levinas, Emmanuel. "Revelation in the Jewish Tradition." In The Levinas Reader, edited by Seán Hand, 190–209. Cambridge, Mass.: Blackwell, 1989.

Levy, Heinrich. Review of *Anschauung und Begriff*, by Max Brod and Felix Weltsch. *Kant-Studien* 24 (1920): 321–25.

Lichtheim, Richard. *Das Programm des Zionismus*. Berlin: Zionistische Vereinigung für Deutschland, 1913.

Lindenfeld, David. *The Transformation of Positivism: Alexius Meinong and European Thought*. Berkley and Los Angeles: University of California Press, 1980.

Lindeskog, Gösta. *Die Jesusfrage im neuzeitlichen Judentum: Ein Beitrag zur Geschichte der Leben-Jesu-Forschung*. Uppsala: Lundequistska, 1938.

Lindner, Gustav A., and Franz Lukas. *Lehrbuch der Psychologie*. Vienna: Gerold, 1900.

Linsky, Leonard: *Referring*. London: Routledge & Kegan Paul, 1967.

——. *Names and Descriptions*. Chicago: University of Chicago Press, 1977.

Loar, Brian. "The Semantics of Singular Terms." *Philosophical Studies* 30 (1976): 353–77.

Löffler, Alexander. "Die Abgrenzung von Vorsatz und Fahrlässigkeit mit Berücksichtigung des deutschen und österreichischen Vorentwurfes." *Österreichische Zeitschrift für Strafrecht* 2 (1911): 131–74.

Lohsing, Ernst. *Österreichisches Strafprozeßrecht: In systematischer Darstellung*. Graz and Vienna: Moser, 1912.

——. *Österreichisches Strafprozeßrecht*. 3rd ed. Vienna: Österreichische Staatsdruckkerei, 1932.

Mach, Ernst. *Die Analyse der Empfindungen*. Jena: Fischer, 1886.

——. *Erkenntnis und Irrtum: Skizzen zur Psychologie der Forschung*. Leipzig: Barth, 1905.

Mackie, John L. *Truth, Probability and Paradox: Studies in Philosophical Logic*. Oxford: Clarendon, 1973.

Marek, Johann Christian. "Zum Programm einer deskriptiven Psychologie." *Grazer philosophische Studien* 28 (1986): 211–34.

Marek, Johann Christian, and Barry Smith. "Einleitung zu Anton Martys *Elemente der Deskriptiven Psychologie*." *Conceptus* 21.53–54 (1987): 33–47.

Marty, Anton. "Descriptive Psychologie: Nach den Vorlesungen des Prof. Dr. Marty." Mimeographed transcript (333 p.) on microfilm, in custody of the

"Forschungsstelle und Dokumentationszentrum für österreichische Philosophie" (Graz, Austria).

——. "Grundfragen der Sprachphilosophie." In *Psyche und Sprachstruktur*, edited by Otto Funke, 75–117. Bern: Francke, 1940.

——. *Untersuchungen zur Grundlegung der allgemeinen Grammatik und Sprachphilosophie.* Halle: Niemeyer, 1908.

——. *Gesammelte Schriften.* Edited by Josef Eisenmeier, Alfred Kastil, and Oskar Kraus. 2 vols. 4 parts. Halle: Niemeyer, 1916–20.

——. *Über Wert und Methode einer beschreibenden Bedeutungslehre.* Edited by Otto Funke. Reichenberg: Stiepel, 1926.

McGinn, Colin. *The Character of Mind.* Oxford: Oxford University Press, 1982.

——. "The Structure of Content." In *Thought and Object: Essays on Intentionality*, edited by Andrew Woodfield, 207–58.

Meinong, Alexius. *Gesamtausgabe.* Edited by Rudolf Haller and Rudolf Kindinger, with Roderick Chisholm, 7 vols. Graz: Akademische Druck- und Verlagsanstalt, 1969–78.

——. *On Assumptions.* Edited and translated by James Heanue. Berkley and Los Angeles: University of California Press, 1983.

——. "The Theory of Objects." In *Realism and the Background of Phenomenology*, edited by Roderick Chisholm, 76–117. Glencoe, Ill.: Free Press, 1960.

Meumann, Ernst. *Einführung in die Ästhetik der Gegenwart.* Leipzig: Quelle & Meyer, 1908.

Milful, Helen. "*Weder Katze noch Lamm?* Franz Kafkas Kritik des *Westjüdischen.*" In *Im Zeichen Hiobs: Jüdische Schriftsteller und deutsche Literatur im 20. Jahrhundert,* edited by Gunter Grimm and Hans-Peter Bayerdörfer, 178–92. Königstein: Athenäum, 1985.

Miller, Eric. "Without a Key: The Narative Structure of *Das Schloß.*" *Germanic Review* 66 (1991): 132–40.

Miller, George A. "Images and Models, Similes and Metaphors." In *Metaphor and Thought*, edited by Andrew Ortony, 202–50. Cambridge: Cambridge University Press, 1979.

Mitchell, Breon. "Kafka and the Hunger Artists." In *Kafka and the Contemporary Critical Performance*, edited by Alan Udoff, 236–55.

Möbus, Frank. "Theoderich, Julia und die Jakobsleiter: Franz Kafkas Erzählfragment zum *Jäger Gracchus.*" *Zeitschrift für deutsche Philologie* 109 (1990): 253–71.

Moench, Dietmar: *Die methodologischen Bestrebungen der Freirechtsbewegung auf dem Wege zur Methodenlehre der Gegenwart.* Frankfurt: Athenäum, 1971.

Morscher, Edgar. "Von Bolzano to Meinong: Zur Geschichte des logischen Realismus." In *Jenseits von Sein und Nichtsein: Beiträge zur Meinong-Forschung*, edited by Rudolf Haller, 69–102.

——. "Propositions and States of Affairs in Austrian Philosophy before Wittgenstein." In *From Bolzano to Wittgenstein: The Tradition of Austrian Philosophy*, edited by J. C. Nyiri, 75–85. Vienna: Hölder-Pichler-Tempsky, 1986.

——. "Judgement-Contents." In *Mind, Meaning and Metaphysics*, edited by Kevin Mulligan, 181–96.

Müller, Aloys. Review of *Anschauung und Begriff*, by Max Brod and Felix Weltsch. *Archiv für die gesamte Psychologie* 31 (1914): 39–47.

Müller-Seidel, Walter. *Die Deportation des Menschen: Kafka's Erzählung "In der Strafkolonie" im europäischen Kontext.* Stuttgart: Metzler, 1986.

Mulligan, Kevin, ed. *Mind, Meaning and Metaphysics: The Philosophy and Theory of Language of Anton Marty.* Dordrecht: Kluwer, 1990.

——, and Barry Smith. "A Relational Theory of the Act." *Topoi* 5 (1986): 115–30.

Neesen, Peter. *Vom Louvrezirkel zum Prozeß: Franz Kafka und die Psychologie Franz Brentanos.* Göppingen: Kümmerle, 1972.

Neumann, Gerhard. *Franz Kafka: Das Urteil. Text, Materialien, Kommentar.* Munich: Hanser, 1981.

Neumann, Gerhard. "Hungerkünstler und Menschenfresser: Zum Verhältnis von Kunst und kulturellem Ritual im Werk Franz Kafkas." In *Franz Kafka: Schriftverkehr*, edited by Wolf Kittler and Gerhard Neumann, 399–432.

Nietzsche, Friedrich. *Werke in drei Bänden.* Edited by Karl Schlechta. 3 vols. Munich: Hanser, 1960.

Northey, Anthony: *Kafka's Relatives: Their Lives and His Writing.* New Haven: Yale University Press, 1991.

O'Shaughnessy, Brian. "Consciousness." In *Studies in the Philosophy of Mind.* Midwest Studies in Philosophy, vol. 10. Edited by Peter French, Theodore Uehling, and Howard Wettstein, 49–62. Minneapolis: University of Minnesota Press, 1986.

Österreichisches Staatswörterbuch. Edited by Ernst Mischler and Josef Ulbrich, 2nd ed. 4 vols. Vienna: Hölder, 1905–1909.

Österreichische Strafprozeßordnung. Edited by Leo Geller, 4th ed. Vienna: Perles, 1894.

Pascal, Roy. *Kafka's Narrators: A Study of His Stories and Sketches*. Cambridge: Cambridge University Press, 1982.

Pasley, Malcolm. "Semi-Private Games." *The Kafka Debate*, edited by Angel Flores, 188–205.

——. "Die Handschrift redet." In *Franz Kafka: Der Proceß*. Marbacher Magazin, vol. 52, edited by Malcolm Pasley and Ulrich Ott, 5–29. Marbach: Deutsche Schillergesellschaft, 1990.

Pawel, Ernst. *The Nightmare of Reason: A Life of Franz Kafka*. New York: Farrar, Straus, Girous, 1984.

Pazi, Margarita. *Max Brod: Werk und Persönlichkeit*. Bonn: Bouvier, 1970.

——. "Franz Kafka, Max Brod und der *Prager Kreis*." In *Kafka und das Judentum*, edited by Karl Erich Grözinger, Stéphane Mosès, and Hans Dieter Zimmermann, 71–92.

Perez, Jizchok Lejb. "Drei Geschenke." *In*: J. L. Perez, Scholem-Alejchem, and Scholem Asch, *Ostjüdische Erzähler*, edited by Alexander Eliasberg, 77–94. Weimar: Kiepenheuer, 1917.

Pernthaler, Peter. "Das Bild des Rechts in drei Werken von Franz Kafka (*Amerika*, *Strafkolonie*, *Prozeß*)." In *Dimensionen des Rechts*. Gedächtnisschrift für René Marcic, edited by Michael Fischer, Raimund Jakab, Erhard Mock, and Helmut Schreiner, 259–81. Berlin: Duncker & Humblot, 1974.

Pietsch, Max. "Schuld und Erfolg im Vorentwurf eines österreichischen Strafgesetzbuches mit Berücksichtigung des deutschen Vorentwurfs und des geltenden Strafgesetzes." *Allgemeine österreichische Gerichtszeitung* 63 (1912): 289–301.

Politzer, Heinz. *Franz Kafka: Der Künstler*. Frankfurt: Fischer, 1965.

Posner, Richard A. *Law and Literature: A Misunderstood Relation*. Cambridge: Harvard University Press, 1988.

Pynsent, Robert B., ed. *Decadence and Innovation: Austro-Hungarian Life and Art at the Turn of the Century*. London: Weidenfeld & Nicolson, 1989.

Quine, Willard V. Orman. *From a Logical Point of View*. Cambridge: Harvard University Press, 1961.

——. *The Ways of Paradox*. New York: Random House, 1966.

Radbruch, Gustav. Review of "Die leitenden Grundsätze der Gesetzesinterpretation," by Oskar Kraus. *Zeitschrift für die gesamte Staatsrechtswissenschaft* 26 (1906): 259–60.

——. Review of *Der Kampf um die Rechtswissenschaft*, by Gnaeus Flavius. *Zeitschrift für die gesamte Strafrechtswissenschaft* 27 (1907): 241–43.

Ramm, Klaus. "Handlungsführung und Gedankenführung." In *Kafka-Handbuch*, edited by Hartmut Binder, 93–107.

Rang, Bernhard. "Editor's Introduction." In: Edmund Husserl, *Aufsätze und Rezensionen 1890–1910*, ix–lvi.

Riffaterre, Michael. *Fictional Truth*. Baltimore: Johns Hopkins University Press, 1990.

Rignall, J. M. "History and Consciousness in *Beim Bau der chinesischen Mauer*." In *Paths and Labyrinths,* edited by J. P. Stern and J. J. White, 111–26.

Robertson, Ritchie. *Kafka: Judaism, Politics, and Literature*. Oxford: Clarendon, 1985.

Rodlauer, Hannelore. "Kafka und Wien: Ein Briefkommentar." *Anzeiger der Akademie der Wissenschaften in Wien: Philosophisch-historische Klasse* 199 (1985): 202–48.

Rodlauer-Wenko, Hannelore. "Die Paralleltagebücher Kafka-Brod und das Modell Flaubert." *Arcadia* 20 (1985): 47–60.

Ronell, Avital. "Doing Kafka in *The Castle*." In *Kafka and the Contemporary Critical Performance*, edited by Alan Udoff, 214–35.

Russell, Bertrand. "Meinong's Theory of Complexes and Assumptions." *Mind* 13 (1904): 509–24; 204–19; 336–54.

——. "On Denoting." Mind 14 (1905): 479–93.

Sanders, E. P. *Paul, the Law, and the Jewish People*. London: SCM Press, 1985.

Scheichl, Sigurd P. "Aspekte des Judentums im *Brenner* 1910–1937." In *Untersuchungen zum "Brenner."* Festschrift für Ignaz Zangerle, edited by Walter Methagl, Eberhard Sauermann, and Sigurd Paul Scheichl, 70–121. Salzburg: Müller, 1981.

Schillemeit, Jost. "Kafkas *Beschreibung eines Kampfes*." In *Der junge Kafka*, edited by Gerhard Kurz, 102–32.

Schirrmacher, Frank, ed. *Verteidigung der Schrift: Kafkas "Prozeß."* Frankfurt: Suhrkamp, 1987.

Schopenhauer, Arthur. *Sämmtliche Werke.* Edited by Julius Frauenstädt. 6 vols. Leipzig: Brockhaus, 1873–74.

Schorske, Carl. *Fin-de-Siècle Vienna: Politics and Culture.* New York: Vintage, 1981.

Schuhmann, Karl. "Husserls doppelter Vorstellungsbegriff: Die Texte von 1893." *Brentano Studien* 3 (1990–91): 119–36.

Sebald, W. G. "The Law of Ignominy: Authority, Messianism and Exile in *The Castle.*" In *On Kafka,* edited by Franz Kuna, 42–58.

Sheppard, Richard. *On Kafka's "The Castle": A Study.* London: Croom Helm, 1973.

Singer, Heinrich. "Zur Frage des staatlichen Oberaufsichtsrechtes." *Deutsche Zeitschrift für Kirchenrecht*, 3rd series, 5 (1895): 60–166; 8 (1898) 30–77.

——. *Einige Worte über die Vergangenheit und Zukunft der Czernowitzer Universität.* Warnsdorf: Stracke, 1917.

Sluga, Hans D. *Gottlob Frege.* London: Routledge & Kegan Paul, 1980.

Smith, Barry "Brentano and Marty: An Inquiry into Being and Truth," In *Mind, Meaning and Metaphysics*, edited by Kevin Mulligan, 111–49.

Smith, David Woodruff, and Ronald McIntyre. *Husserl and Intentionality.* Dordrecht: Reidel, 1982.

Smith, David Woodruff. "Content and Context of Perception." *Synthese* 61 (1984): 61–87.

Sokel, Walter H. *Franz Kafka: Tragik und Ironie: Zur Struktur seiner Kunst.* Munich and Vienna: Langen & Müller, 1964.

——. "The Programme of K.'s Court: Oedipal and Existential Meanings of *The Trial.*" In *On Kafka,* edited by Franz Kuna, 1–21.

Stach, Reiner. *Kafkas erotischer Mythos: Eine ästhetische Konstruktion des Weiblichen.* Frankfurt: Fischer, 1987.

Stanzel, F. K. *A Theory of the Narrative.* Translated by Charlotte Goedsche. New York: Cambridge University Press, 1984.

Stanzel, Frank K. "Teller-Characters and Reflector-Characters in Narrative Theory." *Poetics Today* 2.2 (1981): 5–15.

Stern, J. P. "Guilt and the Feeling of Guilt." In *The Problem of "The Judgment,"* edited by Angel Flores, 114–31.

——, and J. J. White, eds. *Paths and Labyrinths: Nine Papers read at the Franz Kafka Symposium held at the Institute of Germanic Studies on 20 and 21 October 1983.* London: Institute of Germanic Studies, University of London, 1985.

Stieg, Gerald "Wer ist Kafkas Bote Barnabas?," *Austriaca* 17 (1983): 151–56.

Strawson, P. F. *Freedom and Resentment and Other Essays.* London: Methuen, 1974.

Stumpf, Carl. "Über Gefühlsempfindungen." *Zeitschrift für Psychologie und Physiologie der Sinnesorgane* 44 (1907): 1–49.

Sussman, Henry. *Franz Kafka: Geometrician of Metaphor.* Madison: Coda, 1979.

——. *Afterimages of Modernity: Structure and Indifference in Twentieth-Century Literature.* Baltimore: Johns Hopkins University Press, 1990.

Timms, Edward. "Kafka's Expanded Metaphors: A Freudian Approach to *Ein Landarzt.*" *Paths and Labyrinths,* edited by J. P. Stern and J. J. White, 66–79.

Tismar, Jens. "Kafkas *Schakale und Araber* im zionistischen Kontext betrachtet." *Jahrbuch der deutschen Schillergesellschaft* 19 (1975): 306–23.

Tugendhat, Ernst. *Vorlesungen zur Einführung in die sprachanalytische Philosophie.* Frankfurt: Suhrkamp, 1976.

Udoff, Alan, ed. *Kafka and the Contemporary Critical Performance: Centenary Readings.* Bloomington and Indianapolis: Indiana University Press, 1987.

Ulbrich, Josef. *Das österreichische Staatsrecht.* Handbuch des öffentlichen Rechts der Gegenwart, edited by Georg Jellinek and Robert Piloty, vol. 4, pt. 1, sect. 1, pt. 1. Tübingen: Mohr, 1904.

Utitz, Emil. *J. J. Wilhelm Heinse und die Ästhetik zur Zeit der deutschen Aufklärung.* Halle: Niemeyer, 1906.

——. "Untersuchungen zur Sinnespsychologie." Review of *Untersuchungen zur Sinnespsychologie,* by Franz Brentano. *Philosophische Wochenschrift* 8 (1907): 380–92.

——. "Kritische Vorbemerkungen zu einer ästhetischen Farbenlehre." *Zeitschrift für Ästhetik und allgemeine Kunstwissenschaft* 3 (1908): 337–60.

——. "Zweckmäßigkeit und Schönheit: Eine aesthetische Betrachtung." *Philosophische Wochenschrift* 9 (1908): 49–61.

——. *Grundzüge der ästhetischen Farbenlehre*. Stuttgart: Enke, 1908.

——. "Erinnerungen an Franz Brentano." *Wissenschaftliche Zeitschrift der Universität Halle-Wittenberg: Gesellschafts- und sprachwissenschaftliche Reihe* 4 (1954–55): 73–90.

Vietta, Silvio, and Hans-Georg Kemper. *Expressionismus*. Munich: Fink, 1975.

Vogl, Josef. *Ort der Gewalt: Kafka's literarische Ethik*. Munich: Fink, 1990.

Volkmann, Wilhelm F. *Grundriß der Psychologie*. Halle: Fricke, 1856.

Wagenbach, Klaus. *Franz Kafka: Eine Biographie seiner Jugend, 1883–1912*. Bern: Francke, 1958.

——. "Julie Wohryzek, die zweite Verlobte Kafkas." In *Kafka-Symposium*, edited by Jürgen Born, Ludwig Dietz, Malcolm Pasley, Paul Raabe, and Klaus Wagenbach, 39–53. Berlin: Wagenbach, 1965.

Wagner, Nike. *Geist und Geschlecht: Karl Kraus und die Erotik der Wiener Moderne*. Frankfurt: Suhrkamp, 1982.

Warhanek, Karl. "Strafe, bedingte Verurteilung und bedingte Entlassung." *Allgemeine österreichische Gerichtszeitung* 62 (1911): 197–205.

Warner, Martin. "Black's Metaphors," *British Journal of Aesthetics* 13 (1973): 367–72.

Wassermann, Jakob. *Mein Weg als Deutscher und Jude*. Frankfurt: Fischer, 1921.

Watt, Henry J. Review of *Anschauung und Begriff*, by Max Brod and Felix Weltsch. *Mind* 15 (1916): 103–109.

Weber, Max. *Gesammelte Aufsätze zur Wissenschaftslehre*. Tübingen: Mohr, 1922.

Weininger, Otto. *Geschlecht und Charakter: Eine prinzipielle Untersuchung*. Vienna and Leipzig: Braunmüller, 1903.

Wellbery, David E. "Scheinvorgang: Kafkas *Das Schweigen der Sirenen*." In *Vorträge des Augsburger Germanistentags 1991: kultureller Wandel und die Germanistik der Bundesrepublik*, edited by Johannes Janota, 4 vols. 3: 163–76. Tübingen: Niemeyer, 1993.

Welles, Orson. *The Trial: A Film by Orson Welles*. Edited by Nicholas Fry. London: Lorrimer, 1970.

Werfel, Franz. *Bocksgesang: In fünf Akten*. Munich: Wolff, 1921.

Wertheimer, Max. "Experimentelle Untersuchungen zur Tatbestandsdiagnostik." *Archiv für die gesamte Psychologie* 6 (1906): 59–131.

Wieacker, Franz. *Privatrechtsgeschichte der Neuzeit.* 2nd ed. Göttingen: Vandenhoeck & Ruprecht, 1967.

Willard, Dallas. *Logic and the Objectivity of Knowledge: A Study in Husserl's Early Philosophy.* Athens: Ohio University Press, 1984.

Winkelman, John. "Felice Bauer and *The Trial.*" In *The Kafka Debate,* edited by Angel Flores, 311–34.

Wörterbuch der philosophischen Begriffe. Edited by Rudolf Eisler. 3rd ed. 3 vols. Berlin: Mittler, 1910.

Woodfield, Andrew, ed. *Thought and Object: Essays on Intentionality.* Oxford: Clarendon, 1982.

Wundt, Wilhelm. *Grundzüge der physiologischen Psychologie.* 2nd ed. 2 vols. Leipzig: Engelmann, 1880.

——. *Völkerpsychologie.* Vol.1, *Die Sprache.* 2 pts. Leipzig: Engelmann, 1900.

——. *Sprachgeschichte und Sprachpsychologie.* Leipzig: Engelmann, 1901.

——. *Grundzüge der physiologischen Psychologie.* 5th ed. 3 vols. Leipzig: Engelmann, 1902–1903.

Zahn, Theodor. *Einleitung in das Neue Testament.* Leipzig: Deichert, 1900.

Ziegler, Ignaz. *Der Kampf zwischen Judentum und Christentum in den ersten drei christlichen Jahrhunderten.* Berlin: Poppelauer, 1907.

——. *Die Geistesreligion und das jüdische Religionsgesetz: Ein Beitrag zur Erneuerung des Judentums.* Berlin: Reimer, 1912.

Ziehen, Theodor. *Psychophysiologische Erkenntnistheorie.* Jena: Fischer, 1907.

Zimmermann, Hans Dieter. *Der babylonische Dolmetscher: Zu Franz Kafka und Robert Walser.* Frankfurt: Suhrkamp, 1985.

——, ed. *Nach erneuter Lektüre: Franz Kafkas "Der Proceß."* Würzburg: Königshausen & Neumann, 1992.

Zweig, Arnold. "Der heutige deutsche Antisemitismus." *Der Jude* 5 (1920–21): 65–76; 129–39; 193–204; 264–80; 373–88; 451–59; 557–65; 621–33.

——. "Der Antisemitismus und die deutsche Jugend." *Der Jude* 6 (1921–22): 137–50.

Index